REBUILD & THRIVE

Emotional Healing and Foundational Life Skills for Survivors of Sexual Exploitation

AMANDA MOON ELLEVIS

Amandamoonellevis@gmail.com

Printed and bound in the United States of America

ISBN: 978-0-578-39511-1

If you or a loved one has been trafficked, please call the National Human Trafficking Hotline at (888) 373-7888 to get help today.

Advance Praise for *Rebuild and Thrive*

Rebuild and Thrive has been used at Grace House for more than a year as a workshop group class with our shelter residents and as ongoing curriculum for our weekly peer support group. The effectiveness of its ability to walk alongside survivors in taking all the necessary steps toward independence is what keeps this material a crucial part of our program.

—Marjorie Saylor, Director of Client Care at Alabaster Jar Project

In a space and experience that cannot offer a "one size fits all" approach, Amanda Moon Ellevis shares her healing and recovery lessons in a practical and meaningful way in this book. I had the privilege of partnering with Amanda during part of her healing and love her heart to give back and help others from the lens of her own journey. Take those first steps toward healing with Amanda's book.

—Stephanie Renick, MSW, former Program Director Alabaster Jar Project

Overcoming your past, finding yourself, and beginning to dream again is exactly what you will experience. I have been truly inspired, and this is on one of my must-read lists.

—Keelin Washington, National Public Speaker and Survivor Advocate

Within *Rebuild and Thrive* are truths gently told that I absolutely needed to hear from a trusted mentor and friend when I first exited the sex industry, but did not; like so many other survivors, I did not have access to a residential recovery program. Using this book is akin to working closely with a trusted survivor-leader mentor as they guide with the wisdom that comes from lived experience and their hard-earned wholeness and healing.

—Emily Hollerbach, MBA, The Cool Aunt Series

The patterns that lead to sexual exploitation often develop early on in adolescence, and as we have seen with Amanda—it can affect any of our children. I have been amazed as I saw Amanda's healing and growth after the trauma she suffered. In *Rebuild and Thrive,* she gently guides the reader through the process of understanding their personal experiences, leading them on the path to healing. This book will help survivors rebuild their self-esteem and reach higher levels of self-sufficiency.

—Annette Lewis, Contra Costa County Board of Education

For Roxanne

Foreword by Susan Johnson

Dear Reader,

I am overjoyed to introduce you to this book because I have witnessed the resilience, strength, and growth that the author has obtained before writing it. The heart of the author is pure in her desire to positively impact the lives of others who have gone through similar circumstances and challenges, providing them with useful tools. Despite the many autobiographies that have been written by survivors of exploitation, this book is different as it literally addresses life situations, life skills, relationship skills, and coping tactics that the author herself has experienced and utilized. This book is going to impact your life in a powerful way and will be a useful tool to go back to or to share with others.

As a nonprofit service provider for an organization that provides long-term housing and resources to survivors of exploitation and trafficking, I have witnessed firsthand the author's journey toward her own empowerment and goals of self-sufficiency. Each topic in this curriculum is something that she herself dealt with and overcame, and now shares tools that others can apply. If nothing else, this curriculum will also validate your experiences and thought patterns, and possibly reveal unhealthy behaviors that you have adopted as survival skills. It will provide you with useful tactics to assist you as you are working to reframe, rebuild, and work toward your own goals of healing and self-sufficiency.

In our organization, we have adopted this curriculum and provide each person who moves into our residential program with a copy, as it is a relevant road map to their healing journey. My hope is that you and each person that reads it will embrace the concepts and tactics as essential tools on the pathway of your healing journey. Embrace the journey! You will thrive and inspire.

Sincerely,

Susan Johnson
Co-founder & Director
Alabaster Jar Project

CONTENTS

To the Reader

Sexual exploitation is legally defined as *an act or acts committed through exploitation of another person's sexuality for the purpose of sexual gratification, financial gain, personal benefit or advantage, or any other non-legitimate purpose.* You will learn that being a survivor of sexual exploitation can mean many things, but firstly, being a survivor means that there is a long road ahead of you, full of self-improvement, trauma therapy, and hard work.

This book is designed to guide new sexual exploitation survivors through their first fifteen months of healing. Each chapter represents one month, and each month is divided into four sections, one for each week of the month. I have found that the most effective survivor treatment programs include trauma therapy mental health counseling, coupled with practical life skills that help us reach and maintain independence. So, in this book, some chapters will focus on working through the trauma you have experienced as a result of sexual exploitation and other chapters will focus on basic to advanced life skills. Both are equally important when it comes to long-term healing and independence.

I did not write this book to share my story, nor is this book meant to teach nonsurvivor readers about what sexual exploitation is or looks like. Survivors don't need to be taught this. This book was written by survivors for survivors. While it was written from the perspective of those who are in a residential survivor treatment program, the information here can be applied to all choices you make when you enter recovery, whether you are in a program or you are recovering independently.

It was written this way because, unfortunately, many survivors do not finish the entirety of their recovery program. If that happens to you, you can continue to refer to this handbook when making life decisions or confronting trauma. If you become your own best life coach and work the steps laid out here for you, you will never have to go back to exploitation again.

Happy Healing,
Amanda Moon Ellevis
Survivor Leader, Lived Experience Expert

Self-Care and Self-Discovery

1

What Makes You, You?

Congratulations! You left exploitation behind. All the challenges that you have experienced are becoming mere memories that will fade more and more with each passing day as you walk toward self-fulfillment in living the best life you can imagine.

You may have spent many weeks, months, or years in a life where you didn't always have control. Getting to know yourself and doing things for your own pleasure may have been the least of your priorities. That all changes once you leave exploitation. You have many steps ahead of you to take toward independence, but the first step is to strengthen your own identity, because the best foundation for independence is having a strong idea of who you are, what you like, and what you want.

So, who are you? What are you all about? What makes you happy?

As trauma survivors, we may have trouble answering these questions. Often during sexual exploitation, we may not have been allowed to have an opinion at all about anything. Many decisions were made for us, and many of our independent decisions might have been made out of concerns for our safety, not because that is what we truly wanted. We may have forgotten who we are as a person, let alone what we like to eat, what we want to wear, or how we want to complete daily tasks. That is what leaving exploitation changes for us. Now we are looking at a blank page to write on for the rest of our story, and we hold the pen in our hands.

"Who am I?" can be an intimidating question, but simply being an exploitation survivor tells us a little bit about who we are:

- We are smart: Leaving behind the toxic lifestyle of sexual exploitation takes planning, strategizing, and analytical reasoning. Being a survivor shows us that we are capable of creating plans and sticking to them.
- We are resilient: Surviving trauma means that we have stared some very scary situations in the face, and yet we have survived them. We are able to face challenges, take them on, and move forward.
- We are strong: Making the decision to leave exploitation shows us that we can do what would make many people give up or surrender, yet we have the strength to rebuild our lives anyway.
- We treat ourselves with respect: We recognized that sexual exploitation was not healthy nor safe for us, and we made the decision to walk away from it. We respect ourselves enough to choose a different path that suits us better.
- We are brave: It takes a lot of courage to walk away from sexual exploitation, knowing that we may risk our safety in doing so, but we did it anyway because fear is not something that we will allow to hold us back from freedom.

Another way to get a better idea of who we are is to look at what we are interested in. While we may not be able to confidently list all our personal characteristics, we do know what we like and what we don't. Sometimes our interests alone can create an identity.

For example: If someone enjoys playing the guitar and has worked hard at honing their craft, we can say that they are a musician. That is a defining part of their identity! Most people would say that musicians are creative, but we can also say that musicians are sensitive, because they enjoy expressing themselves with music. We can say that they are technical-minded, because it takes some mathematical skill to learn how to play notes and chords on an instrument. If a musician enjoys playing instruments live for an audience, we can say that they are courageous, because it takes courage to perform in front of people.

So, while a person might say they simply like playing a musical instrument, we can infer that as a musician, they are creative, sensitive, technical-minded, and courageous.

We can also separate our identity from others by our habits. What we do every day, sometimes without thinking, can be self-defining. When we look at our habitual behaviors, we can ask ourselves why we do them and learn something about ourselves.

For example: If we read before bed, we can infer that we like to be quietly entertained while we wind down for the night. Many book readers are introverts, so we can also infer that we may be an introvert. And by looking at what kind of stories we read, whether they are mysteries or thrillers or light novels, we can see what kind of person we are because of what kind of books we enjoy and find relaxing.

Wherever you are now, stop and ask yourself:

What are my favorite things?

What is my favorite food? Favorite color?

What is my favorite song? Favorite musical artist?

When I am most happy, what am I usually doing?

All of these interests separate us from the fold. Our identity can be broken down into hundreds of things we enjoy or are interested in.

Take this early period in your journey to get to know yourself. Notice when you are happy and when you are not, and what you are doing when you experience these emotions. Think about what makes you different from others around you or even what you have in common with others. Notice your habits and ask yourself where you learned them. Think about your interests and hobbies and what they say about your identity.

To strengthen our identity, we should make a habit of reminding ourselves about our positive qualities. Every survivor is different, so only you will know what will work best for you, but encourage yourself to pick a few traits you like about yourself and say them, either out loud or in your mind, or write them somewhere you will see them often. You might enjoy using a dry-erase board to write these affirmations or use sticky notes to place your affirmations on your bathroom mirror. That way, when you look at your reflection, you can associate your own image with positive qualities. This will promote a strong sense of self and will slowly define your identity as you grow.

If you have a hard time creating your own affirmations, stick to the qualities that all exploitation survivors possess:

I am smart

I am resilient

I am strong

I am worthy of respect

I am brave

… Because you are.

Prompt Questions:

1. How would you describe yourself to someone who may not know you well?

2. What are your favorite things? Top five favorite movies? TV shows? Musical artists?

3. Do you have a hard time defining who you are?

4. Is it more difficult to define who you are or what you like? Why?

Author's experience:

Even though I had a really full life before I was exploited, my trauma was so strong that I had a tough time defining who I was or what I liked when I entered recovery. I didn't even know what food I liked, or what my favorite color was, because everything was decided for me! My abuser controlled my diet, so I never got to pick out what I wanted at restaurants, and I only had an understanding about what colors looked good on me, not what colors I actually liked.

Now I can say I love hot wings and Japanese food, and my favorite color is purple. I have a hard time talking about myself, but I can say that I am a good listener, I am very creative, and I am loyal to those whom I love.

Challenge:

Challenge yourself to think of three traits which describe you, and list three of your most favorite things.

2

Self-Care

When we set our sights on independence, we will find that our daily schedules will grow, our calendars will fill up fast, and we will constantly be looking to the next step, and the next, and the next, and each step will bring more questions and more to do. Though our instinct may be to work harder and harder, taking less time for ourselves, we will find that when we are overworked and do not spend any time nurturing our personal needs, it will be more difficult to keep up with our goals or maintain our motivation. This is why we practice self-care: deliberately doing activities that take care of our physical and emotional well-being. Self-care will become our tool that we call on, especially when our responsibilities grow and develop.

During exploitation, we may have been made to feel guilty for doing anything simply to take care of ourselves, or perhaps the life we lived beforehand that led to our trauma was overwhelming, because meeting the demands of daily life can be challenging for anyone. Whenever you find yourself facing challenges that you must take on, ask yourself: What small things can I do to make this process easier?

While self-care can be as simple as setting boundaries with yourself—getting enough sleep every night, not hanging out with people who use hateful or degrading verbiage—encourage yourself to create your own self-care activities so that you develop a strong, nurturing relationship with yourself. Doing small, enjoyable, and relaxing things by ourselves (and for ourselves) gives us the refreshment and peace we need in our lives while reminding us that we are worthy of this kind of love and care.

Some activity ideas may include:

- Taking a bubble bath
- Going on a walk
- Watching a funny movie or video that makes us laugh
- Giving yourself a manicure or pedicure
- Cooking something delicious
- Reading
- Listening to your favorite music
- Dancing, singing
- Playing a game or sport (for example, shooting hoops, playing Sudoku)
- Crafting: Scrapbooking, knitting, sewing, crocheting

If you look at the suggestions above and don't see anything that suits you, look at things you have done in the past. What kind of things did you do before to cheer yourself up or relax? Self-care is often something we have done before without realizing, but making those past behaviors into activities that we deliberately make time for can be very healing and improve our overall mood and outlook on life.

As your daily agenda grows, it will become difficult to make time to do these activities often. It is best to find the right activities for you early on in your recovery, so when your days get busy, you'll have no trouble starting in on your self-care. It should become a comforting habit, an effortless activity we do to refresh ourselves.

When we start practicing self-care, especially when we start to develop our own activity ideas, we will experience some benefits. We may experience an elevation in our spirits and overall shift in attitude and outlook, but it's also important to note that self-care helps our relationships in social, educational, or workplace settings as well as improves our stamina and ability to complete tasks thoroughly. If we are constantly on the go with no relaxation besides when we are asleep, we may become agitated and unfocused. We need time to ourselves in order to give other people and commitments the attention they deserve.

Self-care activities should NOT:

- Involve drugs, alcohol, or addictive behaviors: Keep in mind that when giving up addictive substances or behaviors, as most of us should when we enter recovery, it may take a while to get our bearings; but ideally, we should be present, conscious, and sober in order to experience true healing from self-care.
- Involve any form of work: We should not consider any activity we do for employment to be a part of our self-care routine. We must keep work and self-care separate.
- Be forced: While certain activities may be relaxing for others, they can be stressful for us. You should not pick a self-care activity that you don't actually want to do, so make sure your activity is truly enjoyable, easy, and calming.
- Be spontaneous: Planning ahead for your self-care activities, meaning to make sure you will have enough time, space, etc., will be more rewarding than doing an activity spontaneously in which your time may be cut short.

- Be done in place of seeking professional assistance: While self-care is healing, every survivor should make an effort to find the right psychotherapist for their needs and get medical attention from a doctor as needed.

As this period passes, challenge yourself to do at least one activity for your enjoyment and relaxation, even if it's just a single twenty-minute activity. Notice how you feel before and after. Do you feel better, or the same? Would you want to try something different next time? Would you rather give yourself more time or less time than you did? Even if you chose the wrong activity or didn't have enough time during your self-care, your effort will not be wasted, because treating yourself with kindness and love alone speaks volumes about your respect for yourself (and for others).

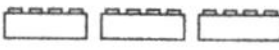

If anyone deserves to give themselves some tender love and care, it's you. Survivors of exploitation often spend many months and years putting themselves last. We might have taken care of our family, our significant others, or filled our responsibility to earn more and more money before we paid any attention to our own needs. We have also fought very hard to leave exploitation, so now it's time to give ourselves a metaphorical "hug" in the form of relaxation and doing one small thing that makes us happy. It might feel silly and awkward at first, but that's okay and totally normal. Soon, self-care will come naturally and be a strong, grounding anchor in your daily life.

PROMPT QUESTIONS:

1. Have you done self-care in the past, perhaps without realizing it?

2. What form of self-care works for you?

3. Have you tried a self-care activity in the past and realized it was just not right for you personally? Why do you think that is?

4. Do you know for a fact that a certain self-care activity won't work for you? Why?

5. How can the choices we make and the boundaries we set in life be a form of self-care? Can you think of any examples of this?

AUTHOR'S EXPERIENCE:

I know some things are not relaxing for me. I do not like Sudoku, and I do not like "peaceful" music. Watching a murder mystery is way more relaxing to me than meditation.

Something I didn't go into detail about in this chapter is how our choices can be a form of self-care. We choose not to do things that will drain us, or we learn to say no when we know something is not good for us.

As you begin employment, your work team is going to ask a lot from you. You don't have to say yes to everything. If they want you to cover their shift but it's your one day off for the whole week, say no! You probably can't get out of doing your work as it is given to you, but you can say no to going above and beyond, and that's not selfish. That's taking care of yourself and your needs so you can eventually be a better employee.

CHALLENGE:

Do at least one activity for your enjoyment and relaxation, and try to remember how it made you feel, and how you felt before and afterwards. Keep in mind that you want to pick an activity that you can do often with little effort!

3

Positive Self-Talk

While gaining independence is empowering, the long road ahead of us can be discouraging at times. Sometimes we can only see the possibility of defeat when we face our challenges, and we start to internalize all that we do wrong or incorrectly. We will put effort forth only to make mistakes, and subsequently think we are not good enough or scrutinize all our flaws and shortcomings. This is especially true for survivors of sexual exploitation, as we often suffered severe consequences for our mistakes, which encapsulated negative views of ourselves, developed an unhealthy perspective of ourselves and our bodies, and shamed our abilities when we did not meet unrealistic expectations or do everything perfect the first time.

Now, if this reflection of your past rings true to you, you might already find yourself shaming your negative attitude and criticizing yourself for not doing a good job at being kind to yourself. Know that you are not alone in this. When we have spent such a long time criticizing ourselves and believing the criticism of others, it is only natural to continue doing so when we try to shift our attitude. It's important, however, to recognize this behavior for what it is—an old habit that never made us feel good—and instead, find our identity outside of nitpicking what we see as flaws.

When we do feel down on ourselves or start to feel insecure about any aspect of our lives, we should try to combat this negativity with positive self-talk, creating a strong inner message that reminds us of all the good things we truly are. We can engage in positive self-talk in many ways. Affirmations alone may be enough to pick our spirits up, repeating to ourselves that we are smart, strong, resilient survivors.

But many of us might find some affirmations feel false or phony at first. After all, if we have spent the entirety of our trauma believing that we are not good enough, rotating between focusing on our shortcomings and struggling to make ends meet in ways that do not empower us, we will find it hard to believe that we are, in fact, good enough, let alone smart or strong. These deep emotional wounds are normal for survivors of exploitation, and they can take a long time to heal. The best way to work toward healing is to take one step at a time. Even if you make small steps, at the very least you're stepping forward.

As time passes and you progress in your journey, challenge yourself to reverse your negative views of yourself into positive views. For every flaw you find, try to find the silver lining. Make an effort to see your pain as lessons which taught you how to become the stronger, wiser person you are now.

Here are some examples of how to turn around negative thoughts:

- I have too much to do = I still have lots of time to improve everything in my life
- I find others around me annoying = I have a hard time empathizing with difficult people, but I will try to anyway
- I am tired = I have worked hard today and deserve rest

- I have a lot of issues = I have learned a lot about myself and others in my lifetime
- I am nowhere near what I used to be like = I have improved immensely
- I am sad = My emotions are strong because I am strong
- I am scared = I am wise and know how to protect myself now
- I am lonely = I am independent and I only let others who are worthy of my respect in my circle
- I am impulsive = I am spontaneous and I know what I want
- I have been hurt deeply by others = I have learned valuable lessons about the value of my trust and safety

This is why we don't identify ourselves as victims of exploitation; we are survivors. Though we have endured some very traumatic events, we see the fact that we lived to tell the tale as more important than the trauma itself. Many individuals have a hard time leaving exploitation, and yet we did it anyway. Our choice to rebuild our lives is what makes us strong, and it speaks volumes about our character, whether we believe it or not.

PROMPT QUESTIONS:

1. We have all been through a lot of traumatic stuff. What helps you stay positive?

2. Have you ever challenged a negative thought before? What was that process like?

3. Do you feel that positive affirmations feel honest or phony? Why?

4. Do you notice that your recovery is easier or harder as you progress? Why?

5. Can you think of one way you can reframe your perception of a challenge in your life? Or if you can't, think of one negative thing that's on your mind and try to reframe it positively.

AUTHOR'S EXPERIENCE:

I will say that looking in the mirror and saying "You are beautiful" over and over does not feel genuine to me. It feels phony, because I am still working on my insecurities and self-confidence. However, I do challenge myself to reframe what my anxieties are. If I am worrying about the worst possible thing happening to me, I ask myself, "What is the best thing that could happen to me?"

CHALLENGE:

Reverse at least one negative view of yourself and your situation into a positive view.

4

EARLY STEPS TO TAKE

By the end of the first month in recovery, you may become eager to start tackling all you need to do in order to gain independence. This is a good sign! While it is important to reflect and regroup your daily life as thoroughly as possible early on, there are a few things you can do to get started within the first few months.

However, remember that every survivor grows at their own rate, and our circumstances are always different. Deciphering which steps you should take early on should be a personal choice, but encourage yourself to look into the following life steps:

Medical Attention

Though many who have suffered trauma have understandable anxieties about hospitals and the medical system in general, it is important to get a checkup once you start rebuilding your life. In the long run, it will help if you get any injury or medical condition you might have as a result of your trauma looked at by a professional as soon as possible. Medical professionals will be able to put these conditions and any subsequent treatments into terms that you can understand and work with. Once they do, you can easily incorporate whatever treatment may be needed with the rest of your healing.

If you are coming out of exploitation without any insurance or employer who would provide it, apply for health insurance through your local Health and Human Services office. You can partner with a caseworker, employed through the office, who will help you navigate this process and take you step by step through everything you must complete to become insured. This can be a monotonous experience, but it is definitely better than getting hefty emergency room bills in the future without being covered.

Mental Health Care

Every sexual exploitation survivor should try to find a mental health therapist who can work through their trauma with them as soon as possible. This does not necessarily mean that something is wrong with survivors or that they are "crazy," but talking to an expert in psychology can help put your emotions and behaviors in terms which allow you to manage them properly. Talking to your friends and loved ones can be healing, but talking to a mental health professional can provide you with workable solutions to your problems.

Finding the right therapist can be tricky. Ideally, you want a psychologist who is easy to talk to, who is trauma-informed and understands the cause and effect of traumatic experiences as well as post-traumatic behaviors, and who introduces you to tools you find helpful in coping with any trauma-related issues. You may not find your ideal therapist right away, and even if you do, you might not see results right away. As long as you stay present and engaged in this process, you will make the right decision and get the healing you need.

Volunteering

Volunteering has a number of benefits for survivors who have no work history and few safe interactions with the rest of the world. First and foremost, volunteering allows you to interact in a work environment with others in a safe way without having to commit to a full-time schedule. It can also give you employment history, professional references, and job skills which will help when your journey requires you to find work.

Consider volunteering at a place where you have interests similar to those who are being employed or served, or where you will be able to gain skills you want to have in the future. Church offices are great places to brush up on clerical skills, libraries have volunteer opportunities all the time, and community gardens allow you to be outside and around nature, which is healing to many survivors. Use your imagination! Call around to any organization that interests you and ask if they have volunteer opportunities available.

Defining Your Social Circle and Setting Boundaries

We don't always get to choose who we interact with, especially when we are in the vulnerable position of leaving exploitation and starting recovery, but we do have the right to privacy if someone from our past, whom we are not living with or interacting with on a daily basis, makes us feel uncomfortable or hinders our daily healing. Consider taking a break from talking to old friends or loved ones who do this. This does not mean you must permanently cut them off, but while you are healing, you may want to spend more time discovering and honoring yourself before you're ready to help heal others who are also being affected by the trauma you survived.

If you are starting your healing in a recovery group or recovery housing, keep in mind that other survivors deserve that right to privacy as well. Stronger connections are formed with trust, and trust takes lots of time to build, especially when our trust has been severely broken by sexual exploitation. Our peers can be our strongest support, but we must be patient with them. We will all share our own version of testimony when we are ready, and we should only do this if we feel safe.

As you move forward with your journey, remember to implement the self-care tools you have learned so far. Remember to use affirmations, whether in written messages or in speaking them to yourself, to remind you that you got this: that you're a strong, smart survivor who is worthy of respect and capable of success. When you feel overworked, remember to practice self-care. When you're feeling down, look at what is making you feel this way and reframe it in a way that helps you grow.

No survivor's journey toward independence is easy, and often as we progress in our healing, more challenges will begin to surface. When we are stuck in those challenges, remember to look both ways: Look forward to your complete independence and keep your eye on the prize. Visualize the kind of life you want and take baby steps toward it until you've met each goal. Then, look at how far you have come. Even though you may not be where you want to be, every single day we spend independently, free from exploitation, is a victory in itself. Celebrate those victories!

PROMPT QUESTIONS:

1. Have you tried any of these steps within the first month of your journey? What was that experience like?

2. How many of these steps are realistic for you to take right now?

3. Have you experienced roadblocks when trying to take early steps in your recovery? Did you ask for help or were you able to overcome the roadblocks on your own?

4. What is a plan to get past the most immediate roadblocks you see?

AUTHOR'S EXPERIENCE:

A lot of the reason I was able to find employment right away was due to volunteering. Because of my exploitation, I had huge gaps in my résumé that I could not explain away. You might be able to explain away a month, but if it's a few months, or a few years, you want to cover your bases.

I was always an active volunteer. Before I was ever exploited, I ran the door at a music venue. I was responsible for checking IDs and taking money for tickets. I got to see free shows and free art exhibits. It was awesome. They never paid me, but I was able to get work references and fill my résumé. So, by the time I applied for my first job when I was in residential treatment, I had no gaps in my résumé and got a job within a few weeks.

CHALLENGE:

Look around and ask yourself if you have taken any first steps toward your recovery. What are the steps you have taken? What step do you think you will take next? Challenge yourself to take that next step!

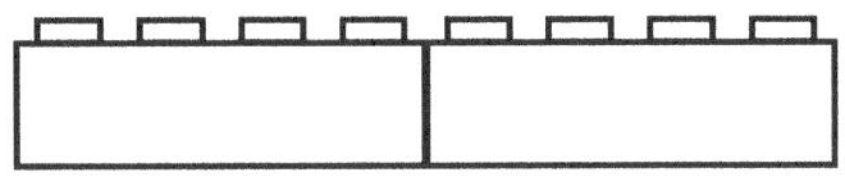

Recognizing, Understanding, and Managing Trauma Behaviors

5

IDENTIFYING TRAUMA SYMPTOMS AND BEHAVIORS

Wherever you are, wherever you're reading this chapter, take a few minutes to notice your surroundings. Are you sitting on a chair or lying on a couch? Can you feel the weight of your body gently pressing you to whatever surface you are resting on? Notice your breathing. Is it slow? Is it rapid? How does it feel to take a deep breath?

By simply observing the world you are in at the most basic level, noting your physical relation to everything around you, or by focusing your attention on your breathing, you are practicing grounding. This is something you can do anywhere, anytime. This will become the backbone of your coping.

As we explore trauma symptoms that are common with survivors, we may feel triggered just by thinking about what the symptoms are and how they might affect us now. If we begin to feel anxious, worried, or feel our mind wander to traumatic memories, we must revert to grounding: Put this book down, take a deep, slow breath, then another, and another, and as you breathe, either count the seconds as each deep breath goes in and out, or start to make observations as you breathe. Say quietly to yourself: *I am sitting, my back touches the back of the chair, the room is quiet, the walls in the room are blue,* and so on, until you are calm and ready to continue learning.

Many who have experienced traumatic events will tell you that those experiences seem to change the way our body reacts to any new form of stress. This is especially true for survivors of exploitation. Survivors are often not strangers to sexual assault and have experienced threats to their life or safety from their abusers or other individuals.Unfortunately, the fear we experience from threats tends to be frequent when we are exploited, and if we also have trouble getting our basic needs met, our fear and stress responses may increase. For the duration of our exploitation, we learned to function in survival mode. Because we had to.

While the benefits of an adrenaline rush (open airways, extra blood pumped to muscles, heightened awareness and focus) may be helpful while we are experiencing an immediate threat to our life, it takes some time for our body to unlearn this process when we start our recovery, and we may find that even small stressors may put us back in survival mode. It takes some practice to manage this, and the first step is understanding what trauma symptoms are and why survivors of exploitation experience them. Of the many trauma symptoms that may occur, following are some of the most common:

Common Trauma Symptoms

Hypervigilance

When you walk into the grocery store, or any public place, do you keep your eye on the door? Do you watch other people present who look suspicious? Do you find that everyone looks suspicious? Do you glance over your shoulder frequently? Are you scanning the room so often that you forget what you're doing, or have a hard time paying attention to what you're shopping for? When someone approaches you, do you jump or are you startled? Do you constantly think you see someone you know that you don't want to see? Do you find that you're scanning the room for your abuser?

These habits we have when we are in public places can be encapsulated into one trauma symptom: hypervigilance. Even once we are in a safe place, we may be fearful that we will face danger again, so we remain hyperaware of our surroundings in order to protect ourselves.

Flashbacks

When something reminds you of your trauma, does your mind start to wander? Do you become overwhelmed with the vivid memory of the experience? Is this memory so strong that you forget who you were talking to, what you were talking about, or what you were supposed to be doing?

Flashbacks often don't feel like they are portrayed in film and on television. It can be as simple as having a strong, disturbing memory that disorients you from whatever activity you are doing. It can be simply annoying, or incredibly scary. When you have flashbacks, it feels as if you are reliving the traumatic event over and over again.

Panic Attacks or Anxiety Attacks

When you get nervous or worried, does your heart beat faster and faster? Does your face flush as all the blood rushes to your head? Do you find it hard to breathe, or do you hyperventilate? Do you have tunnel vision, or does your vision become altered? Do body pains, such as chest pains, accompany this response?

Anxiety can disrupt our daily lives and may lead to panic attacks. We may be feeling like what we would imagine a heart attack would feel like, but it is important to remember this is a fear response. Our brain tells our body that we are in danger when we feel a stressor, but unless we do find ourselves in a life-threatening situation, we must remember that panic attacks pass, and grounding ourselves with mindful observation or breathing may be enough to slow our heart rate. If you do feel like you are having a heart attack, you should seek medical attention as soon as possible.

Isolation

Once you have found a safe space to live, do you find it hard to leave? Would you spend hours or even days in your room if you could? Is this habit coupled with depression? Is your sleep pattern altered, meaning sleeping too much or not being able to sleep?

Isolation is our brain's way of trying to subconsciously protect us from danger. We may have the fear, in the back of our head, that leaving will put us at risk of facing traumatic situations again. It may also be a way to avoid confronting our emotional issues.

Ruminating

When you are alone, do you constantly think about negative things or harp on mistakes you've made? Do you have detailed thoughts about things that may happen if you make a mistake again? Do these negative thoughts repeat in a cycle of one negative thought after another? Do you find this cycle lasting for long periods?

Ruminating is repetitively thinking about the causes and consequences of our actions for prolonged periods of time. Sometimes, those who experience rumination feel crippled by these anxious thoughts and it becomes hard to leave where they are or even move when their brain is going through this repetitive cycle.

Nightmares

Do you find that you often have vivid, disturbing dreams? Are these dreams about your abuser or about exploitation? If they are not, do you have dreams that you are running from something, being chased by something, or otherwise trying to escape a grave danger?

Nightmares are incredibly common for survivors of exploitation. They can interrupt our sleep or cause us to avoid sleep altogether. In the next section, we will explore what to do once you experience a nightmare, but in the meantime, practicing grounding and self-care can help calm your mind and body.

Explosive Anger

Do you find yourself getting disproportionately angry about a situation that wouldn't normally make you angry? Do you lash out at people when it is not necessary? Did this heightened temper coincide with the big life step of leaving your trauma?

Like many stress responses, explosive anger is our subconscious way of protecting ourselves from harm, but instead of running from the stressor, our brain wants to fight it out. We don't want to be hurt again, and so we may attack our problems, or bystanders, head-on without realizing we don't have to fight in that particular situation.

Dissociating

When you are facing a tough stressor, do you simply go through the motions? Do you say all the right things, do all the correct things, but afterwards, you realize you don't even know what just happened? Is your mind so involved in your trauma and potential stressors that you are unaware of what's going on now? Or when you are facing something tough, do you just go completely numb?

Dissociation is when our body is one place but our mind is miles away. This is a defense mechanism we use when current stressors are so upsetting that our brain temporarily shuts off. We start thinking about other things, or simply go numb, in order to survive the stressor at hand.

Psychosis

Hallucinations and delusions pertaining to your trauma would include seeing things that aren't there, hearing things that aren't there, and believing things that aren't true. That last one is tricky, because sometimes we are extra paranoid after trauma, and rightfully so. If you start to experience hallucinations or delusions, you must seek a mental health professional immediately. These are serious symptoms that can affect your health and safety. If all else fails, check yourself into the emergency room.

As survivors, we are strong because we live with the memory and effects of traumatic experiences that most people won't ever have to deal with, and yet we choose to live amongst them in the general public. In many cases, we have looked in the face of near-death experiences, physical assault, poverty and homelessness, or addiction, and even though we might have been scared at the time, we made it past those moments, taking one step forward at a time as those experiences become mere memories. Around our second month in recovery, we all feel like we have a long way to go, but we must not forget that we have also come a long, long way. Simply allowing those experiences to become memories and making choices to live a healthy, independent life is a huge step!

Trauma symptoms come up fast. In order to move forward with our goals, we must become expert in our individual trauma symptoms, both in understanding and recognizing what they are and how to take care of them once they confront us. As you progress in your recovery, challenge yourself to recognize trauma symptoms and behaviors as they surface, and reflect on your past behaviors that might have been symptoms of trauma. What are they? Which ones are more likely to happen to you? If you do become triggered, practice grounding and then self-care until you are at a place where you can move on with your daily life. Working through our trauma can be tough, but it is necessary to gain complete healing. If you haven't started to work with a mental health professional yet, as mentioned in early steps from the previous chapter, this is a place you can find more tools to combat any symptoms of trauma you may experience.

PROMPT QUESTIONS:

1. Go through each trauma symptom and ask yourself if any ring true for you. What trauma symptoms have you experienced? How did you handle them in the moment?

2. Do you have trouble understanding any particular symptom? What about that particular symptom confuses you?

3. In recovery or in other settings, have you ever seen someone else experience one of these symptoms? What happened? What did you do?

4. Why do you think we experience trauma symptoms when our past is behind us?

5. When you are experiencing any trauma symptom, what has helped you bring yourself back into the present moment?

AUTHOR'S EXPERIENCE:

A few of the things I experienced, ESPECIALLY early on in my recovery:

Flashbacks. I was in my room in residential treatment and I was just replaying over and over how my abuser was screaming at me and trying to choke me unconscious.

Hypervigilance. I remember the way it was when I was first at residential treatment; they would drop you off at the grocery store by yourself and meet you when it was time to check out. I was frozen in fear. I was in a new place, and I felt like my abuser could be around any corner. I couldn't even pick out too many things to eat at home. It was really intense.

Sometimes I still have trauma symptoms, but they are much less frequent or intense than when I first left exploitation. And I have so many tools to help me now that I am rarely incapacitated by a symptom.

CHALLENGE:

Challenge yourself to recognize trauma symptoms and behaviors as they surface. Reflect on past behaviors that might have been symptoms of trauma. What are they? Which ones are more likely to happen to you?

6

Emotional Tools

As you have learned about some common trauma symptoms, you have probably noticed that some apply to you and some do not, or perhaps you've experienced some of them but not consistently. (For example, though some trauma survivors have experienced panic attacks, they might not happen all the time.) And sometimes, being stable in recovery is enough to calm most symptoms.

When symptoms do surface, they often occur when we are not prepared to drop everything and do self-care for several hours, and as our recovery progresses, we will gain more responsibilities and have less time to process each overwhelming emotional response. But there are plenty of tools you can use to work through intense emotions without completely halting your activities, or to at least calm your brain and body so that you can go on with your day until you do have time to process what you felt. You have already learned the basic principles of grounding (physical observations of your surroundings, checking in with your body, bringing your attention to your breath) and how important self-care and positive affirmations can be. The following emotional tools will take your coping skills one step further:

Take a Short Break

You may not always have an infinite amount of time to kill, but when experiencing trauma symptoms, it may be helpful to take a five- or ten-minute break. Excuse yourself from whatever activity is triggering you, go to a quiet, private space, and take a break. During this break, do not process your emotions or mentally solve your problems. If possible, don't do anything at all! Within the time you have, try to let all your thoughts and concerns dissipate and focus on your breath, on observing your surroundings, or simply find a spot on the ground and focus your vision on it until you calm down.

We do this because it is very hard to solve problems and think critically when we are experiencing trauma symptoms, but fortunately, if you give it some time, trauma symptoms pass. We should not push ourselves into fight-or-flight mode while we are facing conflict. Wait out your symptoms on your break, and then once your heart rate slows down along with your thoughts, you can sufficiently face the conflict.

Best-Case Scenario and Worst-Case Scenario

A person affected by trauma may confront conflict with a sense of panic, even if we don't outwardly express our distress. If you find yourself jumping to the worst possible conclusion, ask yourself: In this predicament, (a) What is the worst possible outcome? (b) What is the best possible outcome? (c) Is the worst possible outcome something I can deal with? (d) What is most likely to actually happen?

As a survivor of exploitation, you have probably survived some pretty horrible stuff, and yet you got past it all and went on with your life. If we keep this in mind while we look at the outcome we are fearing, we will often find that it's something we are capable of overcoming with flying colors. Also, entertaining the idea that something good or even GREAT might come from what you're concerned about will start to open doors for more positivity to flow into your thought process. But, what we usually find, once we start thinking logically instead of thinking in a panic state, is that the worst possible outcome is more unlikely than we think.

Fact-Checking

When our brain is so used to processing trauma, we often jump to extremes. We may think that we must mentally prepare for bad things to happen, or we start to look for reasons why those bad things will happen, even going so far as to feel that everyone and everything is intentionally working against us.

If you start to feel like this, consider checking your facts. Think about why you're thinking what you are thinking, or what evidence led you to think those thoughts. And ask yourself: If you were in your friend's shoes, would you think that others were working against them? Imagine that you are on the outside looking in at your situation, and question if this is your trauma thought process talking or if what you're concerned about is a rational concern. If the concern is rational, you can take the necessary steps to address the issue, but if it's your trauma or panic mind talking, you will know to shift your focus to calming yourself down by doing basic grounding.

Engaging the Five Senses

This exercise is a great tool to use when you are in the middle of a task and can't really step away to do meditation. When you are feeling stressed, take a deep breath and identify the following:

- Five things you can see
- Four things you can physically, tangibly feel

- Three things you can hear
- Two things you can smell
- And one thing you can taste.

All the while, keep breathing deeply and gently observe your environment. This quick self-check-in is designed to get out of your worrying headspace and into your body, in the present environment.

Useful Distractions

When we are facing a trauma symptom, we might find that there is not much we can do at that moment to address our concerns, or perhaps we are so wound up by our symptoms that we cannot think critically or logically. Instead of focusing on your hardships, engage your brain in something totally unrelated to your present life.

Play a game (Sudoku, crossword, etc.), watch a detective mystery show, do crafting such as scrapbooking, or take on any activity that completely takes your mind off your concern. Taking a step outside of your bubble until you calm down can allow you to come back to your concern or trigger with a fresh perspective instead of a trauma perspective and can help you address your concerns more effectively.

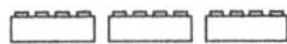

None of these emotional tools are the be-all and end-all of every individual symptom, and you should think critically about which emotional tool or tools will work best for you personally. While those who are prone to rumination may not want to sit quietly for several minutes because it can be hard to quiet their minds, those who often isolate might not want to engage in useful distractions as much because it can lead them to avoiding problems altogether.

Find some time, when you are thinking logically and calmly, to decide what may work best for you and plan to use that tool if you experience a trauma symptom. If the one you pick doesn't work, try a different tool. You might find, as you practice using multiple emotional tools, that your brain gets tired of trying out different things, and the trauma symptom dissipates on its own, simply because the time passes!

The most important thing to remember is that most trauma symptoms will lessen with time. As you progress in your recovery from sexual exploitation, you will get more and more healing under your belt, and though it may be stressful at times, your life will be more functional and less problematic than when you were living a lifestyle where you were constantly taken advantage of. Consider celebrating small victories: When you get through a trauma symptom and get back to a calm state, or when you go a whole day without having severe trauma symptoms, take note of this, give yourself a positive affirmation, and reward yourself with some self-care. Conditioning yourself to view your internal conflict resolution as a good thing not only helps your self-esteem, but it also shows you how smart and capable you are of solving problems.

PROMPT QUESTIONS:

1. Have you tried any of these tools in the past, perhaps without realizing it?

2. Which of these techniques are you more likely to use? Why?

3. What have you done in the past when you experienced a big stressor or trauma symptom? Was what you did helpful or not helpful?

4. What do you usually do when you are confronted with a trauma symptom?

5. Are there any emotional tools listed in this chapter that you know won't work for you? Why do you think that is?

AUTHOR'S EXPERIENCE:

When having anxiety, I like to use:

Best possible scenario and worst possible scenario—because the worst scenario is often not as bad as you'd think.

Fact-checking—because if you stop and think about the logistics of whatever issue is at play, you will realize there isn't always evidence to substantiate your worries.

Five senses—you can do this when you're working, when you're at school, or when you're in an argument. It doesn't take a lot of effort, but the results are very grounding.

These are really practical emotional exercises that you can do by yourself in a quick manner. You don't always have time to sit and do a yoga meditation, especially when you are working, taking care of children, and/or going to school!

CHALLENGE:

Challenge yourself to pick one emotional tool and either write it down or memorize it. Maybe you will use it, maybe you won't. But either way, keep it in mind in case you start to have a panic attack or experience any other trauma symptom.

7

UNDERSTANDING TRAUMA SYMPTOMS

By the time you have reached this chapter, you have made the consistent choice to leave an entire way of life behind you and build a new one, no matter how hard it has been. As you've followed this guide, you've learned basic fundamentals of self-care, grounding, and how to identify certain behaviors as trauma symptoms, which you are learning to effectively manage.

But we might be asking ourselves why we react with those behaviors, or question what made us react that way in the first place. Some of us might even find it difficult to understand whether or not we have actually been exploited, perhaps because of the way others may have normalized their abuse to us. Often, there is a history of neglect or abuse that preceded our exploitation, and the exploitation merely confirmed the negative ways in which we already viewed ourselves. We learned to accept abuse as "normal."

What Does Sexual Exploitation Mean?

To understand why we are affected by trauma symptoms after we have survived exploitation, we must understand what exploitation is: Sexual exploitation is the act of abusing or exploiting another person's sexuality for personal gain, profit, or advantage. This can happen in the workplace, in sex work or escorting, in the pornography industry, on the streets, in the music and entertainment industry, in abusive family life, or even in cults. This process usually involves coercion, meaning that the perpetrator will persuade a person to actively participate in their own exploitation by use of force, threats, or lies. Exploitation abuse is often an extremely nuanced process, which can make it very difficult for a survivor to overcome.

Though we use the word "exploitation" to describe the way our sexuality has been violated, it is important to understand that abusers often try to exploit a variety of our needs and vulnerabilities. They may have exploited our need for housing, income, our addiction issues, or even our needs for emotional support and romantic affection. Exploitation is not necessarily facilitated only by one person, but can be done by a group of people, an institution, or a collective, and some individuals who go into sex work are also exploited by consumers, not necessarily by one perpetrator.

Whoever spots your vulnerability and classifies it as something they can take advantage of for their own gain is an exploiter. This book will explore what abuse is in detail within a few chapters, but for now, we only need to understand that our exploitation probably involved multiple forms of abuse and grasp how that trauma may affect our lives in the future. It can change the way we form romantic relationships, the way we form friendships, the way we work, and can warp our overall attitude and philosophy about different aspects of life.

The trauma behaviors we experience, when we are no longer in exploitation, are often a result of prolonged exposure to trauma in our past. These behaviors and habits commonly linger in our lives even though we may be safe in recovery:

- We become hypervigilant because we have experienced situations in the past where we weren't aware of our surroundings, and something terrible happened to us.
- We experience panic attacks because our brain has become programmed by our trauma to kick-start our fight-or-flight response whenever we come in contact with a stressor, even though the stressor may, in actuality, be insignificant.
- We isolate ourselves to avoid experiencing stressors.
- And flashbacks allow our brains to scan through all the bad things we have gone through to remember how we survived them, similar to how dissociation provides us a mental escape from confronting our fears or stressors.

Sexual abuse can play a role in this, as does emotional, mental, physical, financial, and verbal abuse, and so does having our rights or basic needs withheld by abusers.

If you can find it in your heart to believe this, know that the light at the end of the tunnel is burning brightly. Since exploitation affects every social class, race, ethnicity, sexual orientation, and gender, there are also *survivors* of every possible background who have gone beyond coping with trauma and have become successful, independent people who are constantly changing the world. You are already on that path, though it may not always feel so. Trauma is painful, and sometimes, recovering from trauma is equally painful, but every step we take forward is worthy of positive acknowledgment and even celebration.

It is important to remember, however, that as common as trauma symptoms are for most survivors, they can be serious and indicate the need for professional assistance. Always consult a licensed therapist whenever symptoms become unmanageable.

As this section goes on, remember that your trauma is behind you, even though you may still feel its effects. When your symptoms come up, recognize them and understand why you're feeling the way you're feeling, but challenge yourself to move forward with your daily life, even if it is by mere inches at a time. Inching forward is still moving.

PROMPT QUESTIONS:

1. Without going into detail about your exploitation, what has exploitation changed about either the way you think or the way you act?

2. Is that change something you can live with, or would you like to change that about yourself? Do you see that as something you can realistically change back, or change for the better?

3. Can you recognize when a trauma symptom is so serious that you would need professional assistance? When would that be the case?

4. Is there anything positive about the way your trauma has shaped you?

5. What trauma-related behavior do you want to unlearn, if any?

AUTHOR'S EXPERIENCE:

I have a hard time trusting anyone. I didn't even trust my boyfriend for a long time. We dated for several months until I considered him my boyfriend. So my trauma in exploitation definitely affected the way I dated people.

I have had to make changes in my life because of that. I am really weird about hugs. I am usually okay with people I know, but when it's someone I don't know or don't like, I don't want to hug them. So I usually put my hand out to shake before they can hug me.

CHALLENGE:

Challenge yourself to really reflect on the way your trauma affects your daily life. Examine your quirks and habits now, and try to connect them to your past. Where did those habits come from?

8

SELF-ACCOUNTABILITY

Though sexual exploitation recovery is only beginning to get attention from the general public, despite institutions like human trafficking being as old as civilization itself, there are many organizations throughout the world that have researched and tested what is effective in helping survivors overcome their trauma, and often the process is rigorous.

Most commonly, residential treatment programs will require you to make a variety of commitments that will completely change your daily life. It can be tough and often discourages many survivors from seeking help in the first place. On top of that, for those who actually agree to make all those commitments, housing for survivor recovery is not abundant, and there may not even be a bed available in the residential programs that do exist.

If you find yourself in the position where, for whatever reason, you cannot stay in a rigorous residential program for sexual exploitation recovery, it is best to treat your recovery as if you are your own program director, in charge of your personal healing. This involves planning, holding yourself accountable, and setting up your daily life so that you can get the healing you need while you take all the necessary steps toward independence. Even if you are in recovery housing, you are still in charge of your healing and can cheer yourself on, or at least incorporate your own self-motivation with your program's responsibilities. Ultimately, the work is yours to do, and regardless of where your healing takes place, you are accountable for you. What an opportunity and great realization!

The responsibilities within any recovery program for survivors usually require a complete lifestyle change. Understand that this is not to make your life more difficult. Programs simply want to push survivors to have success within their recovery, and there are many researched and tested methods that have brought survivors that success. Here are a few methods that can help you in your recovery, or at least help increase your odds of not experiencing trauma symptoms:

Fasting from Social Media

All those who have survived trauma and are in the first stages of recovery owe themselves an ample amount of privacy. Not only can it be beneficial to cut off your constant line of virtual communication with everyone in the entire world, but it can also help to temporarily tune out the constant stream of information that social media provides, especially if you are prone to anxiety. One harmless link may lead to another, which leads to another, and before you know it, you can be looking at something that may cause anxiety, set off a panic attack, or cause you to ruminate or dissociate.

The risk here is that you might start researching past abusers or anything about your exploitation, which can take you many steps backwards, as you see old pictures of yourself and toxic people from your exploitation. It's understandably difficult to exist without social media today, but it is certainly possible, and after you fast from it for a couple of weeks, you may find that you have a different attitude toward it in general. It's good for your safety and peace of mind.

If you are not in residential recovery that requires you to fast from social media, consider asking a friend to be an accountability partner for your social media fast. Tell them that you're avoiding social media, explain why, and ask them to encourage you to engage with them (and other safe people) offline, perhaps on the phone instead. Talk about how you can get around social media and still be able to fulfill your steps to independence, and allow yourself to open up to them when you feel like giving up on the fast. The time will come when you will be ready to rejoin social media, but it should be a deliberate, thought-out choice, and having your accountability partner weigh in on that choice will be beneficial to you.

Activity Log and Journaling

Because of the manipulation we may have experienced during our trauma, we might have trouble trusting ourselves and our own perspective, so when trauma comes up, it seems to come out of nowhere. In this situation, what we can do is keep a log of our activities: noting when we experience symptoms like rumination, panic attacks, etc., and paying attention to what we were doing, where we were, and who we were with while we experienced them. This will give us a better idea of what triggers our emotions so we can effectively manage them.

An activity log can also help us analyze when we are content or experience joy to know what activities we should engage with more often, as well as letting us know when we should keep our guard up around potential stressors. Keeping a log can be as simple as journaling what you did that day, who you were with, what the time of day was, and how it made you feel.

Sobriety

We recover from trauma most effectively when we are clean, sober, and free of addictive behaviors. In order to learn how to work through our emotions in a healthy way, we must learn coping skills that don't involve self-medicating. Especially if we have used alcohol or drugs to cope with things that have hurt us in the past, it can be hard to sit with our reflections or painful emotions and not drink or use drugs to feel better. That is totally normal, but we should not depend on substances to fix our emotions. Using them as a crutch will open our lives to dysfunction. It might be difficult now, but in the long run, it will be much easier to learn how to deal with emotions if we are able to do so soberly. This does not have to be a permanent choice, but it can be very helpful while you are actively recovering.

However, going sober is a serious decision, and if you have had a long-term dependence on any mind-altering substance, you should seek a medical professional's advice on how to go sober without compromising your health or safety. You may need additional support for recovering from substance abuse, and should plan how to incorporate that support with your exploitation recovery.

Relocating

Not only does being in close proximity to where your exploitation took place and any abusers, or others who may still be exploited, put you at risk of being reexploited and leave you in harm's way—it will also increase your exposure to triggers. You may be around the same sights, smells, and people who remind you of both the good and the bad parts of your former lifestyle. The good memories might skew your perception of your exploitation or make you miss the old days even though you know, logically, that the overall lifestyle was dangerous. The bad memories can trigger problematic stress responses, or even lead to reexploitation.

Sometimes, a clean break from your past can make a difference in your healing, or at the very least, it can cut down on trauma symptoms. It can be difficult to move away from everything we know and love, but it can also be fun and exciting. Creating your life in a new place is a healing experience for many survivors.

However, relocating is a major life decision and comes with its own setbacks. It is always best to wait until time and money allow it. A great way to relocate is to apply for a residential recovery program for survivors of exploitation in a different area, but if that is not an option, you should have a clear, thorough plan to relocate with the support and help of people you know and trust.

Go Solo

If you are coming straight out of exploitation with an active romantic partner, it is unfortunately very likely that your partner may not have your best interests at heart. Think about it: What romantic partner would watch you go through the pain of sexual exploitation and be okay with it? And even if that person is respectful, responsible, loves you, and has all the qualities you want in a significant other, you may run the risk of being with someone who wants to be depended on by someone who desperately needs their support. As you grow to be independent, you will need this person less and less, and this may make or break your relationship with them. The goal in your recovery is to focus on yourself, and someone who thrives on your codependence to them probably will not willingly support your independence.

However, there are always exceptions to this theory. While you may not want to cut your significant other off from your life permanently, consider taking a break from being actively involved in any romantic relationship activities for the beginning stages of your recovery. Being able to confidently, earnestly love yourself will help you to love others more deeply, and any partner who truly loves you will respect that boundary for the duration of the time you set.

It is important to understand that program directors do not enforce these kinds of rules simply to make you miserable. These lifestyle changes are tested and proven methods that help survivors gain healing. Fasting from social media helps protect our safety and privacy, and we recover from trauma best when we are clean and sober. There are many reasons why each choice is helpful, but in reality, these are simply steps many survivors have taken in the past and have reported as being helpful when rebuilding their lives. If you don't commit to these lifestyle changes permanently, consider trying out these choices for a few weeks, or simply long enough to feel the difference when your mind is clear and you are in a stable environment.

You might be looking at the above suggestions and think that some tactics will be helpful and some won't, or you may even think of other things you can add to your own personal recovery program. The most important person in your recovery is you, so with the support of whoever is in your recovery circle, be it your doctor, therapist, family, recovery program director, caseworker, or close friends and loved ones, design and facilitate your own healing with your best interests at heart. While support is needed for most successful recovery journeys, remember that you are ultimately accountable for yourself and your choices. Recovery can be tough, but once you start taking action in your own journey, you will find that you're more than capable of changing your life.

While this section is not necessarily about trauma recovery, many of the steps outlined in this chapter will help you heal from trauma by putting physical barriers between you and toxic environments or situations in which trauma can worsen. These suggestions are really important!

Prompt Questions:

1. What helps you stay offline? Who in your life can be a buddy who you can contact through a safe phone number or through snail mail?

2. Who, or what, can help you stay sober? Do you need professional help in dealing with substances as a coping mechanism?

3. Which do you think would be the hardest change to make? Which do you think would be the easiest?

4. Can you think of anything else in your life that would help you recover from sexual exploitation trauma? What about that would help you?

5. Which change feels impossible to make, at least at this time in your healing?

AUTHOR'S EXPERIENCE:

I have experience with relocating. I had to completely leave the environment where I lived (Northern California) and move everything down to Southern California. I was far enough away from my exploiter and other toxic people that I could really focus on my goals. In less than a year, I was financially independent.

I also had to stay offline. At the residential treatment program I was living in, we did not have restricted use of our cell phones or the internet, but social media was a big trigger for me, and I kept looking up my past abusers. So, I ended up forfeiting my internet privileges for around eight months, and that was really helpful.

One thing I don't have experience with is drug addiction, and although many people can go into adulthood as casual drinkers, I have learned, from watching other survivor sisters struggle, that there is no such thing as "casual" meth, heroin, or any hard drug use, and if you are predisposed to drug addiction, it is highly likely that you will never be able to be a casual drinker, even though alcohol is totally legal. Think really hard before you make any choices to partake in mind-altering substances, even if it is a legal and socially acceptable vice! If you can, ask a buddy whom you trust to share their opinion on what they think will work for you. Better yet, ask your doctor or therapist.

CHALLENGE:

Challenge yourself to take on one of these lifestyle changes and stick to it. If you are unsure what step to take, and you are not in a residential treatment program, ask someone you trust what may work best for you.

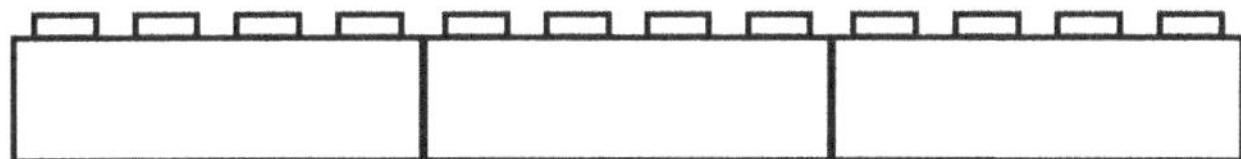

Goals

9

Overview of Goals

You can do a lot of things in exploitation recovery that will lift you to the next level of independence, but goals are what will actually get you there. Put simply, a goal is the desired outcome of our efforts. It can be as large as being a homeowner or having a career in a field that suits you, or it can be as small as cooking your favorite meal for yourself or getting through the day without a panic attack.

Goals are where we are allowed to choose what we want to do, and then break down all our desires into a handful of steps that will get us there. We can track our progress as we go, and clearly see that we have completed each step when certain things that we planned have occurred. That way, we will know that we are on the right path toward what we want to achieve and watch the path get shorter and shorter, until we get to our desired outcome.

For example: You might have the life goal to complete higher education and earn your master's degree because you want to have a well-paying job that requires education credentials, but perhaps exploitation has kept you out of school for a long time. Your academic skills may be rusty, and though you are smart, you might not be able to keep up with classmates who haven't taken a break from school like you have, or at least you may not be able to catch up at the speed you expect to.

Does this mean you can't get your degree? Absolutely not! But with all setbacks you face, you must create a plan that will get you on the path to what you want and keep you on it until you achieve it. This might involve working up to a full course load and not taking full-time units right away when you go back to school, or finding a tutor for certain subjects you know you will struggle with, or even planning on taking certain classes every semester which you enjoy and know you will pass to keep up your momentum so you don't get burned out when things get tough. YOU are in charge of your goal, and YOU know internally what you will need, so when planning your goal, you can put in all the steps you, personally, will need to take in order to meet the goal.

Why Are You Setting Your Goal?

When setting a goal, it is important to keep in mind WHY you're setting it in the first place. If you want to get your master's degree, what will that degree bring you? How will it change your life? Are you choosing to pursue a degree because you want to have that academic achievement for your own sense of accomplishment and self-worth? Or are you wanting all that a college degree will bring you: a good job, generous salary, and therefore, a higher quality of life? Is that what you really want? It may help to reflect on how you will feel once you achieve your goal, or how you want it to feel, in order to understand what you want to get out of reaching that goal. After all, our goals exist to design our ideal life. How should it feel to live your ideal life?

Emotional and Healing Goals

While it is very important to lay out a path you will take toward success and pursue each step in that path, your success can also be defined by your emotional healing. As you learn more about the way trauma affects your life, you will notice new behaviors that indicate that you are healing. Perhaps upon first entering recovery, you may have experienced a lot of flashbacks or nightmares, and after two months of recovery, you may realize that these symptoms changed, either by becoming less frequent, or less intense because of new behaviors, or from focusing on new thought patterns. Ask yourself: What will being emotionally healed look like? What will it feel like? When will you know you're getting better, and when will you know that your mental health needs more attention? Goals for your emotional healing are just as important, maybe more so in the beginning, than other more tangible goals.

Goals are something you may have pursued without realizing it. Leaving exploitation or any other traumatic environment is a goal that requires vision, planning, and taking one step at a time until you have taken back control of your life. You know you've achieved your goal of freedom when you are no longer being exploited, so think back to a few months before you started recovery and were still suffering trauma. What did it feel like? What did it look like? How is your life different now, and what did it take to get to where you stand?

Thinking about how you've achieved past goals, while consciously reflecting on the entire experience and all its feelings, will help you figure out what you will need to achieve goals in the future.

As you progress in this season of your recovery, challenge yourself to visualize your ideal life. If money was no object, nor was education, location, or circumstances, what would you want to do every day? Where would you be? Look to others whom you admire to gain inspiration: What does their daily life look like, and what did it take for them to get there?

The following few sections will cover how to choose your goals and how to break them down into steps, but for now, simply think of what you want to achieve, either in recovery or as a life goal, and ask yourself: What do you want to get out of achieving those goals, and how will that goal change your life?

PROMPT QUESTIONS:

1. Have you ever reached a goal without realizing you had even set a goal? What was that experience like for you?

2. Have you ever consciously tried to set a goal and achieved it? What was that like for you?

3. What is one goal you want to get out of your recovery during your time in residential treatment?

4. What is one emotional or healing goal you may set that you know you can reach?

5. Do you have any goals that you would like to achieve that would take longer than a few years? Have you ever thought about how to get there? What would you do?

AUTHOR'S EXPERIENCE:

My goal is to have my own grant-writing business. I know that to get there, I have to take some pretty significant steps in my life. It involves finishing school, continuing to gain experience at local nonprofits, and earning all the certifications online that I can.

But it's not just the goal of being a grant writer that I want. It is about the lifestyle that career will bring me. I want to have a life where I can support a family of four. It is having recession-proof employment. It's about having a job where I can work from home.

My emotional goal was to work on my anger and reactiveness. I am definitely still working on that.

CHALLENGE:

Challenge yourself to visualize your ideal life. What will it look like? What will it feel like? What will it take to get there?

10

Choosing Your Career and Lifestyle Goals

The last chapter prompted you to imagine the life you want to live, and hopefully, as you've reflected, you found that your ideal life isn't out of reach. If we can survive exploitation, which involves a lot of hard work, intelligence, and a LOT of courage, there isn't much we can't do!

If we are coming straight out of exploitation into recovery, chances are that we don't currently have the job we want, the living space we want, or the overall lifestyle we want, though we probably have a specific idea of what we would change about our current lives. Of all the goals we will pursue, we must think of the ultimate goal as living our best life, then split that ideal life into short-term goals which will get us there.

But you may still have some questions about what career to pursue. Once we are in recovery and start seeing our lives shift, the endless possibilities might leave us without direction. If you are still struggling to figure out which life goals will get you to your ideal life, start looking at what you are good at. When our ultimate goal is to be happy and content with our lives, we should try to center our lives around doing things that bring us joy and that we can do well.

Before we begin, be careful not to get too overwhelmed by long-term goals at this time. Although they are explained and laid out in this chapter, you are not expected to start pursuing career and lifestyle goals at this point in your healing! However, a lot of survivors get through their healing with much more ease when they see "the light at the end of the tunnel," and sometimes that "light" can be a life where you are working your dream job, truly living your best life. Start thinking about the life you want now, though it may be quite a few months before you start taking steps to get there.

Here are some examples of everyday skills and interests that many survivors excel at:

1. Social media: I have a knack for social networking. I know how to get attention with posts and am able to engage many followers.

2. Cooking: I have been cooking my whole life. I can look up any recipe online and make it look better than the picture, and it tastes amazing. I love it when people try my food and ask for seconds.

3. Styling: I have been doing my own hair for years and can easily do what others ask me to do with their hair, or ... I am a makeup guru, or ... I love shopping and always help my friends pick out the best outfits.

4. Caring: I am a good listener. I get joy from helping others, or when I speak positivity into others' lives. I am a natural at taking care of children, or taking care of the elderly.

5. Fitness: I have played sports all my life, and now the gym is my happy place. I enjoy watching my body improve, and working out puts me in a good mood.

6. Management: I have experience running a household or workplace, and people can trust me to be in charge. I am the proud CEO of my life and I like to get things done!

7. Humor: I love making people laugh. I can find the funny side of even the most difficult situations. I write funny posts on social media and love seeing "laugh" reactions.

8. Analyzing: I like watching or reading detective mysteries and trying to solve the mystery before the detectives do. I enjoy problem solving and intellectual conversations that provoke deep thinking.

9. Debating: I usually win arguments. I can be very convincing and persuasive.

All of these interests can translate to marketable skills! Though we may not immediately gain success from our hobbies, we might be able to look at our hobbies, figure out what skills it takes to do those hobbies, and apply those skills to professions that will bring us success and fulfillment.

For example: We may have a knack for social media, and although becoming a social media personality is very competitive, the skills it takes to perform well in social media involve lots of marketing expertise. We can use our eye for marketing to pursue a career in advertising. Or, if social media is your passion, many companies and organizations offer social media management positions. Those jobs are often done from home and can allow you to create your own schedule, or lead to advancement opportunities where you can work on a marketing team, which has the potential to elevate your quality of life.

Another example: Those who gain fulfillment from caring for others may want to pursue a career in medicine, either as a nurse or as a medical doctor, or if emotional support is your strength, you can pursue a career as a therapist or a psychologist.

Another example: If health and fitness are your passions, you may want to pursue a career as a personal trainer, where you will be at the gym, your second home, nearly every day and can make a living by training others' bodies.

But our hobbies don't have to dictate our career path. Instead, we can look at our hobbies, ask ourselves what skills it takes to engage in them, and apply those skills to a completely different career. While we may enjoy cooking but do not want to pursue a career as a chef, we know that cooking involves multitasking, working under pressure, time management, and many other transferable skills. We can use those skills to pursue careers that require them, including a career as a paramedic, a firefighter, a nurse, or even a producer or production assistant in television or live theatre.

By the same token, not everyone who is funny will become a successful comedian, but we know that humor requires critical thinking, seeing situations from multiple perspectives, and a high level of intellect. We can use these skills to pursue a career that requires them, including journalism or professional blogging, litigation or a career as an attorney, or even as a detective or investigative officer. We do not have to pursue our passions as professions, but they can often indicate transferable skills that we possess.

Another thing to consider is that we may not have a career in mind but do have an idea of the lifestyle goals we want to achieve. Maybe we know that we don't want to work a nine-to-five job. Maybe we work best in a graveyard shift! Or perhaps we want to eventually live in a different place than where we spend our recovery. And many survivors find that exploitation has damaged their relationship with their family and they want to have their family back in their life, be it their children or parents or both. With those lifestyle objectives, we can explore what we need to do to obtain it, and pursue careers that will allow us the stability to achieve those goals.

It may also help to make a list of pros and cons for every career and lifestyle you are considering. For every potential lifestyle option, you must consider what benefits the path will have as well as the drawbacks, and be honest with yourself when looking at both sides.

Here are some examples of pros and cons lists for two different career paths:

Pros and Cons of Being a Paramedic

The pros

- Helping others
- Using your skills
- Steady work
- Gaining medical skills

- Living wage pay
- Can support yourself
- Camaraderie with other paramedics
- Fulfilling outcomes
- Being dependable

The cons

- Long hours
- Lots of overnight shifts
- Lots of early mornings and late nights
- Working with difficult patients
- High-stress environment

Pros and Cons of Being a Hairstylist

Pros

- Work in beauty industry professionally
- Substantial income
- Can eventually create your own schedule
- Can make others feel good about themselves
- Use your problem-solving chops
- Normal 9-to-5 schedule allows you to be with family

Cons

- Standing on your feet 8+ hours a day
- Beauty school can be costly
- In school for over a year before you get paid
- Competitive
- Difficult customers

- Pressure on physical appearance
- Must look completely made-up and polished *EVERY* day

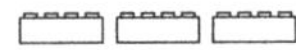

When you look at the pros and cons of every potential career option with a realistic perspective on both the benefits and drawbacks of whatever career you consider, ask yourself:

- Are there more pros or cons?
- Will the drawbacks be too overwhelming to my own personal life?
- Are the benefits worth the drawbacks?
- Will the benefits carry me through the next five years? Ten years?
- Are the drawbacks something I can live with?

If the overall benefits outweigh the drawbacks, you will know you are on the right track.

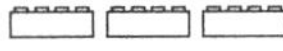

Challenge yourself to:

- Examine your passions and hobbies.
- Reflect on your desires and lifestyle goals.
- And think about what skills it will take to ultimately achieve them.

Ask yourself: How can you apply your skills to different kinds of careers? Continue to explore what it will take to pursue those careers, while keeping in mind that your ultimate goal is to have a lifestyle that will make you happy. As long as you can keep the vision of your desired life in the forefront of all your activities, you will be in a great position to pursue it.

Prompt Questions:

1. What is one skill you already have that can help you in a future career?

2. What is your dream job?

3. Off the top of your head, what are the pros and cons of your dream job? Can you live with the cons? What do you like about the pros?

4. What kind of lifestyle do you want to have? How do you want to spend your time and money?

5. What is your second choice for your career path?

AUTHOR'S EXPERIENCE:

I really wanted to be a hairstylist. I wanted the lifestyle it would bring me, and I thought I would really enjoy cutting and coloring hair. What I didn't think about is (1) school takes up to two years, and that's if you're full-time. I didn't have time to hold down a job while I was going to school full-time. (2) I hate customer service. Every job involves a little bit of customer service, but hairstylists deal with customers all day, every day, or else they don't have a job. (3) I am much better at weaves and hair extensions than cutting and coloring, and to be a weave stylist, you don't have to have a cosmetology license. I wasted a lot of money in loans that I should have never had in the first place. Think really hard before you make any big life decisions!

CHALLENGE:

Challenge yourself to examine your passions and hobbies, reflect on your personal desires and lifestyle goals, and think about what skills it will take to ultimately reach those goals.

11

SHORT-TERM GOALS

Sometimes, the path toward living our best life isn't direct. Many survivors will find that they have the potential to pursue very ambitious careers, but because of financial setbacks or the amount of schooling their career path requires, they will not be able to reap the benefits of their desired career right away. Often, the mere drawback of time will discourage us from even beginning our journey. We need a substantial income NOW. We need to provide for ourselves and our families NOW, not two to six years from now.

Perhaps that is exactly what led to our exploitation in the first place. A person or industry saw that we needed to make ends meet immediately and exploited that need by selling us the dream of complete stability while hiding the fact that exploitation can be dangerous, draining, and will not serve us well in the long run. For many survivors, that deception can become our fuel, because stability is something we are more than capable of maintaining. That wasn't a lie! We just need to find a path that doesn't put our safety and overall well-being at risk and where we are earning money for ourselves, not for someone else.

Truly Short-Term Goals

Later on in this chapter, we will discuss how to turn long-term goals into short-term goals. But before we begin to do that, consider taking on a short-term goal. What do you need to happen by the end of the week?

1. Do you need to sign up for health insurance? Do you need to sign up for food stamps?
2. Do you need to get a radio, CD player, or iPod so you can listen to your favorite music?
3. What about exercise? Will implementing a small workout every day or a few times a week help you get your body moving and make your health slowly come back into focus?

Set one short-term goal for yourself that you know you can complete by the end of the week. Once you meet that goal, celebrate! Then plan for the next short-term goal. This may seem slow going at first, but making short-term goals is really important because it shows us that we are capable of formulating a plan and sticking to it. This will help us as we turn our focus to long-term goals. If we are practiced at meeting short-term goals, then tackling long-term goals will be a piece of cake.

But facing this truth means coming to terms with the fact that long-term success requires working hard for long periods of time. That may mean holding an entry-level job and going to school at the same time. That may mean working in an entry-level position until you slowly work your way up the ladder and go for promotion after promotion.

The key here is momentum: while you're getting all your immediate needs met, taking small but important steps toward your biggest goal will keep it in the forefront of your life. Once those small steps start to add up, you'll see that everything you do to meet your short-term needs is actually part of your long-term goal.

Here is how you break down long-term goals into short-term goals:

1. If you take your long-term career goal and see how close or far you are from it, contemplate what you will need to do for the next few weeks, years, or however long it will take to get there. Map out the steps you will have to take along the way.
   i. Will you need credentials before you can practice this kind of career?
   ii. If so, what kind of schooling will you need?
   iii. How long will you have to be in school?
   iv. Will you be able to support yourself on student loans, or will you need to get an entry-level or part-time job in the meantime?
   v. Or instead of education, will you need more experience in a certain field?

2. Then slowly break down your long-term goal into milestones that will let you know that you are gradually making progress. A year from now, or six months from now, what will happen that would indicate that you've made progress and you're closer to your long-term goal?

3. From those milestones, ask yourself: A few months from now, what will indicate to you that you're on the right track to meeting that milestone?

4. Then break it down further: What will you need to accomplish in the first month of your path?

5. And further: What can you do this week to lead to your goal this month?

6. Finally: Is there something you can do TODAY that would keep you on your path?

Baby steps toward your goal, although they may seem insignificant now, are so important to your path toward success. Not only do baby steps allow you to fuel your momentum but they can also give you the necessary skills, education, and experience you will need to fulfill your ultimate goals.

This works even if your goals have nothing to do with career choices:

- Most survivors find they must heal from trauma, and that can be a goal in itself. What will that healing look like? Fewer panic attacks? A more active social life? Healthy relationships? What can you do in the months leading up to this healing goal to work toward it? Do you need to find the right therapist? How often should you see that therapist? What qualities would that therapist have? How do you put yourself in the position to bring that counselor into your life? Once they are in your life, what work should you do on your own to get long-lasting results?

- If you are separated from your children, your goal might simply be to have them back in your life. What will you need to accomplish in order to do that? What can you do in the months leading up to this goal? What can you do to bring you closer to your goal this week?

- Maybe you don't want to pursue a specific career, but you do know that you want to become financially independent as soon as possible. What will financial independence in your life look like? What must you do to achieve financial independence?

But you may be in a position where you can't pick one long-term goal, or maybe you're still discovering who you really are and don't know what will ultimately bring you happiness and fulfillment. In that case, challenge yourself to create a small short-term goal that you know you're capable of achieving. Setting short-term goals with no long-term objective does a few things for you:

- Short-term goals can help your self-discovery and show you what you may eventually want to pursue as a long-term goal.

- They show you that you are more than capable of setting goals and achieving them.

- They keep you moving forward.

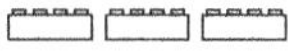

As you pursue these short-term goals, or short-term goals that will lead to long-term goals, reflect on how these goals make you feel. Do they bring you a feeling of purpose and accomplishment, or do they make you want to rethink your overall path? It is normal to get a little discouraged periodically, but be sure to be able to identify when the feelings of discouragement outweigh your overall inspiration.

The following chapter will help you explore how to reassess your goals as you go forward with recovery. For now, simply take what paths you've explored over the last week and break down that goal into milestones, then break down those milestones into monthly goals, then break down those goals to smaller goals, and even smaller goals, until you have laid out your daily path toward your future. And when you can, enjoy the process and celebrate reaching each milestone. These small celebrations are leading up to the biggest celebration of all: living your best life.

Prompt Questions:

1. What short-term goal will help you improve your life and attitude? Can you meet this goal in one week? One month?

2. Why is it important to have isolated short-term goals?

3. How far away are you from your desired lifestyle and career goals?

4. What do you think you will have to do over the next year to reach your goal?

5. What do you think you will have to do over the next month to be closer to your goal?

AUTHOR'S EXPERIENCE:

For school, I know I have about three more years until I graduate. Right now, I am taking one semester of classes toward my general ed. Every time I do the homework, every time I complete an assignment, I am one step closer to my goal of graduating. Each week I spend doing homework and participating in class, I am achieving a short-term goal, and each short-term goal leads to my long-term goal.

CHALLENGE:

Choose one of the following:

1. **Think of your overall lifestyle and career path that you want to pursue and break that down into smaller periodic goals that you know you can meet. Break it down all the way to today. What can you do today that will move you toward your goal?**

2. **Pick one short-term goal and try to meet it by the next time you pick up this book.**

12

Reassessing Goals as You Go

Whenever anyone pursues any type of goal, there comes a point somewhere between beginning the goal and reaching it when they have covered enormous ground but still have a long way to go. At that point, we might start to lose steam, and that lack of self-encouragement can cause us to question our initial goal.

How do we know if we simply need encouragement or if we should change our path entirely?

Sometimes, personal reflection can show you what you truly want from your goals and if you are actually getting those things. Certain factors in our life may make it difficult to keep on track with our goals, while adding new factors might help keep us on track. However, above all else, keep your personal fulfillment in the forefront of every goal you set.

For example: We may want to pursue education at a university level and have the goal of taking the maximum number of credits so we can finish as soon as possible, but financial aid may not be enough to sustain our lifestyle. On top of that, if we are participating in a two-year residential program for exploitation recovery, we have to consider the fact that we will only have our housing covered for two years, and we will need to have an income at the end of that time which can cover our housing costs and other living expenses. Holding down a job may be difficult while we have such a heavy load of classes.

Does this mean that we can't pursue higher education at all? Absolutely not! But we may have to adjust our goals. In this case, we need to design a new goal plan that will sustain our immediate needs while we pursue our ultimate goal. This may mean:

- We might have to take a few less credits for a few semesters than we had originally planned
- And, we might have to obtain an entry-level job in retail, food service, cafe service, or hospitality to supplement our needs with the financial aid we might receive.

Mental Health Goals

Another thing to think about: We might have set the goal that we wanted to get our mental health under control, perhaps to lessen panic attacks and maintain our moods better. But well on our way into this journey, we find that we are not making progress. Perhaps we even find ourselves getting worse, having more panic attacks or anger than we used to have!

Keep in mind that while pursuing our mental health recovery, it often gets more challenging before we get the results we want, but we still must look at our healing plan and consider if we are taking the right steps to gain healing:

- Are we seeing the right therapist?
- Are we seeing the right psychiatrist?
- Are the psychiatric meds we are given working?
- Are we engaging in the right kinds of therapies or the right therapeutic activities?
- Is the therapy we are in too intense or not intense enough?
- Are we taking care of ourselves in the meantime?

We might have to reassess the steps we must take while still keeping our mental health in the forefront of our goals.

Informational Interviews with Professionals

Sometimes there is a big gap between the idea of our dream job and what it actually takes to pursue and maintain that career. There will always be things we cannot see until we are actually working in that field. In that case, it may be best to do a few interviews with professionals in the field you want to pursue. Ask a handful of people the same few questions, not just one person, because you want to get a range of answers.

Some helpful questions to ask them include:

1. What was the level of difficulty of the education leading up to your profession?
2. How is the work-family life balance in your field?
3. How competitive was the job market? How easy was it to find a job?
4. If you could do it all over again, would you make the same career choices?

Again, be sure to ask a range of professionals in your desired field these questions! One person may have a very negative outlook on their career while most other professionals may love it. Or, one person may love their job while most others in that profession hate it. However, it is really up to you how you interpret their advice.

When Our Goals Don't Fit Our Lifestyle

Another thing to think about is when our ultimate goals don't exactly suit us and our overall lifestyle.

For example: We may have the ultimate goal of being a hairstylist, but halfway through our cosmetology training, we may find that we are not as natural as we thought we would be at most hairstyling tasks. Though we have gotten the tutoring we need and put in extra training time on our own, we find that every new technique becomes more difficult. What's worse: We are not having fun anymore. We can't see ourselves working in a salon every day. We don't enjoy customer service, and we find ourselves waking up with dread every day that we have to go back to the beauty school.

In this case, we must understand when the overall feeling of dread goes beyond being discouraged by the challenges we are facing. If we are temporarily discouraged? That's okay. Not every part of the training process will be extremely exciting and fun. But if we don't even want to be at beauty school because we don't enjoy hairstyling, we probably won't enjoy being a hairstylist after all.

At that point, we must consider how many hours we have put into our schooling:

- If we have just begun our education and aren't even halfway through, we might want to work with a financial counselor to figure out how we can take care of the financial debt we may carry if we choose to leave, then change our path and move on to the next goal.

- If we are more than halfway through and still don't want to be a hairstylist, it might be in our best interests to finish training, take our final board exams, and find a job in the industry that may use our skills but won't involve styling hair every day. Perhaps being a salon receptionist, a makeup artist for film and television or the stage, or a beauty blogger or vlogger may be more in line with our desires.

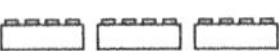

How do we know if we need encouragement or if we need to change directions?

When we find ourselves at the crossroads where we are second-guessing our goals, we must check in with ourselves by asking: Why did we set this goal in the first place, and are we actually getting those things from the goal that we initially wanted?

- Did we want the income that it would bring us?
- Did we want the lifestyle it would bring us? In other words, would we be around the people, places, and things we like if we enter this field?
- Were we trying to make others proud by pursuing this goal? Or is it more important that we are making ourselves proud?
- Finally: Is this goal turning out to be everything that we wanted it to be?

From your answers, if you feel that you need to reassess your goals, go back through the information you have learned in this chapter and redesign your goal plan while keeping in mind the ways you might have to recover from changing your goals, taking into account what you will need to do to change paths. If this goal, though it may be challenging, is something you would like to continue pursuing, you might simply need a boost in the right direction.

Here are some ways to get a boost in the right direction:

- Use the buddy system: Tell someone you know and trust that you are pursuing your goal, why you have chosen that goal, and ask them to hold you accountable for taking steps toward that goal. A little friendly encouragement goes a long way!
- Take a step back and work on short-term goals: Whether you work on your short-term goals as a way to reach your long-term goal, or you simply want to start over by creating and completing daily goals for yourself, it may be less overwhelming to think of goals you can accomplish in a short time rather than focusing on major life decisions. This doesn't have to be forever—just until you feel more confident in your goal-completing abilities.
- Self-Care: It is NEVER a good idea to make major decisions from a place of anxiety and worry. If you have the time and freedom to do so, practice some self-care, and don't think about ANY goals while you do so. Clear your head, comfort yourself, and then go on with your day. The answer will come to you at the right time.

If you're still struggling with whether or not you should keep your goal or reassess all your goals, ask yourself: Can I be happy if I keep this goal today? Will it make me happy a year from now? What about five years from now? Will it better my life in more ways than it will bring challenges?

As long as you keep both your long-term fulfillment and your immediate needs balanced, you'll make the right decision.

PROMPT QUESTIONS:

1. Do you have a deal breaker—that if one thing came in the way of your goals, you would completely change your path? What would that deal breaker be? Your kids? Money?

2. What would make you completely rethink one goal you have?

3. Have you ever had to change paths in the middle of trying to meet a goal? What happened?

4. What can keep you on track to meet the goals you have set for yourself, even in the face of challenges? What can be your inspiration?

5. How can you tell if you just need some encouragement or if you need to change directions completely?

AUTHOR'S EXPERIENCE:

I was seeing a really good therapist, or so I thought, until one day she made a comment about what I had been through that made me uncomfortable. I didn't know what to do. I ended up going MIA and not seeing another therapist for over a year. I wish I had found my new therapist sooner. She's been great and we have worked through a lot of my issues together, including my distrust of therapists.

CHALLENGE:

Challenge yourself to pick a goal you are working toward, and think of whether or not keeping that goal will make you happy today, days or weeks from now, a month from now, or a year from now.

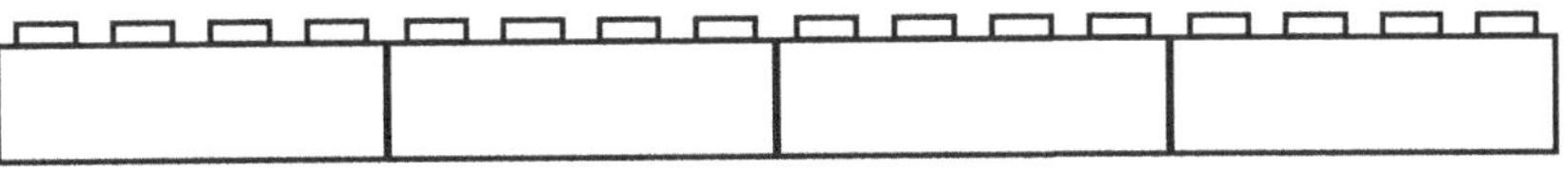

Practical and Organizational Skills

13

Organization —Taking Control of Your Daily Life

If we have spent the majority of our trauma under the control of our abusers, in an endless cycle of hotel rooms, or without a home at all, we might have forgotten how we like to organize our lives. It's hard to keep things ordered in the way we prefer if our living quarters, our daily schedule, and basic needs are constantly changing, and often we had to organize things the way our abusers or others preferred without putting our personal needs first. Around our fourth month of recovery from exploitation, we may not be in the exact situation we have always dreamed of, but we can certainly stabilize our lives to be organized, comfortable, and homey, and it can bring peace.

Having a well-ordered life not only makes us feel more at home and independent but also sets us up for success. If we are constantly working on our goals, improving our lives and healing our minds of trauma, the last thing we want to deal with is disorder, and if we take time to settle everything, from our schedule to our living spaces and basic needs, we will be in a better frame of mind to focus on what really matters most in our journey: our growth.

We can begin to organize our entire life by organizing our living space. Even if we are not in our ideal home, we can still make our spaces comfortable for the time which we are in them. We do not have to keep everything as tidy and clean as a museum, and often, if our abusers were especially controlling, it might be liberating to leave things a little messy, so the important thing is keeping control of your own space:

- Keep messes contained
- Know how to fix messes if they occur
- And form organizational habits that are easy to maintain.

This is a great example of how our short-term goals come into play! Try setting a goal to take control of what space you do have, and put a time limit on it. Do you want to master your spaces in a week? In two weeks? What would that look like? What would that feel like?

Transient Survivors

However, it is also understood that most survivors experience homelessness at some point in their recovery, or that for some time they do not have access to a safe, stable home. We know that it is unrealistic that survivors from a transient situation would be able to apply the same home organization principles to a homeless lifestyle. If you haven't done so, call the **National Human Trafficking Hotline at (888) 373-7888,** and simply absorb this information until you are able to apply it. The next few chapters will have more information that will be useful to you.

Here are some good practices for organizing your living spaces:

- **Purge your belongings**
  It may be helpful in the beginning if you put everything you own into three categories: one group of things which you absolutely must keep, one that you might want to keep but are unsure, and one group of things you can live without. For the first and third group, it's easy: keep the necessary things and throw away or give away what you can live without. For the "maybe" pile, mull over whether or not you need each item for a set amount of time. If you don't use the item within a week, a few weeks, or a month, you should consider tossing it. You can do this as frequently or as seldom as needed, but it is a great idea to start all of your organizing with one big purge.

- **Keep a memento box**
  If something in your "maybe" category doesn't get used every day but it holds a lot of GOOD memories (not memories of exploitation), consider keeping a small memento box of items with memories that you can tuck away and pull out when you want to remind yourself of good things that you once had or anything that symbolizes goals which you want to achieve.

- **Put like things with like things**
  Simple enough, right? Keep shoes together, clothes together, dirty clothes in a dirty clothes basket together, important documents in one place, cleaning supplies together, and toiletry items together. You might even want to color code your belongings within each group if that helps you organize it better.

- **Build a five-step routine**

  Sometimes the most difficult part of organizing on a regular basis is knowing where to begin, and that's where things get out of control! In that case, it might be helpful to formulate a five-step routine. Pick five quick things you can do to tidy up, and do them on a regular basis.

  Some ideas: Put dirty clothes in the laundry basket, put trash in the trash can, flatten or fluff bed covers, put makeup/hair products away, vacuum, wipe surfaces, gather any used dishes, clear desk space, etc.

- **Set your spaces up for success**

  The idea is to set up your living spaces so that you will be able to leave in a hurry and be able to locate and use everything you need in order to leave the house quickly, quietly, and easily. When money and time allow, consider obtaining items such as shoe racks, shelves or plastic containers, tables or desks in order to help keep track of all your belongings.

- **Group housing tips**

  Although some group homes are more secure than others, it is wise to keep your valuables, including medication, money, and important documents, contained where no one else can access them. If you must be away from those items for any reason, consider obtaining a lockbox where only you will have a key.

  If you share a bathroom, consider keeping your toiletry needs in your own room where no one will have access to them. You can use a shower caddy (obtainable at retailers during back-to-school season) or a small plastic/waterproof box or basket to hold your items and take them back and forth to the bathroom.

- **Decorate even the smallest of spaces**
  Try to make your space feel like home. Even if you don't have a lot of money, you can make decorations to personalize your spaces. This will make a huge difference in your comfort and your ability to stay in your recovery home as long as you need to. Small decorations will make you feel at home.

Remember to make it your own! YOU know what will work for YOU. Even if you don't use every tip listed here, or if you have completely different organizing strategies altogether, it is simply important to get control of your spaces in whatever way works. A clear and ordered space will always help with healthy functioning and improve our emotional peace.

In the following three weeks, we will learn (or relearn) other organizational skills, but we will also learn practical skills that will help us in our daily life. If our goal is to be completely and totally independent and self-sustaining, we should build our independence on the foundation of easy and intelligent ways to take care of ourselves and everything in our lives.

Prompt Questions:

1. Would you consider yourself to be a tidy person? Why or why not? Be honest.

2. How is organizing your own personal living space different when you are sharing a home or in group housing?

3. What helps you keep your spaces neat and clean?

4. What is the best part of cleaning? What is the worst part of cleaning?

5. Why is cleaning important to your healing?

Author's Experience:

Decorating my living space always makes me feel better about cleaning.

I am usually a messy person, so I have to work harder to keep my spaces clean. This comes into play when you are couch hopping or a guest in someone else's home. You must keep things tidy.

Also, I was technically homeless for a long period of time. When I was able to stay somewhere, I kept my belongings and areas very clean so they would not want me to leave sooner rather than later. The cleaner your spaces are, the less likely that you will be asked to leave, and you will have a sense of accomplishment for reaching and maintaining that goal.

Challenge:

Challenge yourself to think of a five-step routine to keeping your space clean and then act this out. Try to do it every day for one week.

14

Time Management

For most people, time management classes are boring lectures about stuff we already know but simply choose not to practice. We know that we can have more freedom if we properly manage how we spend our time. We know that being more efficient will lead to more opportunities and advancement in our lives. We know, we know, we know!

If you think about it, most survivors are on a rigorous schedule during their exploitation. They are constantly watching the clock and monitoring their time during their exploitation activities. It is something we, as survivors, already understand, and to "teach" us about time management is redundant, and perhaps insulting.

So instead of preaching from the time management gospel to survivors, who by their very nature fundamentally understand the importance and practices of time management, in this section we will refresh ourselves on tips to improve our time management, ways to practice our skills, and the resulting benefits.

Benefits of time management:

- **Helps you get results faster**
  If we manage our time to actively work on our goals each day, we will be able to meet each goal more efficiently. We will also be able to track our progress, so even when we have not yet met our goal, our time management will allow us to celebrate each daily milestone as we work toward results. But the truth is: The more persistent we are at managing our time, the sooner we will get to our desired outcome.

- **Helps in work skills**
  At work, if you are efficiently engaged with all your duties and can properly manage how you use your time, your supervisor will notice. This can lead to more responsibilities, and potentially more promotions.

- **Manages stress**
  When you have all your ducks in a row and can track all your progress, you will have more time to RELAX! Knowing that you are consistently progressing toward your desired destination in life will put your mind at ease and allow you to slow down when you need to.

Ways to practice your time management skills:

- **Time yourself**
  It's simple: Track how much time it takes for you to complete a task, and the next time you set out to do this task, try to

beat your time. Independent competition with yourself can lead to self-improvement.

- **Multitasking**
  Some tasks have a long wait period, especially household responsibilities like laundry, running the dishwasher, and other tasks. While you wait for one task to complete itself, try to line up your time so that you can complete multiple tasks at once. You will get lots done before you even realize it.

- **Use a whiteboard**
  Whiteboards can be great places for you to leave yourself reminders, especially if you have a lot to accomplish every day. Some whiteboards even come in calendar or weekly form, which can help you keep track of your appointments, goals, job interviews, or whatever is important to you.

- **Use a calendar**
  Put your calendar on the wall somewhere you will see it often and record upcoming events in it. Try not to fill it to the point that every single day is filled with something different; you want your eyes to quickly find the important stuff.

- **Use a daily planner**
  Most cell phones will have a daily planner app where you can plan your activities and even set reminders and alarms when important events come up. Take advantage of this! If you don't have a cell phone, there are many traditional daily planners still available, or a blank notebook can even be used. Design it yourself!

- **Set your living spaces up for success**
  It is ideal to organize your living spaces so that you can leave at a moment's notice and be able to find everything you need in a timely fashion. Organize all your belongings, especially your clothes, shoes, makeup, hair care, and daily needs, so that you can find them, use them, or grab them, and leave quickly and quietly. You never know when a job interview or any kind of impromptu appointment will come up!

- **Allow yourself free time**
  When you manage your time, allow yourself time to RELAX! Stacking your day so full that you don't even have time to relax, other than when you're asleep, can lead to burnout. Consider rewarding yourself with free time or self-care when you have a busy day. We don't always take breaks because we are lazy. Sometimes, we take breaks to regroup, calm our minds, and reset ourselves so we will have more energy to complete tasks later on.

Places to practice time management:

- **Cooking**
  Cooking always involves time-sensitive tasks, but more importantly, it involves completing multiple time-sensitive tasks at once so that everything comes out hot and fresh at the same time. If you like cooking, use this activity to practice multitasking, timing yourself, and planning.

- **Household tasks**
  Getting things done around the house can also help us practice time management with low impact so that when it really comes time to apply your skills, you'll be ready.

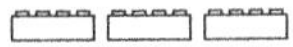

Though many of us survivors have learned time management in unhealthy situations, where exploiters or abusers were forcing us to stick to a rigorous schedule whether we liked it or not, we may find that time management in healthy, stable settings is much more comfortable. At this point, we are not thinking about anyone's opinion but our own. This is our chance to take something from a time in our lives that was toxic and make it truly useful and beautiful.

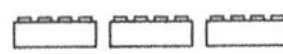

After you brush up on your time management skills on a consistent basis, you will use your time most effectively without even realizing it. It will become a part of you, a necessary tool in your toolbox that can help you no matter what situation you find yourself in.

Prompt Questions:

1. How would you rate your time management on a scale of one to ten, with ten being the highest? Why?

2. How can time management help you in the workplace? How about in an educational setting?

3. What is one way that you can practice your time management skills?

4. What is one time management skill that you are good at?

5. Are there activities you engage in where you know you are wasting time? Are these activities something you can make time for, or do you feel like you have to do away with them? Why?

AUTHOR'S EXPERIENCE:

I am pretty good about time management. I would always time myself when doing tasks in the bakery where I worked. Because of timing myself, I ended up going faster and faster and became a dependable person at work.

Time management also comes into play when planning out your week. Maybe you can't sit there and time all the tasks throughout your day. But it might be easier if you plan daily activities. Give yourself enough time, and be honest with yourself about how much time you will need.

CHALLENGE:

Keep track of how much time you spend on each activity that you take part in. Don't worry about making yourself go faster, just observe how much time you take to do things.

15

Cost-Effective Living

It may be difficult to go from earning fast money that is diverted to enormous costs or even an exploiter's account, to going into government assistance programs and learning to save, but successfully saving money so you can improve your life may be what keeps you firmly planted in your independence. In this chapter, we will discuss ways to facilitate cost-effective living so that you can have all your needs comfortably met as you work toward your goals.

As you work toward finding steady employment, your bank account will grow, but if you get used to saving what you can when you have less money, you will learn good habits that you can follow when you're in a better financial position. If you haven't done so already, apply for food stamps and cash assistance through your local Health and Human Services office, though some states will allow you to do so online. If you are homeless or living in a shelter, keep in mind that you may have to prove your transient status through documentation from a local organization that can vouch for you.

Here are some ways that survivors have successfully saved money that you might consider trying for yourself:

Dollar Discount Stores

- Food: Most dollar discount stores (Dollar Tree, 99 Cents Store) carry canned and nonperishable foods. Some even have fresh fruits, veggies, meat, and dairy. At one dollar per item, you can go wild!

- Hygiene needs: Dollar discount stores also carry basic toiletries such as deodorant, shampoo, body wash, lotion, tampons and pads, and more. Often the brands will be generic, but some dollar stores will carry small amounts of name brand items. Keep in mind that discount stores also carry other feminine needs like makeup, hair products, and pregnancy tests.

- Cleaning products and household items: Some cleaning products can be up to $6 per item in a regular retail store. At a dollar store, you can get the same type of product for only $1, so instead of buying one item for $6, you can get six items. Toilet paper, paper towels, and other items are also discounted to $1, including laundry detergent and fabric softener. The dollar store can be your best friend, and you can come home with a plethora of useful household needs without breaking the bank.

Ridesharing Apps

- If you don't have transportation, rideshare apps, such as Uber and Lyft, can help you make some necessary trips without having to depend upon others for rides. You can use rideshare apps to get to necessary appointments or last-minute job interviews. It's also VERY useful when you have to travel a long distance with a heavy load. (A week's worth of grocery shopping? Call a rideshare!) Survivors have used rideshare apps to pick up a heavy load of groceries or even to move small amounts of furniture to a new location.

- If you don't have a debit card: As with all virtual purchases, rideshare apps require you to use a credit or debit card number, and will not accept cash aid cards from government programs. If all you have is cash, you can purchase a Visa gift card or MasterCard gift card from convenience stores or grocery stores, register the card with your zip code, and use the card as if it were a debit card.

- Safety: Because rideshare apps require you to interact with strangers, it's important to keep safety in mind. Whenever you take a trip, let a friend or person who is close to you know where you are going, when you will be going, and when you should be expected back. If you can, match the license plate of the driver on the app with the car that picks you up. And while being as polite as possible, do not share any personal information with your driver (in other words, do not give any clues that where you are going is your home or any sort of private residence).

  Although emergencies are extremely uncommon with rideshares, if your life is threatened in any way, call the police. You can always follow up later with the rideshare's customer service.

Public Transportation

- No one likes riding the bus, but think of what you will save, and better yet, the independence it will bring you! When rideshare apps offer you a ride for $20 and you can take the same trip for $2 on the bus, you'll learn to love public transportation. While you may want to save important trips for rideshares, daily trips can be made with the bus or train for significantly less money. A monthly pass can save additional money if you have a set schedule or regular appointments where a monthly pass would make sense.

- Plan accordingly: Buses and trains are notorious for being late. Whereas a regular trip may take five minutes in the car, it can be twenty minutes to an hour by bus. Always allot extra time when you are traveling by public transit, and if you can, plan your trip online before you head out the door. That way, you can see exactly when you will arrive at your destination. Remember: It is better to be an hour early to an important appointment than five minutes late!

- Safety: As with rideshares, you want to keep your personal safety in mind. Be aware of your surroundings at all times. If an emergency occurs on the bus or at the bus stop, get the attention of the bus driver as soon as possible. If that does not work, call the police.

Thrift Stores

- Work and interview clothes: Thrift stores rarely have the most up-to-date trends, but they can have clothes that are appropriate for job interviews, which can appear conservative and cover any tattoos we may have received in exploitation. Dress for the job you want! What should a person wear to be in the position you are trying to achieve? It is highly likely that your local thrift store will have something that matches that goal. There are also some organizations that provide interview clothes for job seekers, but in case there is not one in your area, try to find some interview clothes at your local thrift store.

- Functional needs: If you are in a new area for your recovery and are not accustomed to the weather (it is either much warmer or colder than you are used to), you will get the best deals on good-quality clothing at thrift stores. If you need a warm coat and heavy boots, or rather significantly cooler clothing, your local thrift store will have exactly what you are looking for.

- For furniture or household appliances: If you need a common household item, like an iron and ironing board, or even a television, consider looking for it at your local thrift store, because it will be much more cost effective. If you need furniture in a pinch, also consider searching for it at a thrift store.

Reusing Containers

- Recycling at its finest: Reusing any containers that you use, after washing them with soap and warm water, will keep you from needing to buy Tupperware and other plastic containers over and over again. Be creative! Your next food jar can become a container for hair ties, makeup brushes, food items, and many other needs if you open your mind.

Food Bank

- Food banks are notorious for only providing canned foods, but many up-to-date food banks can provide you with fresh fruits and veggies, dairy, and even fresh meat without any cost to you whatsoever. Contact your local food bank today to see if they provide both nonperishable AND fresh foods. You don't have to use your local food bank often, but in a pinch, it can be very helpful.

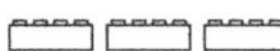

Though it may be discouraging to shop at food banks, use food stamps, or go to Goodwill for clothing needs, especially if we have lived a lifestyle where we were used to getting fast money on a regular basis, we have to remind ourselves how important it is that we support ourselves in a sustainable way that won't put us in danger. When you feel discouraged by this change of lifestyle, remind yourself that it is not forever, that giving up all this progress you've made so far is not worth becoming reexploited, and that you're actively working on ways to improve everything about your lifestyle.

PROMPT QUESTIONS:

1. What items can you save money on? Why?

2. What needs do you think you will have to splurge on? Why?

3. What has helped you save money in the past?

4. How would you rate your saving habits on a scale of one to ten, with ten being the highest? Why?

5. Why would you need to splurge on some things but save on other things?

6. What helps you stay positive when you're making choices to save money? What keeps you inspired?

AUTHOR'S EXPERIENCE:

I would save on getting to work by taking the bus, but if I was going to an interview, I might want to get a rideshare so I don't show up sweaty or disheveled.

My income has greatly improved, yet I still shop at the dollar store all the time. That's where I get my laundry detergent, bubble bath, and deodorant. However, for face wash or any skin care products, I splurge and get the name brand products.

I also have problems with thrift stores because it is hard to find professional clothes in my size, so work clothes are something I would splurge on.

CHALLENGE:

Watch what you spend for one week and try to keep track of what you can save.

16

Worst-Case-Scenario Survival

Cutting toxic habits, people, and activities out of your life does not mean you will reach success immediately. It often means that more struggles will surface, and it can be incredibly discouraging for any survivor to go from getting fast money to having their life completely devastated. Getting a fresh start can be liberating, but it does not come without its fair share of challenges.

Over half of all sexual exploitation survivors are homeless, or have been homeless at one time, so if you are reading this book as you are living out of your car, or if you are couch surfing, or for whatever reason have not yet been accepted into group housing, you are not alone.

In this section, we will explore the worst-case scenario: working your recovery while you are homeless. We will discuss how to survive under undesirable circumstances in case you ever find yourself homeless, so you can have a sense of normalcy in your life as you continue toward your goals, until your circumstances change.

- **Good housekeeping habits**
  If you have the privilege of temporarily staying in someone's home, it is always a good idea to leave your living quarters better than you found them. This will not only increase your chances of being able to stay there again, but cleaning your temporary living quarters is also a great way to thank your gracious neighbors for letting you stay there in the first place. Remember to make your bed, fold blankets if you are staying on a couch, and assist your host with any cleaning they may need help with.

- **Parking overnight**
  If you are living out of your car, be cautious when parking overnight in suburban areas, for neighbors can call the police on you for doing so. If you have nowhere else to park and you're not near a rest stop, consider parking in a retail location's parking lot. Although it's not ideal and you must keep your safety in mind, use a quick Google search to find what retail locations in your area will allow you to park in their lot overnight. Organizations like Dreams for Change have safe parking lots where homeless individuals with cars can park overnight.

- **Gym membership for hygiene needs**
  Gyms usually have showers available for members, so if you are able to obtain membership to a gym, you not only get to use their equipment and machines for exercise, but you will also be able to use their shower for your hygiene needs. Consider taking a duffel bag with your shampoo, body wash, and even toothbrush with you while you exercise, and use the shower facilities once you are through.

- **Laundromat**
  When you need to wash your clothes, consider using a laundromat. Coin-operated laundries will usually have detergent and fabric softener for sale. Remember to save extra coins for the dryer cycle, especially for large loads, because clothes often take twice as long to dry as they do to wash. If you can, stop by the local dollar discount store to pick up detergent, fabric softener, stain stick, and dryer sheets for the low price of one dollar apiece.

- **Holding important documents**
  Keep important documents, such as your Social Security card or birth certificate, or any paperwork from Health and Human Services, together in a secure location. If you are living out of your car, it may be wise to keep all important documents locked in your glove box.

- **Volunteering**
  Volunteering can give you a sense of purpose and it allows you to give back, but perhaps most importantly, it also provides you with work experience that you may need when applying to jobs. Consider volunteering at a place where you would eventually like to work, or at an organization that is close to your heart. If you make a good impression on your supervisor, ask their permission to use them as a work reference on your next job application.

When things get difficult and you feel discouraged by all the brand-new challenges you are facing, gently remind yourself that you actually have a lot of control over your life now. YOU decide when you need to do everything you want to do, how YOU spend whatever money you have, and how YOU choose to take care of all your belongings. All the glamour that may come with a fast-money lifestyle in exploitation does not erase the danger you were in and the fact that your life was dictated by both your former customers and especially by any exploiter. This phase of your recovery will not last forever, and everything you do during this worst-case-scenario period will bring you closer to its end, as well as prepare you for the next set of challenges.

Prompt Questions:

1. How can you maintain a sense of normalcy in the worst of circumstances?

2. Have you had to take any of the steps laid out in this section? What was that experience like?

3. If you do find yourself in a tough situation, what can keep you going?

4. Do you have a backup plan in case you ever end up in a tough spot again?

5. What is it about worst-case-scenario survival that inspires you to not go back to it if you can help it?

Author's Experience:

I was exploited twice, and between both times, and after I left for good, I did not have a stable environment. I slept in cars, I showered at gyms, I went to laundromats. There were a lot of things I had to do in order to stay safe and continue pursuing my goals. Eventually I got into a residential program, but I know if I am ever in a tight spot again, I will know how to take care of myself.

Challenge:

Try to devise a worst-case-scenario plan. Think of what might bring you to that place in life, and using the information in the chapter, devise a way to maintain a sense of normalcy when you are in a tough spot.

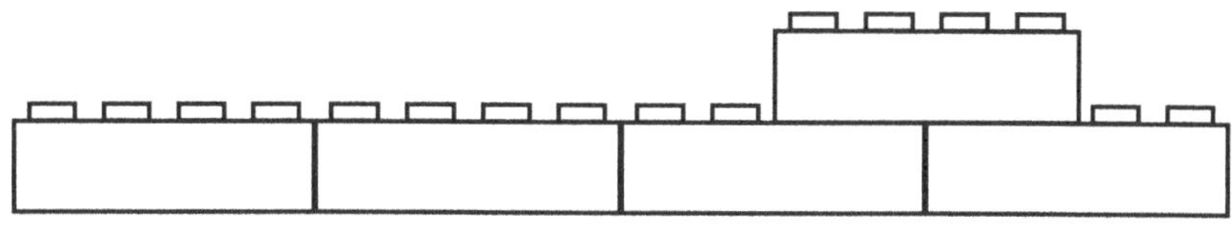

Social Relationships

17

A Look at Past Friendships

When you reflect on friendships you've had in the past, what comes to mind? Where did you meet your closest friends? How did they treat you? How did you treat them? What did you like about them and what lessons did they teach you about friendship?

How did exploitation affect those friendships? Did you lose friends? Did you keep them at a distance to protect them from what you were experiencing? Did any of your friends reach out and try to help you? Or did it feel like they abandoned you?

And what about friends that may have gone into sexual exploitation with you, or who were instrumental in you staying there? Were there healthy or unhealthy aspects to those friendships?

Many of us who have lived through sexual exploitation can say that we were tough, tougher than we ever were in our entire lives, because we had to be! Our lives were at stake. We rarely interacted with people we could trust, and the people we thought we could trust often turned out to be the least trustworthy of all. No matter if we were exploited in our early teen years or well into adulthood, exploitation changed us: our habits, our personality, and the way we form relationships.

We learned the hard way that we can't be open and vulnerable with everyone. There are many people out there who genuinely have no problem taking what we share with them and using it against us. When that happens, we often feel like we can't trust anyone, possibly even our loved ones. And the truth is we can't trust everyone. We must protect ourselves.

But going through life with our fists up, ready to fight off anyone who gets too close to us, can lead to a very lonely, unfulfilling life. As humans, we are social creatures, and when we have plenty of people in our lives who are there to give us support and receive support from us, or even better, to grow and spend quality time together, our mental health will improve substantially and we may be more likely to succeed in all areas of our life.

The good news is that surviving exploitation gives us some advantages in forming new relationships, as we now have more wisdom and discernment than before, and we can use the skills we have already learned to rescope how we form social relationships. We have been through so much that we DO need special protection so we don't fall into any sort of abusive relationships or toxic friendships again, and the best person to protect ourselves is ourselves.

Past Social Relationships

In this section, reflect on what has and hasn't worked in past social relationships:

- What qualities do you want your close friends to have?
- How can you reflect those qualities yourself?
- What hasn't worked in past friendships?

- When friendships were broken, what was your role in that bond being broken?
- How can you use what you learned from your trauma to sharpen your discernment in choosing who you open up to?
- What does it take to be a good friend?

Challenge yourself to look at the people in your life, perhaps in recovery or residential treatment housing, and see what qualities they have which would make for a good friend. And more importantly, think of what YOU have inside yourself that would be important when it comes to forming a long-lasting bond with a person or group of people you can grow with.

Your own style of friendship makes you a unique friend. While we should all aim to hold ourselves to a certain set of principles in social relationships, the principles we choose to lead our lives must come from within, and the unique ways we interact with others and support others are what will inevitably draw the people who are meant to be part of our lives into solid relationships with us.

PROMPT QUESTIONS:

1. Did exploitation change any of your friendships? How so?

2. What sort of qualities do you want friends to have? How can you reflect those qualities in yourself?

3. What kind of friendships, or social relationships, will you avoid? Why?

4. How can you use what you learned in your trauma to sharpen your discernment in choosing who to open up to later?

5. What does it take to be a good friend?

Author's Experience:

I lost a lot of friends when I went into exploitation, and then came a lot of friends whom I depended on when I was trying to get better. When I finally did get better and reach independence and all that, even more friends fell off the map. Those friends wanted or maybe even needed to be depended on, and when I didn't depend on them anymore, they never wanted to see me as an equal in the first place.

I have a handful of friends who did survive all the way from my childhood. They were friends who always had good boundaries. That doesn't mean they shut me out, but they did keep me at a healthy distance. I am at the point now where I keep others at a healthy distance as well, so those people remain good friends of mine.

When choosing who I wanted to bring into my life in the future, I had to look at how independent they were. The more independent they were, the less codependent they would be with me, and the more appreciative they would be if I did something special for them.

Challenge:

Challenge yourself to reflect on past friendships and social relationships. What has worked in the past? What friendships didn't work in the past? Why do you think that is?

18

Recognizing Healthy Friendships

As sexual exploitation survivors, we have experienced some of the deepest, slickest emotional manipulation that anyone may ever face. Often our abusers, and sometimes fellow exploited individuals, coldly and calculatedly figured out how to befriend us and build up our trust, only to use us and break us down. When we have seen such an ugly side of human nature, we may not trust anyone again. And honestly, we shouldn't blindly trust everybody, but if we keep our wits about us, we can use our smarts to tell who will become a good friend, or confidant, or someone we can count on and give support and receive support from.

Some survivors find that balance is the key to solid social relationships. You don't want people in your life who are constantly bringing you down or "checking" you, but you also don't want someone who is too clingy or dependent on you, so much so that they won't be honest with you when you need their honesty. Ideally, we want people in our lives who will lift us up, yet be real with us when we want their honest opinion. And the way to find good friends with balance in their relationship with you is to bring that balance when we are seeking them:

- **Be open yet controlled:** Be transparent about how you feel and what you think, but keep a gentle guard up, and don't share intimate details too early on.

- **Be honest but subjective:** Be real with them about your opinions without dragging anyone through the mud. Give them a fair shot when they want to know what you think.

- **Be a good listener, but make sure they're listening too:** Listen actively to potential friends, because they will tell you everything you need to know whether they know it or not. But every so often, ask yourself: Are they remembering things about me that I share with them? Do they add on and comment on what I say, or do they simply switch the conversation back to themselves?

- **Celebrate your likeness but honor your differences:** It is important that you have lots in common with potential friends, but keep in mind that opposites attract! You can learn a lot from people who are different from you. Variety is the spice of life.

- **Spend quality time but keep your space:** Give them quality attention when it's important, but allow yourself (and allow them) to have time to regroup and process your time alone.

Especially if we are in close quarters with other survivors and those with us in recovery, we will have many opportunities to meet new people and many opportunities to decide how much we will let them into our lives. Use balance to decide how close they should be. Here is a quick cheat sheet of red flags to keep in mind when deciding how open you should be with others:

RED FLAGS

- **They glorify the lifestyle of sex work:** When you are in recovery housing, you are there to leave exploitation behind. It's okay to mildly joke about it enough to feel comfortable with each other, but if someone is constantly telling stories about their glory days while being exploited, and that makes you uncomfortable, keep your distance.

- **They ask really personal questions without knowing you well:** Asking you questions to get to know you is very common. However, asking personal, intimate questions too much, too often, or too early is a sign that you must keep your guard up. (For example: Asking you how much money you made during exploitation is a very INAPPROPRIATE question.)

- **They are especially friendly when they need something from you:** Do they ask you to do things for them, or buy things for them, or straight-up ask you for money? And are they only nice when they need something? Do they react foully if you can't give them what they want? Keep your distance.

- **You feel yourself avoiding spending time with them:** You find yourself making excuses not to hang out, or you realize you're cutting conversations short. That's your gut telling you to keep your distance from them.

- **They disregard your opinion:** They take control of plans so much that they don't listen to what you want to do, or they ask your opinion yet go against it. That shows that they don't value what you think. Big red flag!

- **They are too competitive:** They make rebuilding their lives a game with you, and they want to make sure that they are on top. Pushing each other to succeed is one thing, but trying to throw each other under the bus is another.

- **They complain about your friendship qualities:** They make you feel bad for not having enough time or attention to help deal with their problems. This is especially a red flag if they don't even give you what they're asking of you.

You can also apply these red flags to potential romantic relationships. If a potential partner is overly curious about your former sex work days, asks too many personal questions, is always needy, disregards your opinions, or brings you down more than they lift you up, you might want to keep your distance from them. We will discuss romantic relationships in detail within a few more chapters.

And it goes without saying, but recovery housing is simply a test kitchen for your independent life. That being said, you can practice all these techniques now so that you can apply them accurately when you're out in the world making new friends. Just keep in mind that you need to keep this information, and self-check in, quietly to yourself. You don't need to cut everyone down when you feel like they are being a toxic person, because it's not important that they know they are in the wrong; it is only important that you know.

Challenge yourself to keep a mental log of all your interactions with everyone in your life. Are there more positive qualities than negative qualities? Do you want to be around these people or do you simply feel like you have to? Of course, in recovery housing, we do have to be around certain people whether we like it or not, but it is up to us how close they get to us.

Prompt Questions:

1. What are good signs in potential friendships? What qualities would good friends exhibit?

2. Do you have examples, either from your past or from other people you have observed, of good friendships? What made them good?

3. Do you have examples from your past where friendships did not work out well? What was that like for you?

4. What are red flags with potential friends who are survivors?

5. What are red flags with potential friends who are not survivors?

6. How can you use balance to shape potential friendships?

AUTHOR'S EXPERIENCE:

In treatment housing, I was around a lot of other survivors who glorified sex work/exploitation. That was really hard for me, because in the beginning, I had a hard time leaving that lifestyle behind. I just had to avoid those people. I kept a healthy distance, and when those conversations did come up, I subtly changed the subject.

CHALLENGE:

Challenge yourself to think of three qualities you want a potential friend to have, and three qualities that you don't want them to have.

19

INTERPERSONAL CONFLICT RESOLUTION

It is common for arguments and conflict to come up while you are sharing a house with other survivors, or any group of people. Sometimes, those conflicts are so irritating that they take up the majority of our focus in healing. And how backwards is that? We want to heal and improve our lives, yet we are constantly worrying about what's directly around us … usually over things that don't even matter!

It happens to the best of us.

The good thing is that we can use this time, in whatever living arrangement we are in, to learn how to resolve conflicts easily, so that when we move on to our independent lives, we are skilled and savvy and we find solutions to problems where everyone can be happy. We are no longer in the toxic environment of sexual exploitation, so now we can handle disagreements maturely, like adults.

And keep in mind: When you move out of treatment housing, it is not likely that you will live by yourself; you will probably be living with roommates and must use the same skills when dealing with anyone you may live with in the future. So, it is best to get started on your problem-solving skills now, because you will always, always need those skills! Here are some fundamentals of conflict resolution to keep in mind when you find yourself in a conflict:

- **Listen carefully:** Make sure you know what the other side wants and why. It may even be helpful to repeat back what they say, so that you understand it fully and so that they know you understand it.

- **Think before you react:** You don't want to make impulsive choices that can harm your relationship with the other person, harm them, or harm yourself. Try to take your time to really process the conflict before offering any solutions.

- **Take ownership of your role in the conflict:** It is amazing how far an apology will go. Saying "I am so sorry, I messed up, that's my bad," will show the other person that you are not simply trying to screw them over and that you accept some responsibility in the conflict. (Seriously, how can you argue with someone who is telling you that they know they are wrong?)

- **Correct the problem, not the person:** Try to separate yourselves from the issue and look at the issue itself. What needs to be fixed? It is easy to get riled up and attack the person you disagree with, but that doesn't correct the problem. What's really bothering both of you, and how can you fix it?

- **Compromise, compromise, compromise:** If possible, try your best to find a solution that everyone can live with. This might result in some sacrifice on your end, and if you're struggling with that, ask yourself: What is the value of the sacrifice? Does it mean that the conflict will be resolved and you no longer have to deal with it? That's a good deal!

- **If necessary, give yourself a "time-out":** We cannot resolve conflicts properly if we are heated and our emotions have escalated. Sometimes, it's best to give yourself a five- or ten-minute break, cool off, and come back and get the conflict resolved. During this break, do not overthink the problem or anticipate your next attack. Simply breathe and let the stress in your body depart.

- **Thank the other person:** Even if you are about to walk away from a conflict and you're irritated at each other, thank the other person for their time in trying to solve the problem. As with apologies, gratitude can go a long way.

It is easy to let interpersonal conflicts get the best of you when you are in a group living environment. Know that your journey is bigger than the house you are in. There will be a time when you are further along in your healing, and you'll look back and feel cheated that you spent your time at the residential program in conflict with housemates, when you could have been working hard to improve your life skills, or saving money, or furthering your healing. You don't want petty conflicts to interfere with that, because your focus should be on yourself.

And remember that no conflict with another person in the house is worth getting terminated from the program for. You do not want things to escalate so rapidly that you will do something you regret and get kicked out of the home. Stay away from physical altercations or raising your voice at anyone. If you find that a person is getting physical or aggressive with you, get a staff person's attention to help deal with the problem.

When you are in an argument or conflict with someone, ask yourself, "Am I learning anything from this conflict? Is it helping me grow? Can I live with a compromise in this situation, where I don't necessarily get EVERYTHING I want but I get enough that I can go to bed at night and feel good about how I handled the situation?" The answers to these questions will show you the value of the conflict itself.

Prompt Questions:

1. How have you handled conflict resolution in the past? How has it worked for you or not worked for you? What would you have done differently?

2. How can you de-escalate an argument?

3. How can you let the other person know that you are on their side, not against them?

4. Why is it important that the other person knows you are on their side even when you haven't found a solution right away?

5. When will you know if an argument is going nowhere and that you need to put it on hold or leave the argument altogether?

6. What is your plan for what to do when an argument is going nowhere and escalating to an unhealthy/unsafe level?

AUTHOR'S EXPERIENCE:

The main thing that will make me stop an argument is if there is yelling, name-calling, or physical aggression. If someone escalates the argument to that level, it is best to leave and come back to the conversation later in a less aggressive environment, or not at all.

Beyond that, I always felt like it was important, when having a tough conversation, to persuade the other person that I was on their side. When we could work together instead of against each other, we solved problems a lot more efficiently.

CHALLENGE:

Devise a plan you will use when confronting potentially uncomfortable conversations. What will you do if things escalate? How will you get the other person to know that you are on their side? Write this down, or discuss this with someone you know and trust.

20

How to Share Your Past in a Healthy Way

Surviving exploitation is such a jarring, life-changing experience, and yet such a nuanced event which many people do not understand. In a way, it makes us who we are and shapes the way we look at the world. Sometimes it may feel like it separates us from other people, so we might find it difficult to explain why we are different to the nonsurvivors in our life.

Sharing Is NOT Mandatory

Before we get into how to address your past, understand that it's totally okay to NOT share about your past. You don't owe anyone the truth, especially if their only reason for asking is pure curiosity. Sharing your story is a very personal choice, and sharing it or choosing not to share it does not make your survivorship any more or less valid. You do you, and saying "None of your business" is a perfectly acceptable response when someone pries too much.

If you do feel the need to share about your past to anyone for any reason, just keep in mind that you will get a different reaction depending on how you share about your past. For example, if you tell people that you were once a "hooker," people might judge you and assume you made poor choices in life. Even if you say you used to be a "stripper" or "exotic dancer," you may not extract the same respect that you would if you said something completely different, which we will share later in this chapter.

It's unfortunate that most laypeople are not educated about sexual exploitation and that they may unfairly judge us for our "choices," when in reality, we may not have been given a choice in our exploitation at all! But the reality is that many people do judge survivors that way, not always maliciously, but perhaps they simply don't understand what it means to be a survivor. However, if you explain to people that you were trafficked or exploited, they are more likely to view you as a survivor of some really terrible circumstances than as someone who made bad "choices."

So, if we don't say, "I was a hooker," or, "I was a stripper," or a "hoe," what do we say?!

There are many things we can say, and you should use your own discernment on what explanation or statement works best for you, but try to think of a phrase or explanation that empowers you, or at the very least does not make you appear like a potential criminal.

Here are some ideas:

"I am a survivor of sexual exploitation."

"I am a survivor of human trafficking."
"I am a survivor of the sex industry."
"I was a victim of a violent crime."
"I am a trauma survivor."
"I have been through a lot and am in the process of rebuilding my life."

These are all statements that do not incriminate us or warrant unwanted questions about the past.

Potential Scenarios

In what circumstances might it help to explain your past, or how your past may explain your current circumstances, to someone? Again, if someone is just curious, it is up to you whether you share or not; but in some situations, it may be helpful to explain just a little bit about your past:

- **When a friend asks you to a party or to go "out":** If you are now in sober living, making sober life choices, or in recovery housing where you are mandated to remain clean and sober, parties and other settings where alcohol is provided may be a huge trigger. You can explain to your friend that you're taking a break from alcohol to improve your health, and offer to meet them in a different setting, like over coffee or breakfast. Here, you might not have to say anything about your past exploitation.

- **Needing extra help with school:** If exploitation has kept you out of the education system for a while, you might need some extra help in school. You can tell your teacher or a school counselor that you were a victim of a long-term crime and that you might need a tutor because it has been so long since you have been in school. This is a great opportunity to ask for tutoring services.

- **With doctors:** If a doctor has a medical concern related to your exploitation, you may want to be open with them. Explain that you were trafficked or exploited, NOT that you were a sex worker, and that might lead him to do certain necessary tests to bring you back to good health. These are important details that your doctor should know.

- **With psychologists or psychiatrists:** With mental health professionals, it's always important to share that you were exploited, because it will help them diagnose and treat you. It may also explain some possible diagnoses, including PTSD, insomnia, or depression and anxiety. Note that you want to find a therapist whom you can be open with, and if you feel like you can't open up about your past with them, you should do your best to find another therapist.

- **With teachers, professors:** You shouldn't have to explain your exploitation to an educator. However, if your recovery program requirements interfere with your ability to perform in class (class ends after your sober living or treatment housing curfew, or you need access to a computer that you may not have in your living environment, etc.), you may want to explain to your teacher that you are in recovery and need to make some adjustments to your learning program.

- **With employers:** Again, you should not have to explain to your employer that you were exploited, and as many laypeople are not educated about exploitation or trafficking, we strongly suggest that you not tell them about it because they might unfairly judge you for it. However, if you need to adjust your work schedule to meet recovery housing program requirements, you might want to let your employer know you are in recovery housing with strict requirements that you must meet, and that your schedule needs to be adjusted accordingly or else you may not have a place to live. It may help to have your program write your employer a letter explaining these needs.

- **With coworkers, classmates, and other peers:** Proceed with caution when deciding how to frame your past to your peers. While it may educate others on exploitation, assume that they won't understand all the details, and be very careful what you say. Try not to say things like, "I used to be an escort/stripper," and try to say things more like, "I have had some difficult times in my life that taught me a lot," or, "I was exploited from a young age, so now I'm rebuilding my life to be more suitable to my needs."

- **With other survivors:** There are ways to share about your past in a healthy way to others who have been through similar trauma, but be sure not to share details that might trigger others or make them judge you. Stay away from talking about how much money you earned and specific names of people from your exploitation, including your old stage name or sex acts you may have been exploited to do.

When Is It Best to Not Share at All?

When deciding when to share about your past, always ask yourself if sharing will truly improve your relationship and communication with this person. Will it help or will it simply bring up more questions? And ask yourself if, in your gut, this person feels like a safe person. Remember that your past experience was personal, and no one else needs to know if you don't feel like sharing.

Repairing Family Relationships

Most of us who have survived sexual exploitation have realized that we have many relationships from before our exploitation that may need some repair. We may never get the chance to repair our relationships with some friends or familiar faces. But what is worse is when we have damaged relationships with our parents, our siblings, or our children. Those relationships, if all parties involved are living emotionally healthy lifestyles, are worth fighting for.

However, trying to insert yourself back into old family relationships without doing the work needed to heal can be at best awkward, and at worst painful, especially if one or more of you want to metaphorically punish the other person for how they have hurt you or led to you being hurt. Because of this, it is best to stay safe and on the surface until the other parties are more comfortable. Small talk is boring, but it could be your key back to your family. If you do have the chance to talk to them, try talking about the weather, current events, what you watch on TV or what you are reading. Do not feel like you have to prove to them that you have healed or changed your life. Actions speak louder than words.

Even so, it is worth noting that not all families are created equal, and some families have toxic qualities that may lead to a person being trafficked. If that is true for your family, it may be best to keep your distance for your own safety and to improve the quality of your recovery. Again, actions speak louder than words, and it may be helpful to observe formerly toxic family members for a while before you dive into repairing your relationship with them.

Remember that you are so much more than your past! Your survival from exploitation says way more about you than your experience of being exploited. If you feel uncomfortable sharing your past in new settings, or how your past affects your current situation, simply stick to key phrases:

"I have been through a lot ..."

"I am a trauma survivor ..."

"I am in the process of rebuilding my life ..."

Prompt Questions:

1. Is sharing about your past something you will do in the future, even to friends and family? Why or why not?

2. Who is a safe person you can practice sharing your story with?

3. What words will you use if you share your story with other survivors? How about nonsurvivors?

4. What words will you NOT use? Why?

5. Are there any relationships that began before your exploitation that you would like to repair? Who are those people in your life? Why are those relationships worth repairing?

6. Think back to those relationships worth repairing. Who were you in that relationship? What was your role? Why was your role important?

AUTHOR'S EXPERIENCE:

If I am talking to another survivor, I am not shy about using slang. It sometimes creates a common ground, especially if the survivor is a new survivor and the language is fresh in their head. However, when I first made a police report, I used a lot of slang and I regret it, because after the fact, I felt like it made the officers think of me as a criminal, when I was actually coming to them as a victim of a crime.

A lot of survivors choose not to share about their exploitation to their family or potential romantic relationships. I can understand maintaining privacy from your family, as I do not share many details with my family, but I could not be in a serious relationship with anyone who didn't understand my past. Early on in the dating process, I would share about my past, and the potential partner's reaction would tell me if I could date them seriously or not. If they wanted all the gory details about sex work, I knew that they were not a safe person and I could not date them in a serious way, but if they instead thanked me for sharing, and said what a strong person I was for overcoming my past, I could pursue them as a serious relationship. We will go over dating in a later chapter. This is just an example from my experience.

CHALLENGE:

Challenge yourself to decide what you should say when sharing about your past with someone you have never met. What would you say, and how would you say it? Write it down, or say it in your head. Bonus: Practice saying it out loud to someone you trust who already knows about your past.

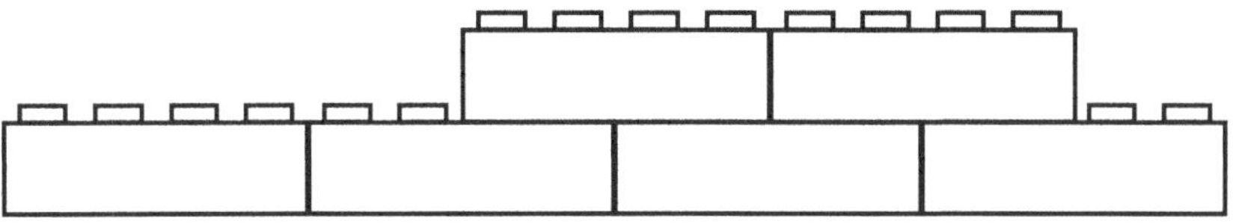

Understanding Abuse

21

Our Past Relationships

Although everyone's experience is different, many survivors come out of exploitation feeling like we have been tricked. There are even movies called "Tricked" and similar titles that ask the same question: If these individuals are so smart and capable, how could they fall victim to so many lies?

How did we end up in recovery anyway?

Sometimes we fall into exploitation through a phony modeling agency. We may have signed contracts we didn't read. We may have developed an online relationship, yet once we meet our online romantic partner, we realize they aren't who they said they were, and then we are stuck with an exploiter. We might have been kidnapped. We may have started out as a sugar baby, but one thing led to another, and we started exchanging sex work for money. There are many ways we may end up in exploitation, and as stated before, every survivor's story is different.

But perhaps we became exploited because these lies weren't so easy to articulate. Often, exploitation abusers will test the waters, pushing you mere inches, until inches become a mile. Many survivors report that their abusers normalized the idea of exploitation in subtle ways.

Maybe it started with lying about where they work or what they do for a living, and after that lie is debunked, they will admit that they're a pimp, but will try to make you think that it's not a big deal. They may then say that many people do it all the time, that you just don't see it or can't pick out other escorts and pimps in a crowd, though they can.

Looking back, you may see all of this leading up to the biggest lie: that your life will be fantastic if you allow them to exploit you. If they started with that big lie, you probably would have run for the hills. But sexual exploitation abuse is so nuanced, detailed, and well thought-out that every bit of information which an exploiter shares with a potential exploitable person is carefully planned as to when and how they will share it.

If this knowledge is new to you, there are a few things you must understand:

- You are still intelligent: If you were not smart, your abuser wouldn't have had to come up with an elaborate plan to trick you into exploitation.
- Your exploiter isn't smarter than you: There are many resources for traffickers and other abusers to devise a plan from, even reference books written by former pimps in prison. Your abuser didn't reinvent any con that hasn't been done a million times before. Often, it is merely a matter of luck.

We can also learn a lot about ourselves by looking at past relationships. Challenge yourself to explore what your relationships were like before your trauma:

- Why or why didn't your relationships work?
- Do you see a pattern in any of your past relationships?

Often, these relationships may be very different than our relationship with our abusers. Maybe our abusers were offering something in a relationship we've never had before (sexual attention, promise of income, emotional openness, edgy lifestyle, etc.). Or maybe it is the opposite: that our abusers were providing relationship qualities that were comfortable and well known to us, that being with them felt like home.

In this chapter, we will explore abuse and abusers for only two reasons.

- One, to train ourselves to recognize emotionally abusive behaviors in others so we can protect ourselves.
- Two, to understand abuse so well that we are able to forgive ourselves for what we have been through.

Once we have a better understanding of how we were tricked, coerced, and controlled, we can start to see ourselves as human beings who have overcome severe trauma, who never intended to be exploited. While many outsiders may think survivors made bad "choices" in the past, you will see that coercion and manipulation hardly leave survivors any choice at all.

Even if you didn't experience an abusive emotional relationship during your trauma in exploitation, if you did not have a pimp or boyfriend who exploited you as an abuser and were simply "renegading" or being exploited on your own without any third-party control, the information in this chapter can still be useful in future relationships, because often, when an abuser learns that a potential victim has already been exploited in the past, they have a completely different set of rules they play by, and it will be important to recognize what their tactics are so you can keep yourself safe.

As always, use grounding to center yourself if the information here is overwhelming, and take a break from reading if you need to. The goal is to learn mindfully, not trigger trauma behaviors.

According to Polaris Project, a reputable national source on human trafficking research, there are several vulnerabilities that may lead to one being sexually exploited. Read this list and ask yourself, "Does that sound like me at the beginning of my exploitation?"

Those who are vulnerable to trafficking (and exploitation) often:

1. Have an unstable living situation
2. Have a history of domestic violence
3. Have a caregiver or family member who has a substance abuse issue
4. Are runaways or involved in the juvenile justice or foster care system
5. Are undocumented immigrants
6. Are facing poverty or economic need
7. Have a history of sexual abuse
8. Are addicted to drugs or alcohol

Other vulnerable people include:

1. Those with preexisting mental health conditions, especially those that are not treated properly
2. Those with eating disorders
3. Those who experienced sexual abuse in early childhood
4. Those who have been sexually assaulted early in their adolescence

Maybe the entire list of vulnerabilities doesn't speak to you, but if you have just one of the above-listed qualities in your life now, or before you were exploited, you can be susceptible to sexual exploitation.

Remember that we have the potential to prosper in our lives beyond whatever we initially thought we could. If you compare how you are now to how you were when you started recovery, and all the qualities and skills you have gained up until this moment, imagine what you can achieve going forward in that same amount of time while you're learning more about your past self so you can shape your new life. You're on the right track!

Prompt Questions:

1. Take a look at the list of vulnerabilities that would make one susceptible to sexual exploitation. What are, or were, your vulnerabilities?

2. On a scale of one to ten, with ten being the highest, how vulnerable were you to sexual exploitation? Why?

3. How were your relationships outside of exploitation different from the relationships you had during exploitation?

4. Why is it important to understand abuse and abusers?

5. If your anxiety or trauma symptoms get triggered when studying abusers, what will you do to calm down and get back into the moment?

AUTHOR'S EXPERIENCE:

I didn't get true healing from exploitation until I understood how abuse worked. After learning about abuse, I was not only able to forgive myself for everything I went through because I finally understood it, but I was also able to protect myself from abusers in the future. Once you know the signs, you can spot a potential abuser very early in the relationship.

CHALLENGE:

Challenge yourself to explore what your relationships were like before your trauma. Why did or why didn't they work? Do you see a pattern in any of your past relationships?

22

Abuser Patterns and Techniques

While we aren't always in a position to turn back the clocks and investigate exactly what happened, how it happened, and why everything happened the way it did during our exploitation, it can bring us healing to take a step back from the whole situation and look in as an innocent bystander. We can do this in many ways. We can journal. We can reflect on who we were before our trauma compared to who we are now. We can participate in an array of trauma therapies with a licensed therapist. We can ask for spiritual guidance from someone we trust.

One thing that has brought many survivors healing is to study sexual exploitation in order to understand what their abusers were actually doing during the periods of abuse, and to then analyze why they did what they did when they were traumatizing them. It's not a fun topic, but it can help you see yourself as someone who deserves forgiveness and healing once you have a better idea of how abuse works.

Survivors must consider participating in extensive trauma therapy because of the variety of ways they are abused. Not only do they often experience verbal abuse, physical abuse, sexual abuse—both from their exploiter and sex buyers or consumers—they also experience financial abuse (withholding the money YOU earned and not allowing you to spend it even if you need it for necessities like food or rent, or not telling you how much you have earned), cultural abuse (outing them to others who are not familiar with their involvement with sex work, or not allowing an international survivor to learn English or isolating them from those who speak their language), and psychological abuse.

We will cover the extent of psychological abuse reportedly used by sexual exploitation abusers in this chapter. Most of these tactics are deliberate choices designed to coerce and control the specific victim they have chosen, but it's important to understand that many of these tactics are merely byproducts that come naturally after other tactics have played out. Also, remember that not every abuser uses every single tactic. They may find that certain tactics are more effective for certain victims. It is also important to understand that most tactics either escalate or decrease, depending on the progress of the abuse in the relationship.

Common Sexual Exploitation Predators' Psychological Abuse Tactics

Love Bombing

Showering you with gifts, physical attention, sexual attention, using loving language, building up your confidence and self-esteem, being encouraging concerning your insecurities. Love bombing creates a plateau for the abused victim to compare the relationship to when the abuse increases and the relationship is not going well. Victims may find that once they've suffered serious abuse, they desire the loving parts of the relationship and remain in the abusive relationship to get tiny glimmers of that love. Normal affection is common in all new relationships, but over-the-top, overly affectionate behavior in the beginning of a relationship should be alarming (if your partner does not know you well, yet they still say they love you, or they bomb you with love in other ways).

Micromanaging

Micromanaging may start as a person asking you to text them when you're going to sleep or waking up in the morning. It will usually progress to strong suggestions as to what you should do, what you should wear, what food to order at a restaurant, how you should spend your money if you are allotted any spending money, and may involve suggestions concerning your hygiene habits. At its peak, micromanaging will have an abuser managing every minute of every day and every single behavior you express. The micromanaging commands may become so intricate that you cannot possibly comply with all of them, which will give an abuser more reason to harp on any and all habits.

Patronizing and Belittling

Patronizing language can come off as honest and helpful when it is really meant to insult you passive-aggressively. (For example: "Baby, I know you tried your hardest, but you're just not smart enough to do my job.") An abuser might also belittle you, your personality, your interests, or your accomplishments. (For example, comparing your dreams of becoming an artist to a little kid putting drawings on their mom's refrigerator.) Abusers might even use passive-aggressive pet names to insult you (such as names that insinuate that you are overweight, unintelligent, unattractive, or all three). However, when you have an adverse reaction to these names, they might say that you have no sense of humor or can't take a joke.

Patronizing and belittling are meant to lower your self-esteem in ways that are hard to notice. If you gradually develop a negative self-image over time, you are more likely to depend on your abuser, or at least remain in the relationship, because you might feel that everyone sees you in a negative, undesirable way, and have a false sense that your exploiter is the only one who will accept you.

Gaslighting

Gaslighting is the term used to describe when an abuser attempts to warp a victim's sense of reality, and to put it bluntly, make them feel like they are "crazy." It can start as small things: Saying something and later denying that they said it. In sexual exploitation, it may be telling you that you both have a certain amount of money, but later, they may say that you spent it all when you know for a fact that you didn't spend so much. It may be saying that you won't have to do certain sex acts, and later telling you that you have to do these acts. However, when you remind your abuser that they said you wouldn't have to, the abuser will deny ever saying that you didn't have to in the first place. Sometimes, people just lie, but when lies turn into more lies and it becomes a pattern that makes you question your own sanity, you may be a victim of gaslighting.

Depriving You of Food or Sleep

Sexual exploitation predators will come up with all kinds of reasons why exploited individuals can't sleep, why they can't eat, supposedly because they want their victim to lose weight or stay up late/wake up early because they need to attend to sex work clients. However, the real reason sexual exploitation abusers deprive you of food or sleep is because when you lack the energy you get from eating and sleeping, your drive, willpower, and your ability to think for yourself diminishes, making you easier to control and ultimately exploit.

Introducing a New Drug

Sexual exploitation predators are notorious for introducing highly addictive drugs to the individuals they exploit. If their victims become dependent on the drug, they will be dependent on the abuser to supply them with drugs. In addition, if a victim gets a drug conviction on their record, they will ultimately have a harder time finding legitimate work, which also makes them easier to exploit.

Humiliation or Public Embarrassment

An abuser may try to humiliate you in public (or in front of people you know) not only to lower your self-esteem but also to assert their control over you. If they publicly embarass you, yet no one comes to your rescue, and they get away with it, you may gradually feel that no one will be able to help you at all. A sexual exploitation predator may also intimidate you in public so you feel that law enforcement, or other public officers, are not on your side, and will reinforce that feeling by threatening to turn you in to the police for sex work if you do not do what they tell you to do.

Playing the Victim

If you try to confront an abuser about a concern you have about their behavior or your relationship with them, they will often turn the tables on you and blame you for making them behave badly or for ruining the relationship. For example, you might confront an abuser about physically abusing you, yet they will insist that you provoked them, and if you didn't provoke them, they wouldn't have to abuse you in the first place. This may escalate into an abuser expressing emotion by crying or having a nervous breakdown right before your eyes, which results in all the attention being on them so that you are distracted from your initial concern. As a result, none of your concerns are ever addressed, so the abuser can proceed to treat you however they want to.

Blaming

Whenever something goes wrong, an abuser may try to convince you that it's your fault, even if it is something that has absolutely nothing to do with you. Their debit card doesn't work? Somehow, it's your fault. The car won't start? Your fault. Not only does this lower your self-esteem, it also makes you believe that your mere existence is problematic. As a result, you become more dependent on your abuser.

Apology Gifts

Often when an abuser hurts you in some way, they will surprise you with a gift. The gift can be as small as your favorite drink from a coffee shop, or as big as flowers or jewelry. This will temporarily distract you from why you may be upset with them, keeping your abuser in the game with you longer. It is a form of love bombing, and may also be used to warp your sense of reality. (*If my abuser does such nice things for me, why was I so mad in the first place?*)

Isolating You from Friends and Loved Ones

Abusers will isolate you from your friends and family in a number of ways. They may do so by force: by simply telling you that you can't see them or preventing you from seeing or communicating with them for various reasons. Or, they may try to assassinate the character of the people you love. They may tell you lies about them, belittle them to you, or otherwise try to make you no longer feel the same connection you once had with them. Perhaps someone has reached out to help you. If the abuser finds out, those loved ones may become his primary target for character assassination. If an abuser can isolate their victim from everyone the victim loves, they will have fewer people in their life who can help them, and the victim will become easier for the abuser to control.

Teaching You or Forcing You to Recruit

Exploiters, especially sex trafficking predators, will teach some of their more seasoned exploited individuals to recruit new potential victims. However, this is not a friendly promotion. Exploiters know that if they convince you to recruit new exploited individuals, you will overstep into criminal territory, and you may even receive pimping and pandering charges from law enforcement. The more charges you have on your record, the more difficult it will be for you to find legitimate work, and the more you will depend on exploitation, and him or her, to support you.

If you do find yourself in a long-term relationship in which you feel you are being manipulated, controlled, and deceived, use fact-checking as a primary tool for keeping yourself safe. Make note of the things that happen to you and anything that someone told you that you later found out to be untrue. Keeping an informal journal can help you keep your head above water until you can seek help. Because abusers depend on your trust in them and distrust in yourself, you must strengthen your trust in yourself as much as possible.

Why do sexual exploitation predators psychologically abuse their victims? In short, an exploitation predator will play extensive mind games with their victims to ensure that they will continue to do sex work so that they can remain financially stable. If an abuser completely cripples their exploited victim's mental and emotional well-being, including everything from their self-esteem to their grip on reality, their victims will be more inclined to do whatever they say, ensuring that nothing can interrupt their lifestyle.

If anyone you are romantically involved with uses any of these tactics with you, they do not have your best interests at heart. The following section will discuss how to recognize these tactics and how to safely remove yourself from a potentially abusive situation before any abuse may occur, but for now you simply must recognize all of these signs as red flags, including everything from public humiliation to signs as subtle as love bombing.

But, simply recognizing abuse for what it is does not make emotions disappear, and understanding that our partner has abused us does not mean we didn't put a lot of effort into the relationship ourselves. We invested lots of time, money, and work into being with this person, and our exploiter may have told us how much they loved us so many times and in so many ways that we had no reason not to believe him.

So how can someone love you, yet do all these horrible things to you?

They can't. Love does not hurt you in any way, be it mentally, verbally, or physically. Love doesn't try to control your life and what you do with it at the expense of your personal goals and overall safety.

However, an exploitation predator might love what they get out of their relationship with you. They may love the money they take from you. They may love being able to control another human being. They may love the power they feel over you. They might love the lifestyle that the money they take from you allows them to have.

But someone who truly loves you would never exploit your sexuality for their own profit.

Period.

Prompt Questions:

1. Have you experienced any of these tactics in your past, or during your exploitation? At the time, did you consciously know what was happening? What was that experience like?

2. Which abuser techniques happen early on in the relationship? Which techniques happen later in the relationship? Why do you think that is?

3. If you have experienced any of these techniques, what did it feel like at the time? And, knowing what you know now, why do you think that is?

4. What is the ultimate objective of abuse to an exploitation predator, or any other abuser? Why would that be important to them?

5. Have you ever felt like you should take any of the blame for potentially falling for any of these abuser tactics? Why or why not?

6. Which of these abuse tactics don't feel like abuse at all?

AUTHOR'S EXPERIENCE:

My abuser used almost all of these techniques. I had a preexisting mental health condition, so he often used gaslighting to make me think I was going crazy, or that I was having mental health issues yet again. He would do things to me, like punch me or slap me, then later when I would confront him about it, he would say that he didn't know what I was talking about, that I must have imagined it. That worked until I got a black eye, which is a little harder to explain away. But if I remember correctly, his lies just got more intricate and crafty. To this day, it is difficult for me to recognize if the abuse really happened. I do have some pictures of the abuse, which helped.

When I would catch him in a lie, he would then blame me for "making" him abuse me. And when I would get really upset or he thought I was going to rat on him, he would shower me with gifts, usually new clothes or travel accessories. He definitely love bombed me in the beginning, and would occasionally love bomb me throughout the years. I fell for it for a long time, until I just couldn't stand it anymore. There was definitely a pattern of him trying one tactic, and if that didn't work, he would try a different abuse tactic.

CHALLENGE:

Challenge yourself to think of one abuse tactic that you have experienced in the past. What is it? How did it make you feel? Do you think you could spot it if it happened in the future?

23

Facing Potential Abusers in the Future

Abusers come in all shapes and sizes. Exploitation predators may appear to be close friends or potential romantic partners. Abusers can parade themselves as talent agents or someone who can further your career in some way. They may even be a relative or someone close to your family. So how do we tell if a person is just a normal person or a person that will try to abuse and control us further down the road?

Simply recognizing abuse tactics when you see them begin is often enough to protect yourself, as long as you remember that tactics will appear mild in the beginning before they escalate. If these mild behaviors even resemble abuse tactics that may develop, they should still indicate your need to be cautious.

In the previous chapter, we discussed what specific abuse tactics are, though you may have noticed some tactics do not happen right away (for example, depriving you of food and sleep usually doesn't happen until later in the relationship). But some tactics do happen early on and should be seen as a red flag.

- **Gaslighting**
  Early in the relationship, gaslighting may look like mere inconsistencies in their story. A potential abuser may say they are in a certain line of work or live in a certain area, but upon further investigation, you might find that is untrue. An abuser will usually have some easy explanation, but if it has a hint of dishonesty or doesn't ring true, you can consider this a red flag.

- **Micromanaging**
  If someone you are getting to know suggests that you call them at certain times, or text them when you wake up or when you go to sleep, and the suggestions turn into commands, and those commands increase and expand, you may be dealing with someone who is controlling, and a potential abuser.

  Your first line of defense here is to try to set boundaries with them and explain that you do not want to be with anyone who is controlling your day-to-day choices. But if that's not enough to curb their controlling behavior, you should try to distance yourself from them.

- **Love Bombing**
  It is normal for a new romantic partner to be affectionate. What is not normal is if this person's affection is disproportionate to the amount of time you have spent getting to know them. If a person asks you to move in with them or talks of marriage before you really know them, you should see it as a red flag, NOT as a romantic gesture. Try to set boundaries with them about where you're at and what

you want or don't want from them. If that doesn't work, you may want to distance yourself from them.

It is always a good idea to stay present when forming new relationships and consider every potential relationship mindfully. Often, trauma survivors may see all potential relationships as possible abusive relationships, but usually, time helps heal that paranoia, and the further you get in your healing, the easier it will be to see a potential partner for what they are at base level. We will go over dating and romantic relationships in more detail during Chapter Forty-Nine, but for now, simply absorb this information about potential abusers and hold it in the back of your mind.

What happens when you do come face-to-face with an exploitation predator?

Possible Scenario

You've met a guy and you have gone on a handful of dates. He's nice, he's funny, and you two are all-around compatible with each other. Since you see things going a serious direction with him, you decide to open up with him and tell him about your past in exploitation, knowing that he won't judge you for it. However, instead of comforting and accepting you, he asks you, "Why did you stop?" He then goes on to explain that sex work is not a big deal, that you shouldn't be ashamed of what you've done, and then starts to let you in on the underground sex industry in his area that, somehow, he is very familiar with. Though you like him and don't want to cut the relationship off right then and there, you realize that he is an exploiter.

What You Can Do

Even if a person seems nice and safe after a few dates, there are ways to tell if you are dealing with a potential abuser. If you open up to a potential romantic partner about your trauma, but instead of receiving your emotions with comfort and acceptance, they try to convince you to reenter sex work, you should try to leave as quickly and quietly as you can. It would not be wise to have an emotional reaction to someone who can potentially cause you harm, so remain polite, and gradually ghost them from contact with you.

This is why the language we use is important when we are expressing our past exploitation to others. Saying "I once was an escort" or "stripper" or "hoe" potentially invites unwanted conversations about the sex industry, whereas saying "I am a survivor of exploitation," or, "survivor of human trafficking," lets others know where you stand, and that you already do not view working in the sex industry in a positive way.

Opening up to anyone about your trauma should be a calculated, well-thought-out decision on who is worthy of that information and how you share it with them. This is not because you should be ashamed of what happened to you, but you must protect your privacy in order to keep yourself safe. This intimate conversation is a personal choice, so you must consider how the information will be received and if it will change your relationship with the person. Again, simply telling someone, "I used to be a hoe," or "I was a stripper for a long time," may make them see you as a criminal or someone who still romanticizes the lifestyle of exploitation.

Instead, consider telling a person who is worthy of your trust, "I was trafficked when I was growing up," or, "I was exploited and taken advantage of in the past." Not only do those statements avoid unwanted conversations about sex work, but they also present you as someone who has grown past the abuse you suffered. Again, this is not because we should be ashamed of our past, but because we must protect ourselves.

In the growing survivor movement, many of us wish that we lived in a society where none of us were judged for our past exploitation, but because the general public is still greatly misinformed about sexual exploitation, we must remain mindful of how we share our story, if for no other reason than to protect ourselves and for our personal safety. If we say the right thing to a survivor who is struggling, we may give them the inspiration they need to turn their life around, but if we say the wrong thing to the wrong person, especially by saying the wrong words to a potential predator who will then try to reexploit us, we may be putting ourselves in danger.

Although some abuse tactics are harder to uncover than others, as they do not involve direct abuse, remember that under no circumstances whatsoever should anyone defend or validate their physical abuse to you. **No one should ever, ever put their hands on you in anger**, especially not someone who you are trusting enough to form a relationship with them.

Finally, remember that if you see a potential relationship show the slight hint of abusive behavior, try setting boundaries in the relationship, stating what you want and need in the relationship and how you do or do not want to be treated. If the potential partner does not respond well to these boundaries, you must distance yourself from them.

PROMPT QUESTIONS:

1. What is one tactic, from the last section of this chapter, that you know you would recognize if someone acted that way toward you in the future? Why would it be easy to spot now?

2. How have you coped with confronting abuse in the past? What would you have done differently?

3. Could you spot the difference between an abuser and someone who just has poor communication and coping habits? What would that difference be?

4. What would you do if you found yourself in a potentially abusive relationship in the future? How would you set boundaries with them to test the waters and see if they are responsive to them?

5. What advice would you give a friend whom you think is in a potentially abusive relationship?

AUTHOR'S EXPERIENCE:

After I left my trafficker, I ended up in another yearlong relationship with a domestic violence abuser. It is sad to admit, but I thought, "At least he doesn't sell me for sex." In my mind, that was a step above what I had already been through, when in reality, it was almost worse. Had I studied abuse before I ever met him, I would have picked up on some key red flags right away!

You really never know when you'll run into someone abusive, or when a friend or someone you love might be in an abusive situation. I put a kibosh on several potentially abusive relationships as I matured, but while I worked in a grocery store during my recovery, a handful of people knew what I had been through, and they ended up asking me for advice, if not for themselves, then for other coworkers.

CHALLENGE:

Plan on how you would set boundaries with a potential abuser in the future. Ask yourself, "How would a good person react to boundaries? How would an abuser react to boundaries?"

24

Forgiving Yourself

Think back to before you were exploited, before you were a teenager, before you hit puberty, when you were a young child, and ask yourself the following questions:

- What did you want to be when you grew up?
- What dreams did you have?
- What things did you want to achieve when you became an adult?

Chances are that you had no idea you would be exploited, or at least you didn't imagine that exploitation would become a huge part of your life for any amount of time, and even if you did foresee yourself going into the sex work industry in some way, you probably had no idea how dangerous the lifestyle actually was.

When we leave exploitation, we have a chance to make the young child we once were proud of who we have become, because who wouldn't be proud of someone who faced extreme adversity, yet got their life together and moved onwards and upwards? In order to get that gratification, however, we must first understand that though we may have played a role in our own exploitation, we were extremely victimized and exploited, if not by one individual exploiter, then by many collective predators. Perhaps the sex industry itself is what exploited our need to survive in a tough world.

Survivors of all kinds of trauma often find themselves to blame, at least partially, for what they went through, and though it's important to take ownership for our actions, it's also important to see ourselves separate from the trauma. Now that we understand what abuse is and how it works, we can see how we may have been coerced and taken advantage of at different times during our trauma.

Sexual exploitation is bigger than our own story. It happens to all kinds of people all over the world in a myriad of ways. So, we must ask ourselves: If that same abuse happened to someone we love, would we blame them, our loved one, for everything that has happened to them? Or would we simply want to reach out and help them?

The unfortunate thing we know now is that many people exist in the world who either don't know how much harm they are causing exploited individuals (johns, tricks, sex industry consumers or clients), or they simply don't care, and that's a scary thought: that there are people out there who will take advantage of vulnerable people and don't feel bad about doing so, or at least they don't feel bad enough to change their behavior. Some of us learn this lesson sooner than others, but by the time anyone has survived abusive trauma like sexual exploitation, we know that true evil exists in the world.

What does this knowledge mean to us? We are free! We will never have to fall victim to exploitation abuse again. From now on, the relationships we choose to keep in our lives will be honest, worthy of our trust, and will help us grow instead of taking us backwards. We will know this because we can use the information that we have learned this month to prescreen any potential close relationship for abusive or exploitative behavior, or catch it later down the road.

What Does Forgiving Yourself Look Like?

Even though survivors have done nothing "wrong" by getting entangled in exploitation—especially those of us who were physically forced into exploitation—a lot of us still hold on to the guilt that comes with it. We may feel guilty for getting into a bad situation in the first place. We may feel guilty for turning our backs on our family, our children, our future. We may feel guilty for the acts during exploitation. However, it is important to recognize that the strongholds pulling us into and keeping us in exploitation are powerful, as we can see when we study abuse tactics used by exploitation predators.

Forgiving yourself is not easy, and it is not an overnight process. Forgiving yourself is the choice you make every day. You may spend many months or years learning to forgive yourself for everything that happened. Part of that is understanding your own vulnerabilities and recognizing where you were taken advantage of. Another part is accepting what you cannot change. It happened. It was rough. However, it was in the past, and you never have to go through it again.

A third component to forgiving yourself is making the commitment to yourself that you will never put yourself through exploitation again. This is when all that you will learn in this book will come into play: We understand abuse so we can keep ourselves safe. We learn how to set goals and stick to them so we won't have as many vulnerabilities to exploitation in the future. We are taking all the necessary steps to make our lives better, so we will never have to go through the pain of exploitation again.

Learning about abuse can be as overwhelming as it is rewarding, so if you haven't done so lately, please participate in your favorite self-care activity and use some positive self-talk to let yourself know how proud you are of yourself for overcoming all you have, and to tell yourself that because you're wiser, good things lie ahead.

Prompt Questions:

1. What does forgiveness mean to you?

2. What is your experience with forgiveness?

3. What would make your eight-year-old self proud? What would make your eighty-year-old self proud?

4. If a close friend or loved one went through exploitation, how would you react? Would you blame them or scold them? What would you do?

5. Do you feel that you are worthy of forgiveness? Why?

6. Do you forgive yourself for what you went through? Why or why not?

AUTHOR'S EXPERIENCE:

When dealing with major issues like abuse, it is wise to ask yourself, "If a good friend were in the same situation, what would I say or do to help them?" That always helped me find compassion for myself.

CHALLENGE:

Take some time to practice self-care.
This is a tough chapter, and you may need it.

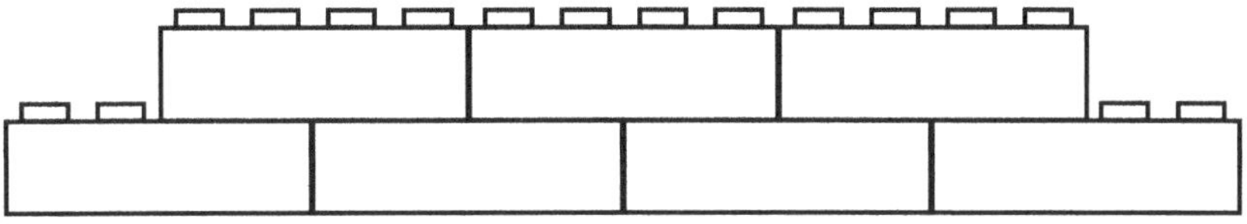

Pursuing Education

25

Pros and Cons of Pursuing Education

Many survivors find that exploitation has interrupted their education path in some way, whether they were exploited as teens and didn't finish high school or their higher education was cut short due to the circumstances of their exploitation. We can't change the past, but fortunately surviving trauma gives us a chance to re-explore education with a more mature mindset, if that is the path we choose.

So *is* that our path?

If we haven't finished high school, we must consider that many entry-level positions, even in retail, may require that we have a high school diploma or GED, and while getting our GED may seem like a simple fix, it does require some studying as you must pass the exam with a certain percentage of correct answers, which differs by state. Gaining our diploma after not having been in school for some time may not be easy either, but it can be a more gradual entry back into a school environment. We can do this through independent study programs at our local adult school, or even online in some cases.

If you are stuck halfway to finishing your college education, or if you have finished your bachelor's degree but find that you will need postgraduate education to pursue a career in the field you choose, yet you're still stuck with the bare minimum budget of a new survivor, you must consider how to meet your immediate needs while still being able to stay on track with your education goals. This may mean holding down a full-time, entry-level job with a partial load of classes, or vice versa, and this may also mean that you must pursue scholarships and/or financial aid.

Time is also another important factor to consider. How long can you afford to not work, or is there a way you can pursue education and work simultaneously? There are only a few survivor-centered residential programs that extend beyond two years, so you must have an idea how to support yourself after those two years if you are pursuing secondary education, and although in a perfect world, we would get a paid internship after a year or so of college, it doesn't always work that way.

For some survivors, education is not an immediate need, and we may find that supporting ourselves financially will take all of our focus as we set our sights on employment. This chapter may still interest you because it will talk about turning your student brain back on, and at the very least, it will give you some useful information about pursuing education, just in case you change your mind once you're set with employment. You don't have to go out right now and sign up for classes, just keep your ears open.

Challenge yourself to look at both the ultimate future and the immediate future:

- Will you need to advance in education to make it through the next year?
- What about the next few years?
- How about ten years down the road? Will you be happier if you advance your education in another decade?

What about your life goals? What do you want to do ultimately, that you would be happy doing every day of your life? What kind of education, formal or informal, will that require?

You don't have to have the answers right now. Just think about it.

Prompt Questions:

1. Is education something you will need to pursue independence?

2. Is there anything about school that interests you?

3. Is there anything about school that brings up fears for you?

4. Will you have to balance school and work at the same time?

5. What will help you stay focused in school while you are busy keeping up with other goals?

AUTHOR'S EXPERIENCE:

When I was in recovery, I was very focused on getting a job, saving money, and moving out of residential treatment, so school was the furthest thing from my mind. I also hated school because I did not have a great experience in high school, as many people don't. I did attempt to start junior college while I was in recovery, but because I was very concerned with making enough money to move out of the residential treatment program, the timing was just not right and I did not start school till quite a few years later.

A few years out of recovery, I discovered that if I was serious about getting a job in grant writing or working for nonprofits, I would have to have to have at least a bachelor's degree. But enough time had passed in my recovery that I was in a better place to start school, as I was about six months into my new job. It was very easy to add in a couple of classes and increase the number of classes as I went. You just have to figure out when the time is right for you!

CHALLENGE:

Challenge yourself to look at both the ultimate future and the immediate future. Will you need education to advance yourself through the next year? What about the next few years? How about ten years from now? Will you be happier then if you advance your education now?

26

Navigating Your Education Options

Though sometimes it feels like exploitation has set us behind the pack of most other people, surviving exploitation provides us with a fresh start to our lives. Maybe we haven't been in the education system for the last couple of years or so, but from where we are at, we can start simple, then gradually build up to meeting our goals.

This section will help you decide which education paths you might choose. It will also include some tips on how to get there financially. Again, if you're not interested in pursuing education at this time, simply keep your ears open! This may help you down the line in your recovery if you change your mind, or it may be helpful to share with other survivors who need this information more than you do.

Below are some pros and cons for the most common education choices one may make at the beginning of their exploitation recovery journey. Consider every option with an open, discerning mind and think about what may or may not work for you:

GED: Pros and Cons

Pros: With a GED, you can apply for most entry-level jobs without question. It will make applying for trade schools easier as many require a GED at minimum, though regulations vary from state to state.

Cons: Some upper-level schools and jobs require a diploma and will not accept a GED. The test is also difficult and takes some studying, so some people prefer to get their diploma, because it will make their higher education more accessible. And without a diploma, you may not be eligible for financial aid, depending on what state you reside in.

Diploma: Pros and Cons

Pros: With a diploma, you will not have any issues applying to most entry-level jobs and secondary education institutions, because diplomas are widely accepted for applications. You may also like having the sense of accomplishment of finishing something you started long before your exploitation.

Cons: Earning your diploma may require you to spend more time in the classroom than you would if pursuing your GED. Instead of one big test, you will have a greater number of smaller tests. And if you haven't been in school for a long time, it might be difficult to navigate the whole process on your own and still live up to the standards of a full-time student right off the bat. If this is still your goal, grab a tutor and buckle up for the ride!

Trade School (Cosmetology School, Medical Assistant Programs, Automotive)

Pros: Save time! Trade schools usually only require that you spend a specified number of hours in school, followed by a licensing exam. This process can take as little as two years or less, and then you will be employable in the field. Also, there are often job opportunities during your time at the school, depending on what field you're in. For example, in cosmetology school, though you may not have your license, you are still eligible to hold front desk and receptionist positions at local salons, which will give you valuable shop experience.

Cons: Trade schools are notorious for students dropping out before they finish. If that happens to you, that's a huge waste of time and money. Trade schools are a huge expense, and whether you get a job in the field or not, you will be expected to pay back any student loans you have incurred once you leave the school. You also must be aware of fraud with trade schools—many are good and reputable, but there are so many that are scams. Do your homework and research before signing up.

Community College, Junior College

Pros: Save money! Not only is the tuition significantly less than a four-year university, but the whole structure of junior colleges is designed to help students who are not familiar with college figure out how to learn effectively and navigate the experience by themselves. At the end of two years at the junior college, you can use your associate's degree to find a job, or you can transfer to get your bachelor's at a four-year university. Win-win!

Another "pro" for community college is that there are many resources available at community colleges, such as career testing, free tutors, educational planning, and sometimes even mental health support.

Cons: As of the year this is written, there is no way you can graduate with a bachelor's degree from a junior or community college. If you are pursuing a bachelor's degree, you must transfer to a university after meeting all the requirements at the community college level. Also, if networking is a big part of your desired job field, you may want to move on to a university after junior college to increase your ability to network with other like-minded individuals.

University

Pros: At a four-year university, you can earn your bachelor's degree. Four-year colleges are also a great place to network for professional opportunities. Some say that a bachelor's degree is the new equivalent of the high school diploma. Employers consider it the new minimum requirement for most professions!

Cons: Universities are expensive! It's best to try to complete as much as you can at the junior college level first, or apply for scholarships and/or financial aid. Also, universities often have higher expectations for their students than community colleges. It might be difficult to dive headfirst into a university if you are not an experienced student or haven't been back to school for a while.

Paying for School

Sometimes paying for school is the only thing holding us back from even beginning to pursue education. It's best to talk to your school counselor about what fee waivers and other financial assistance programs you are eligible for, because it varies from state to state. For example, in California there is a waiver you can sign up for that covers the entire cost of tuition at the community college level for eligible students. Other waivers help students from different ethnic backgrounds and financial brackets.

You may even be eligible for grants, or government-awarded monies, which can cover anything from tuition to the cost of living. After applying for school, check out FAFSA.gov to see what you are eligible for. As always, applying for scholarships, even small ones, can help pay costs while you attend school.

If loans end up being part of how you need to pay for your education, try to borrow as little as possible, but remember that with better career options for the future, you will also have better means to repay the loans. The repayment periods are usually fairly generous.

It also does not hurt to get a part-time or entry-level job while you're at school to help meet your financial needs. If you don't know where to begin looking for work, try working at your school! Many colleges and other schools have lots of job opportunities right on campus.

Considering your personal circumstances with clear discernment, what sounds like the best plan for you? Is school something you can work into your recovery? Is it something that must be put on hold until you are financially independent? Or is education going to be your big break in reaching true independence?

PROMPT QUESTIONS:

1. What is the first step in your education journey that you will need to take?

2. What is your ultimate goal with your education?

3. Is there a different educational option that you haven't thought about before that interests you?

4. What is your plan for how to pay for school?

5. What is your experience with education, before or during exploitation?

6. Do you think your experience with education would be different now? Why or why not?

AUTHOR'S EXPERIENCE:

I was lucky enough to have finished my high school education and have taken a few college classes before I was ever exploited, so the next step was to continue taking classes at the junior college level until I could transfer to a university.

Money was a big thing that held me back. Because of student loans I took out for a trade school, which I never graduated from, I was not eligible for financial aid until they were paid off. However, I did qualify for a tuition waiver, and I am planning on applying for scholarships by the time I transfer to a university.

CHALLENGE:

Challenge yourself to write down your ultimate goal with your education, and put that note where you will see it every day. Keep your eye on the prize!

27

Turning Your Student Brain Back On

Our brains were wired in a very specific way while we were exploited. We often were trained to follow orders from our exploiter, be money-hungry or even money-obsessed, and we often had to shield our ego from the sexual abuse we were suffering. Learning new things was often not a priority for us, because surviving was our main priority.

But the brain is a beautiful and wonderful organ, designed for growth, not just survival, and whether we can see it now or not, we can rewire our brain to do whatever we want it to. It just takes some practice. If we are setting our sights on education, we just need to get back into the student frame of mind, and there are plenty of things we can do to help our mindset.

Below are a few things you can try to get your brain back into learning mode. Consider trying one or two of these things to start rewiring your brain for education:

Flash Cards

Though many of us have already spent time in school learning our times tables, we might be a little rusty. Get your hands on some flash cards and start memorizing some multiplication basics.

Bonus challenge: Once you get refreshed on basic math, try to move on to foreign language flash cards. You can make them yourself with index cards! On one side, write the English word, and on the other side, write the same word in a foreign language. Then test yourself. It might be helpful to learn some basic words in another language, and it will definitely begin to rewire your brain!

Word of the Week

To expand your vocabulary, find a word you've never used before, look up its meaning, write it in a place where you will see it often, then use this word as often as possible. Change the word once a week and watch your vocabulary expand!

Reading for Pleasure

Many survivors in active recovery read a lot of devotionals and self-help books, like this one. Do you read anything simply for pleasure? Try reading a book just for fun! This will change your relationship with reading and will improve how quickly and effectively you read.

Setting Weekly Goals, Planning and Organization

As we pursue education and start working to support ourselves, our schedules will fill up. Use the information you learned in Chapters Thirteen and Fourteen and keep a strict schedule of all your weekly tasks and goals you want to achieve. While you're signing up for school, you might want to start with financial aid goals and meeting deadlines with open enrollment. If you get the hang of your weekly schedule now, it will be easier once you start preparing for exams, tests, and goals within the classes you will take.

Another important change you might need to make is how you talk to yourself. If you had an abuser in the past who told you over and over that you were stupid or incapable of taking care of yourself, know that you are not alone ... and that anyone who said that to you is WRONG. You have made it through a large portion of your recovery, and you're still going! That takes a lot of courage, persistence, and mental strength, which are all things that will help you in the education system!

Remind yourself of some of your best qualities through affirmations:

- I am smart: if I have the mental strength to escape exploitation, there's no reason I can't accomplish my education goals.
- I am strong: I am in it to win it; school is nothing compared to what I've already done.
- I am improving my life: education will give me so many opportunities that I didn't even know were possible.

Education is a huge blessing. It will be tough at times, but it won't be anything you can't handle. You've already been through so much! Compared to surviving exploitation, school should be a piece of cake.

Prompt Questions:

1. Without going into detail, are there any skills you acquired through your exploitation, or on your journey to recovery, that may help you when facing education?

2. What part of your brain haven't you used since before your exploitation? What kind of thinking will you need to exercise?

3. Is there any part of learning that you enjoy? Why or why not?

4. How does "turning your brain back on" prepare you for school?

5. What will help you stay positive when you face challenges in school?

AUTHOR'S EXPERIENCE:

In my exploitation, I had to have good time management, which helped me a lot in school, but I was constantly in defense mode, which caused me a lot of anxiety when starting school. I never liked school, but I always loved writing, so one of the things that helped me was picking a word of the week to expand my vocabulary. When you start school, new words are going to come up all the time, and it is good practice using these words in casual conversation.

I also really surprised myself at how well I remembered my times tables. Knowing your multiplication is the bread and butter of all math classes, and flash cards definitely helped me.

CHALLENGE:

Set one weekly goal for your education, whether or not you are already in school. Do you want to complete orientation for the next semester? Do you want to get an A on your next test? Set this goal by writing it down, and put it somewhere you will see it every day this week.

28

Student Maintenance and Organization

Like any other long-term commitment, your education will take some management, maintenance, and endurance on your part. You must keep an open mind while you pursue all your classes, and must use your best judgment while picking your classes, studying for them, and choosing your focus in school. This section will discuss some long-term needs in school and how to resolve any major issues as you pursue your education goals.

Studying

In class, pay attention to what your teacher wants you to know about whatever subject he or she is teaching. When taking notes, make sure to write down any key points the teacher highlights AS WELL AS anything that is especially confusing to you, so you know what you will need extra time to learn on your own.

It is best to study at home for one hour per unit of the class you are taking. Even in trade school, you will have to study for periodic tests as you pursue your license. Studying can involve practical procedures, as in hands-on learning, or memorization of information. Both are important, though some classes will involve more memorization than practical know-how, and vice versa.

Using flash cards to remember information can be very helpful. There are smartphone apps you can use that will generate flash cards for you, or you can make your own out of index cards. This can be useful in learning new language, new terminology, and even formulas. Be creative!

And as always, be sure to practice self-care after a long study session. Not only will this provide you some mental relief, it will also train your brain to know that after studying comes relaxation, so you will be more likely to want to study again!

When Do Professors Cross the Line?

As there are good cops and bad cops, good doctors and bad doctors, there are good professors and bad professors, and as a student, you must be wise in differentiating between the two and then dealing with possible bad professors.

For example: Some professors may have you in their class for only two weeks before they tell you that you don't have the gift that would allow you to pass their class, and that you should save yourself the trouble and drop the class.

Why is this a bad professor?

Because what he or she is actually saying is that they don't have the ability to teach you the subject, which in turn means they are probably not the best teacher. So what do you do? You can either get a different professor in the same subject, or if that's not an option, you can grab a tutor and work twice as hard as when you began the class. Prove that jerk of a professor wrong!

Another example: A teacher starts to casually flirt with you, then becomes more obvious about it as he flirts with you in front of the class. He might even start degrading you and tell you that someone as pretty as you doesn't need an education; you can just be a sugar baby or marry into a wealthy family. (Sound ridiculous? It happens more often than you'd think. Some teachers take advantage of students whom they view as vulnerable.)

In this situation, do whatever you have to do to get a different professor. If you allow this kind of mild harassment to slide, it will only progress. Get a different professor, and it may be wise to report this kind of behavior to school management or authorities if you feel that it has crossed the line. Chances are this may happen to other students, and those professors need to know that their behavior is not okay. Check out Chapter Seventeen on social relationships to brush up on how to share your past in a healthy way.

As survivors, we should always be careful about how we share about our past exploitation and who we share it with, not because we should be ashamed of it but to protect ourselves and our personal safety. This includes other students and your professors. If you are in recovery housing and your recovery's restrictions interfere with managing your schoolwork, it is better to frame your concerns as recovery-related rather than mentioning what you are in recovery for. Do not go out of your way to tell other students or professors about your exploitation until you are sure that they are a safe person who will not judge you for it or take advantage of you because of it.

Avoiding Burnout

Sometimes we are much more ambitious at the time we are picking our classes than when we are struggling with our class load. When picking our classes, we must take into account how long it has been since we have last been in school, and keep in mind that we are still working on our own personal recovery as we pursue education. It is best to not overload yourself in the beginning and gradually build up to having a heavy load of classes instead of starting off with your most difficult subjects. This way, we are less likely to drop classes halfway through the semester.

So how do we know if it is actually best to drop a class or change directions?

Check in with yourself every couple of weeks and ask yourself: How am I doing in my classes? Do I still like what I'm studying? Am I likely to pass this class?

In the first few weeks, you might want to push yourself a little extra in order to get yourself going, but if you're halfway through, or more, with your classes and you are struggling too much and not enjoying the classes, you might want to think about changing directions. However, if you're close to the finish line and are unhappy with your classes, you should always do your best to at least finish. It's better to get an average grade than to get an "incomplete."

If you are really struggling with a subject that is necessary for you to complete in order to reach your academic goals, talk to your school counselor or even your teacher about finding a possible tutor or learning center which would help you with your goals.

And as always, it is SO IMPORTANT to practice self-care. You must set aside some time to take care of yourself while you pursue any goals, but especially your academic goals. Your brain needs some time to relax in order to be fully functional while working toward your education.

Challenge yourself to reflect on your own personal needs while pursuing school:

- What boundaries will you set with your teachers, fellow students, and with yourself?
- How much studying is too much?
- What will help you focus on your goals?
- What will help you unwind when you need to?

One of the most important things to remind yourself is why you are pursuing education in the first place. It's not necessarily to be a perfect student or get perfect grades and impress your teachers. It is to better your quality of life. Keep that dream in the forefront.

Prompt Questions:

1. What would happen in your life that would indicate to you that you were burned out from school?

2. What will you do if you find yourself suffering from burnout?

3. Have you ever had an experience with a teacher or professor acting inappropriately? What was that like? What did you do during that time?

4. Have you had experience with a bad teacher in the past? What made them not a good teacher? How did the class turn out?

5. How does a good teacher act? How does a bad teacher act?

6. How can you incorporate self-care into your school schedule?

AUTHOR'S EXPERIENCE:

Right after I left exploitation for the first time, I enrolled in the local junior college, and in my very first class on the first day of class, the professor made a sexist comment to me IN FRONT OF THE WHOLE CLASS. Even though I had been through way worse during my exploitation, I knew that what he said to me was inappropriate for a professional teacher to say to a student. I reported him, and then changed my class.

I hate to say it, but to avoid burnout, I do the bare minimum that is expected of me. I show up to class and do my homework, but I do not do extra-credit assignments unless my grade is falling behind. And, I also incorporate self-care into my weekly schedule.

CHALLENGE:

Challenge yourself to come up with a plan if (a) you find yourself in a bad teacher's class, or (b) you start to suffer from burnout. What will you do? What steps will you take to resolve the issue?

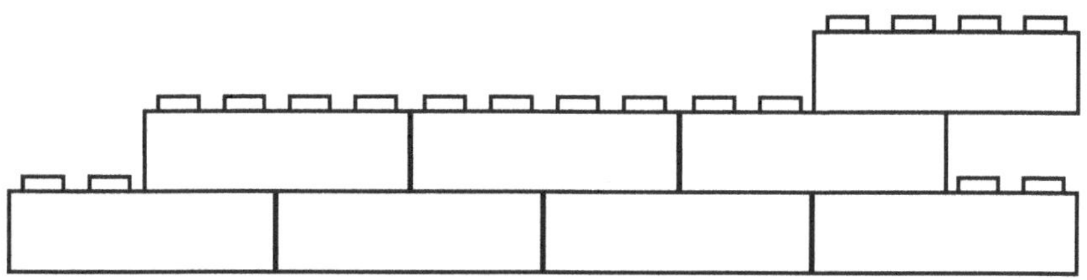

Pursuing Employment

29

Finding the Right Employment Path

It takes a combination of different components to successfully change your life from your past in sexual exploitation to an independent lifestyle. You may aim to have a mentally healthy lifestyle, great emotion and behavior management, and a solid plan for independence. But one thing is clear: **Stable employment and supporting yourself is incredibly important in your journey to succeed and remain free of exploitation for the long term**. Even as we study in school to further our education, it is important to remember that we are working hard in school to ultimately prepare ourselves for future professional employment.

Now, some of us who have formerly been exploited in the sex industry may have a unique attitude about work, since what we did for work basically violated our privacy for large amounts of cash, not to mention it may have been advertised to us as a quick, "easy" job. Working outside of exploitation may not initially bring in as much money as we used to earn, but remember four key things about non-exploitation employment:

- We will get to keep all our money and will not have to give a portion (or all of it) to an exploiter.
- Legitimate work is not illegal, as some exploitation jobs are, and therefore our earnings cannot be seized by the police.
- We will have total control of our work ethic and earnings.
- We will not sacrifice our privacy, dignity, and self-respect for a paycheck.

If we get a high-paying, idealistic job while we are still working on our recovery, we should consider ourselves very lucky, because the boundaries of our treatment path do not always allow us to work the 9-to-5 jobs of our wildest dreams. And while we should always keep our sights on our ultimate career path, this month we will focus on entry-level positions that you will be able to obtain with little to no training or experience, while still working your recovery program.

Below are some entry-level employment paths which can support you while you work your program. If you are not sure what kind of employment to seek, here are some ideas of what may fit for you:

Clerical and Administration

If you can type fast, have great organizational skills, and are good on the phone, clerical or administrative work could be an awesome path for you. The downside is that most offices only hire one secretary, which means getting an administrative assistant gig is very competitive, and they often require a bachelor's degree, even if you don't use any skills you acquired in college on the job. The plus side is that you will most likely have a normal Monday to Friday, 9-to-5 schedule, which has its benefits, a dress code vs. a uniform, you won't be on your feet all day, and you will likely have holidays, evenings, and weekends off.

Though most smaller offices have only one administrator per office, many offices have several layers of roles requiring administration. These roles often offer great experience in a fully professional environment.

Serving/waitressing

Those who work well under pressure tend to thrive in the service industry. If you are setting your sights on the medical field, where you will deal with time-sensitive work and helping difficult patients with ease, you can learn a lot of the same work ethic while serving. The downsides to serving include long hours on your feet, potentially serving difficult people, and probably being required to work holidays, evenings, and weekends. The plus side is that, depending on where you work, you can make great tips. That's cash in your pocket at the end of the shift, which most people who work do not have!

Retail/Grocery

Grocery and retail are often huge stores with lots of employees, which means you are often given lots of hours, and many grocery stores are protected by unions, which can mean better benefits, and that you have your union to potentially advocate for you to your employer. The downside is that you will most likely be required to work evenings, weekends, and holidays, and since some retail chains have a large employee body, you may not have a direct relationship with your employer. Some might consider that a good thing, though, because it allows you to learn your job without direct pressure from your superior.

Barista

Working at some popular coffee chains may require you to have exceptional customer service skills, even in the face of some nasty, ruthless customers, while still being able to meet daily deadlines and keep up with drink and food orders. Many consider this a challenge. But again, if you thrive under pressure, this can be a good gig for you as you will be able to shine, and you can potentially receive weekly tips. Here, though, you will be expected to work nights, early mornings (before dawn), weekends, and holidays.

Food Service

Fast food is very fast-paced with high expectations, and so is working in a kitchen. The upside is that you will get lots of hours if you keep up with your coworkers, and food service experience is universal, meaning that the skills you learn at one job can absolutely be applicable to similar future jobs. In fact, getting your food handler's card can be useful (and a plus for potential employers!) to any future jobs. Hours may be unpredictable, though, and you may work evenings, weekends, and holidays.

Working in a kitchen (line cook, sous chef) is an excellent path to consider if you are bringing a criminal record with you into recovery. You won't be dealing with the public, and you can gain skills that become a trade which you can take to other potential jobs. If you have facial tattoos from exploitation, many kitchens have relaxed regulations regarding tattoos. Some of the most famous chefs in the world have many!

Call Centers

The great thing about call centers is that you won't be seen, and that the majority of your work will be over the phone. If you have face tattoos received in exploitation that have prevented you from gaining employment, this might be a good option for you at certain locations. The downside is that you will have to work long hours at inconvenient times, and you may have to provide excellent customer service to very rude customers.

Factories, Machine Shops

Some employees thrive in factory or assembly-line settings and some don't. Though a plus is that you will not be dealing with customers or performing any customer service at all, you may be on your feet doing repetitive things for long periods of time, and you may be expected to complete strict hourly or daily deadlines. Even so, you may be free from working holidays, weekends, and nights, depending on where you work.

Temp Agencies

Temp agencies are businesses where agents will connect you with temporary jobs. On the plus side, you will probably be able to get a job fast through a temp agency, and those jobs may lead to permanent positions! But there are a few catches. For one, though the jobs may lead to permanent placement, permanent placement is not guaranteed, and you may find yourself job-hopping and changing jobs weekly. The other catch is that temp agencies are businesses. They make money off of getting you hired, usually a few dollars on every hour. So while a future employer may put the starting rate at $18 per hour, you may be making much lower than that, with the rest of your earnings going directly to the temp agency. If getting placed in a job immediately is your priority, go for it! Just be aware of the few potentially negative factors.

Volunteering

Obviously, volunteering for the rest of your life will not bring you any substantial income, but as mentioned in greater detail in Chapter Four, a great way to figure out what kind of job you want is to volunteer at a place similar to where you will ultimately want to work. Usually, the interview process for volunteering is very minimal and relaxed, and staff can often work with your busy recovery schedule. Sometimes you can even find volunteer jobs that will give you a small stipend for your volunteer shift, although that is rare.

But if we want to be a doctor, we can't just volunteer to be one, so here are some ideas for volunteer positions that will give you a feel for the industry you desire to be a part of:

- Medical field: Nursing home/retirement home volunteer
- Administrative field: Front desk at a church
- Mental health field: Support staff at a rehab or domestic violence facility
- Service industry: Soup kitchen helper

Volunteering is also VERY important, because it allows you to gain legitimate work experience to add to your résumé, and if you nurture a good relationship with the organization which you're volunteering with, you may be able to use them as professional references for future employers. Although the above suggestions coordinate with future career goals, you do not necessarily need to find a volunteer job in the specific field you want to work in. Just find something that you wouldn't mind volunteering at for a few hours per week and gain some experience there.

Use your imagination! Remember from Chapter Eleven, we learned how to set our sights on what we want, or our goals, and from there, create a step-by-step plan for how to get there. This is where that knowledge really comes into play! Even if your ultimate goal may take many years of education, you can consider entry-level employment as a very important step toward obtaining that goal! And even if entry-level employment doesn't pay as much as we would like, it can absolutely pay well enough to provide an independent lifestyle.

Challenge yourself to take your ultimate employment goal and break it down into steps to get there, from how many years it will take, to each coming month, to each week, right down to the very day you are reading this chapter. What can you do today to move you toward your goals?

The next few weeks will cover all you need to know to get a job, from writing a résumé to acing an interview, but for now, simply reflect on what kind of job you ultimately want, and speculate what you need to learn, gain, and grow to get there.

PROMPT QUESTIONS:

1. What are your concerns about entering the workforce? Does your past in exploitation play a role in finding a job?

2. What kind of jobs have you had (not related to exploitation) in the past? What was your experience like then?

3. Which entry-level job appeals to you? Why?

4. Brainstorm your needs in employment. What are they? Will you need to be able to get there by public transit? Do you need more hours or fewer hours? Do you wish to avoid customer service jobs? Explain.

5. What is your ultimate employment goal, the one goal that will bring you ultimate fulfillment in your life? What will it take to get there?

6. Which entry-level job can prepare you for your career goals?

AUTHOR'S EXPERIENCE:

I had a lot of aspirations when it came to employment, but I knew that even if my ultimate goal was finishing school and getting a job in my desired field, I had to obtain an entry-level job in the meantime to support myself while I pursued my goals. At the time, I didn't mind customer service, so that was the first place I looked. I worked at several places, including a church office, Walmart, and a grocery store. The grocery store was union organized, so I was able to get good benefits and lots of hours, so that is where I stayed for almost three years.

CHALLENGE:

Challenge yourself to take your ultimate employment goal and break it down into steps that will get you there, from how many years it will take, to each coming month, to each week, right down to the very day you are reading this chapter. What can you do today that will move you closer to that goal?

30

Job Searching

In this section, we will cover how to find a job, including:

- How to pick a good job to apply to
- How often to apply
- And how to write a résumé

If you haven't already, strongly consider finding a volunteer position to hold while you are looking for a job. This allows you to continue working so there are no gaps in your résumé, and may provide you with strong professional references in case you need current references for the jobs you apply to.

But, remember that you are in charge of your own job-finding strategies. YOU know what will work best to find YOU a job for which you are a good fit. Just keep the following information in mind when working on your job search.

Searching for the Job

As we have already learned, we have lots of options for entry-level jobs that each have positive and negative factors. So, besides figuring out what kinds of jobs would be a good fit, what should we consider when picking a job?

- **Location:** Can you get to the job site by public transit? Or if you have a car, is it a reasonable distance to drive every day? Is the job site in a safe part of town?

- **Hours:** You won't always know what hours you will work before you are hired, but for some jobs, you can infer when you will work. For example, if you work at a coffee shop, you may be required to work before sunrise on a daily basis! Can you handle that schedule? Can you work night shifts? Keep business hours in mind when picking the job.

- **Recovery compatibility:** Ask yourself if this job is something that you can work along with your recovery, considering both the hours that you must devote to your recovery outside of the job, and if the job itself will trigger you in any way. Also consider, if you are in residential treatment, what kind of jobs will they allow? In my experience, recovery housing programs usually do not let you work at bars or dispensaries.

  Keep in mind that many working adults partake in drinking and sometimes other drugs as well, though this is outside of work hours. Can you handle being around those kinds of people and their conversations at this stage in your recovery? Or do you need to find a more conservative job setting?

- **Uniform and Dress Code:** Can you comply with a strict dress code? Are you willing to cover tattoos and take out piercings on a daily basis? Can you afford a full wardrobe that the job may require you to have? Do you have any problem wearing an employer-issued uniform?

- **How MANY hours:** Are you looking for a part-time job or a full-time job? Do you have enough free time to work full-time? Or on the other hand, can a part-time job truly support your lifestyle?

Résumé: A résumé is a document that presents your work and education history, references, skill set, and contact info in an organized, readable fashion. Even if the potential employer only requires an application to apply for the position, you may want to put together a résumé so that you have all your job history, education history, and professional references together in one place. Some job applications also allow you to digitally upload a résumé, which makes the application process go a lot faster.

Résumés have several important sections:

- **Name and contact info:** Phone, email, and city of location. Make sure your email is appropriate and mature! Usually just a name and a few numbers works.

- **Job history:** Here, you want to include the name of the company you worked for, when you worked for them, what your job title was, and a few of your responsibilities at that job. (Here, you can use volunteer jobs and don't necessarily have to mention that they were volunteer jobs. Just state the organization, your title, and some of your volunteer responsibilities.) You can also list the location of the job and your supervisor's name if you feel it's necessary, but you don't have to. It is a good idea to use Google or other search engines to help with this. If you don't have access to a computer, ask someone who does to help you!

Keep in mind that you only want to list the most recent or relevant work history, and usually only include three or four examples.

- **Education history:** If you graduated from high school, college, or have achieved your GED, list that here. If you have not completed any of that but are currently in school, say which school you are at, what you are studying, and that your "degree" is in progress.

- **References:** Here, list anyone (and their contact info, usually just their phone number, but you can include their email) who can advocate to future employers that you are a good worker. These references should be people who supervised you in a work setting, even if that work setting was volunteer work. Try not to use family members or friends, unless you have worked with them in a professional setting. However, you can have personal references, especially if you do not have any professional ones, but make sure they know about your character, work ethic, and other qualities.

> Another option here is to put "References available upon request," in case you need some time to arrange professional references. But be sure to let each person you plan to use as a reference know that that is your plan, and ask their permission beforehand!

Remember that résumés should be as short and concise as possible. Try to fit it all on one page! And feel free to also Google some examples of résumés online. But it is important to make your résumé personal and professional, so be creative and use what YOU think will get YOU the job.

Cover Letters

A cover letter is a personalized letter to your employer explaining why you are the best candidate for the job. It usually accompanies a résumé. Cover letters aren't usually required for entry-level job applications. However, including a cover letter with your résumé when applying for upper-level positions may give you a better chance of obtaining an interview.

Feel free to Google a few examples of cover letters online, but your potential employer will tell you all the information you need to include in your cover letter under their advertisement for the available position. Do they want a team player? Mention that you are a team player in your cover letter! Do they want potential candidates to have customer service experience or technical experience? Include that in your letter!

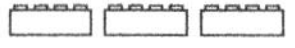

How often should you apply to jobs?

As long as you don't have a job, FINDING a job should be treated as your job, because it really is a lot of work. It is best to get your résumé written, and then start applying anywhere you can. You can find potential employers through employment networking sites, such as Indeed.com or Monster.com, or you can simply do an internet search for the business you want to apply to if you have something in mind, since most official business websites have a "careers" tab with information on how to apply to them.

The most effective way to find a job is to set a number of jobs that you will apply to per day, and meet that goal every day until you find a job. Usually applying to ten jobs per day is a round number where you will start seeing results. By the end of a week, you will have applied to more than fifty jobs. That's a good start!

If you feel like one job would be a great fit, and you really want that particular job, you might even want to call that hiring office and check on the status of your application. Doing this, especially on your best behavior with the most professional language you can muster, may leave a good impression on whoever is in charge. Just be sure that you talk to the person who is in charge of hiring, as you do not want to waste anyone's time who is not in charge of hiring you.

This section, challenge yourself to find five jobs you want to apply to. You do not have to apply to them right now; simply research what it will take to get an interview with them. Do you need to submit a résumé, or is it simply an online application? Is the actual job location a good fit for your mode of transportation? And most importantly, can you see yourself working there every day for a long period of time?

PROMPT QUESTIONS:

1. Last chapter, you were guided to brainstorm what your needs are for your employment. Now, thinking more realistically, what are those needs? Are they the same as before, or did they change?

2. Have you ever written a résumé before? If so, what was on your résumé?

3. What do you think is most important to include on your résumé?

4. Who can you use as professional references on your résumé? Why are they a good fit?

5. What kinds of job applications would you need to include a cover letter with? Why?

AUTHOR'S EXPERIENCE:

Although I was applying to customer service jobs, which usually do not require that you submit a full résumé, I still wrote out my résumé and made a Google Doc with all the important information. That way, when I was applying to jobs online, I could just upload the doc into the application, and it automatically filled out all the information for me.

If you see a job posting for a company you have never heard of before, do your best to Google it in order to see if it is really a place you want to work. Websites like Glassdoor.com may even have former employee reviews, where you can hear what it was like to work at the company.

CHALLENGE:

Group activity: Write your résumé, including the sections laid out in this chapter. After everyone is finished, try to read them together, and exchange constructive criticism so that everyone can improve their own résumé.

Independent activity: Challenge yourself to find five jobs that interest you, research them, and see if you have what it takes to apply. Bonus if you send in an application!

31

ACING AN INTERVIEW

Getting an invitation to an interview is as exciting as it is nerve-racking. That invitation means that your potential employer sees that you may be a good match to their company, which is a great sign! The downside is that speaking in front of people who hold opportunities in their hands can make one very nervous. What if you mess up? What if you say the wrong thing, or say something that doesn't make sense?

The key to acing the interview is to have a clear-cut plan in mind and prepare all you can for that plan, while being natural and rolling with the punches. This means walking into an interview knowing what kinds of questions will be asked and being prepared to answer those questions, knowing your résumé inside and out so you will be able to explain any of the items listed on it, and making sure to look and feel your best so you will be relaxed and calm during the interview. Here are some things to keep in mind when preparing for an interview:

- **Do your research!** Know a little bit about the company beforehand, at least what the company is and what they do.

If you can, figure out what their mission statement is (no need to memorize this, just know what it is) and become familiar with their goals as a company. Interviewers may ask you what you know about their company during the interview, and you don't want to be stumped!

- **Interview attire:** As the old saying goes, "Dress for the job you want, not the job you have." When deciding what to wear, lean toward professional, not fashionable, because your personality should show through your strong answers to questions, not necessarily through how you look. Be sure to dress conservatively for every kind of job, even if you will dress less formally for the actual job. Limit cleavage and short skirts/shorts, and if possible, cover any tattoos and take out face piercings. You might not have to once you get the job, but for an interview, it is a good idea to look more professional than usual.

- **Rehearse before you get there:** Hiring managers are going to ask you about gaps in your résumé, why you left your previous jobs, and other slightly uncomfortable questions. You want to have an answer for everything. Think ahead to what they might ask and prepare a short statement to explain. For example, if they ask, "Why were you out of work for a number of months at X time?" you might say that you were moving out of the area, focusing on family emergencies, or making a transition to the next stage in life. And when you're thinking ahead, think of any follow-up questions to that answer, and imagine what you should say then. Also, they will want to know your best skills and attributes! Keep your best work qualities in mind and memorized.

- **Arrive EARLY:** Don't simply arrive to an interview in the nick of time. Arrive a few minutes early. Before you even go into the building, take a moment to breathe, collect your thoughts, and get into a relaxed state. If you are late to an interview, you are subject to them asking you to leave, and you may not get a chance to interview at all.

- **Answer honestly, but remember that the interviewer does not need to know all the intimate details of your life:** The interviewer does not need to know that you are a survivor or in recovery. They do not need to know ANY intimate details of your life! Simply give them smart, concise answers that focus on your work ethic, responsibility, and skills.

- **Criminal background:** If you have a criminal background, know the laws in your state regarding the employer's right to ask about your criminal background. For example, in California, employers may no longer ask if you have a criminal background before they offer you employment. Upon extending an offer, they may make the offer conditional and a criminal background check may be required. This is common and is not reflective of their impression of you. If a company runs background checks, they are required to do so for all potential candidates. You will not be singled out. If that is the case, consider sharing your criminal background in a professional way, so that when they extend the offer, they hear it from you first. At the very least, though, be prepared on how to respond should they offer you the opportunity to give an explanation.

- **NEVER speak badly about any past employer:** If you say that your last boss was terrible and go into detail about what made him/her such a lousy boss, the first thing your interviewer will think is that you're going to be hard to work with and that you don't get along well with authority. Remember, if they ask you about past employers, they are not trying to find out more about your last employer; they are trying to learn how you deal with management. Stay positive as much as possible.

- **Be natural:** If you don't know the answer to a question, be honest! You can say something like, "I'm sorry, I probably have to think about that one a little more."

- **KEEP YOUR EYES AND EARS OPEN!** Remember that to an extent, you are interviewing the employer too. If the interviewer is rude, or if the environment seems chaotic or simply not a good fit, keep that in mind when later choosing to accept or not accept the job.

- **Watch out for pyramid schemes:** Also keep in mind that some pyramid schemes disguise themselves as employers in order to scam individuals into buying into their company. Do not take any job offers that require you to buy something in order to work for them! If they want you to buy knives in order to sell them, get the heck outta there! If they want you to buy makeup products in order to sell them, politely leave the interview! People ruin their lives and credit taking part in pyramid schemes, also known as multilevel marketing companies, or MLMs. Buying an employer's product with money you don't have is not worth it.

- **Ask them a question:** Lots of employers ask if you have any questions before they end the interview. This is a great opportunity to show them that you are truly interested in the job. Some examples of questions to ask are:
  "What will a typical day look like for me?"
  "What do you expect most from your employees?"
  "What are the next steps in this process?"

- **Always thank the interviewer for the opportunity and for their time:** If you feel it's appropriate, send them a thank-you email afterwards, but always thank the hiring manager in person before you leave the interview.

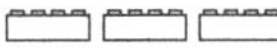

Here are some standard interview questions that are often asked. Keep them in mind when preparing for an interview:

- "Why do you want to work for our company?"

- "What are your greatest strengths as an employee?"

- "What are your greatest weaknesses?" *(This is a trick question! Try to turn one of your weaknesses into a positive, but whatever you do, do not go into detail about your weaknesses. Try filling in the blanks: "I am really working hard on how to improve my ____________, and I am doing this by ___________.")*

- "Why are you leaving your current job?" *(If your current job on your résumé is a volunteer position, explain to the interviewer that you like your current job, but that they are not offering enough hours at this time.)*

- "Describe a time where you faced a difficult situation and explain how you solved that problem." *(This is a really common question. Have a few scenarios memorized so that you aren't stumped when you get to this question.)*

Challenge yourself to do a mock interview with a buddy. Give them a list of questions to ask you and try to answer those questions as professionally as possible. You may surprise yourself with your answers! And even if you don't do well the first time, take note of where you are struggling, and practice more for next time.

Applying for jobs is certainly stressful and can make one very anxious. But keep this in mind: When we have struggled through exploitation and all it brings us, including poverty, abuse, mental illness, addiction, and many things that others can't even begin to imagine surviving, getting a job is like a blip on our radar, especially compared to all the other things we have accomplished.

PROMPT QUESTIONS:

1. What are your thoughts regarding employment interviews? Do they excite you? Do they make you nervous?

2. What interviews have you gone to in the past? What was that experience like for you?

3. What do you wish you would have done differently in past interviews?

4. What are the steps you should take to prepare for an interview?

5. What will you do on the day of an interview?

6. Can any skills you acquired during exploitation be useful when trying to ace an interview? Why or why not?

AUTHOR'S EXPERIENCE:

During my exploitation, I knew I had to stay one step ahead of whoever I was with at all times. That came in handy when it came to interviews! I always Googled the employer before I even showed up, and I had prepared answers for any questionable items on my résumé.

One thing that I learned was that if they asked a question that I didn't know the answer to, it was best to be honest. I said, "I am not sure. I will have to think about that one a little more." A few times, that honest answer got me the job!

CHALLENGE:

Challenge yourself to do a mock interview with a person you trust. Give them the list of questions listed here in the chapter, or come up with your own questions. Try to answer those questions as professionally as possible. You may surprise yourself with your answers!

32

Employee Maintenance: Keeping Your Job

Once you have a job you like, you must work hard to keep that job as long as you can, for it will take you to the next levels of independence. No, you might not have this job forever, but as long as you have it, you want to gain new skills, develop good habits, and nurture your relationship with your direct supervisor, just in case you need to use them as a reference for future potential jobs, or in case they have the opportunity to promote you.

Toward the end of this chapter, we will also discuss how to deal with difficult people on the job, and how to tell when you should move on to a different job, if the job you're at is not an ideal place for you to work. But first, we will talk about good employee habits and principles.

Being a good employee starts with good habits.

- **Show up on time every day:** Always show up on time, if not a few minutes early. If, for whatever reason, you are running late and know for a fact that you will not make it on time, it is always good to call your manager to let them know that you are on your way and just running behind. Make sure that you make this call clearly ahead of time so that your employer can anticipate your arrival. However, don't make a habit of being late!

- **Time management:** When working, allow for more time than you need to complete each task. It is better to complete a task early and move on to the next task than to be late finishing every task. It might even help to time yourself doing certain tasks which you will repeat often, and constantly try to beat your time in the future. Just keep one eye on the clock and watch yourself improve.

- **Active listening:** Make sure you listen to your supervisor and that they know you are listening. Sometimes it helps to learn new tasks by repeating back the directions you have been given. If you do make a mistake and forget their instructions, make it clear that you are so sorry you messed up and either reiterate that you do know how to fix the mistake or ask how you should do the task differently. If you need to, and if it is allowed, consider trying to write the important stuff down. Don't be afraid to set yourself up for success!

- **Take responsibility for all your own actions:** If you do mess up, or if something goes wrong at work and it is your fault, or you have some responsibility in the problem, speak up and own your actions. A simple apology, especially if you are a new employee, can go a long way. Your boss might not expect perfection, but they will always expect you to be honest, and if you are actively working to improve the problem with your boss, it will look a lot better to them than seeing you throw someone else under the bus.

- **Excellent customer service:** While not every entry-level job will require customer service skills, you want to treat any interaction you have with other employees, clients, or supervisors with excellent customer service. Use your manners, say please, thank you, and I'm sorry, and always treat everyone with courtesy and respect.

- **Always be improving:** It is always a good idea to constantly find ways to improve your work ethic within the job you have. How can you work faster? Or more efficiently? How can you learn more about your job every day? Your employer will appreciate each improvement you make in your work.

What if the job is not working out?

Sometimes you get halfway through training in a new job and can already see that this job is not a good fit for you. Maybe it sounded good in theory, but doing the actual work is way outside of your comfort zone! In this case, ask yourself if you really spent enough time trying out this job. If you've given it a good try over a few weeks or a month and it's still not flowing, you have a choice to make: Do I continue pushing through this job until it works, or do I start looking for a new job?

You can even ask your supervisor if they think you'll pick it up in time to progress in the company or if they think you're not a good fit.

If they say you're not a good fit, don't be discouraged! Thank them for their honesty and make the decision to stay or leave yourself.

Two Weeks' Notice

If you do have to leave a job, some of us might want to walk off the job in the middle of the shift and never look back. However, you never know if you're burning a bridge that you should actually keep, and it is important to leave every job in a professional way if possible. Try giving two weeks' notice for your resignation, which is a simple letter giving your employer two weeks to figure out how to replace you and get their company back up running smoothly in your absence. Remember to keep this short: All you need to include is that you are leaving the position, when your last day will be, and thank your employer for the opportunity (even if it wasn't a good one). This will ensure that you can keep your employers as a solid reference and that you can get all of your pay and exit materials in a nice, organized fashion.

Mistreatment of Employees

If you feel that you are truly being mistreated by an employer or there is blatant harassment toward you, either contact your Human Resources representative, or HR rep, or if you work for a union, contact your union rep to file a grievance. They should be able to help you mediate this problem, and can possibly grant you a transfer to another location or department. If you do this and the problem is still not resolved, strongly consider finding another job. You do not want to work in a place where harassment is accepted. This may not be a good work environment for you (or anyone)!

Challenge yourself to answer the following questions, and speculate how you would be able to handle these tough questions in a professional setting:

- What makes a good boss?
- What makes a good employee?
- What is the best way to handle conflict on the job?

PROMPT QUESTIONS:

1. What makes a good boss? How would you spot a good boss in the future?

2. What makes a bad boss?

3. Have you ever had experience with a bad boss/manager/supervisor in the past? What did you do? What was the outcome of that job?

4. What makes a good employee?

5. What is your plan for handling conflict on the job?

6. How do you know if a job is simply not working out?

AUTHOR'S EXPERIENCE:

When I was in residential treatment, the first job I found was a serving position at a restaurant, and I had never done anything like that before, but I figured, why not? Well, not even two weeks into working, I found I was not keeping up with the other servers. And the managers wanted me to work a lot faster. The problem was I was going as fast as I possibly could! I figured at that point, I would be better off if I found a different job. I ended up working in retail instead.

You don't want to stay in a job where you know you will be miserable. No, no job is perfect, but I knew deep down that I was not cut out for serving. Serving is a hard job!

CHALLENGE:

Challenge yourself to speculate about what you will do if you have a bad boss, a bad work environment, or conflict on the job. How can you handle it?

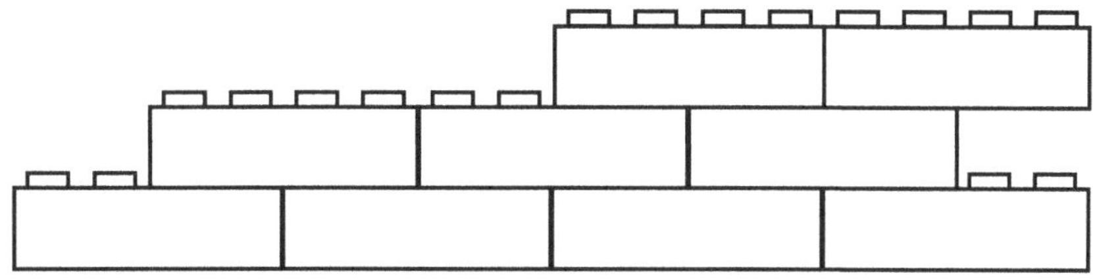

Housing

33

Confirming Your Household Needs

When we have a past of exploitation, where we survived homelessness, or our need for shelter was exploited by people who ended up harming us, we tend to value housing more than most. Now that we are in control of our lives, WE get to decide where we live and how we want to live. Even if we aren't in the most ideal situation, we will have more control over our environment, and that can be a clear representation of all we have achieved thus far. This month, we will look at how to obtain housing, how to make sure we have safe housing, and how to maintain our housing situation once we have it.

While our ultimate dream may be to be homeowners, our ability to be homeowners may vary from state to state, and we might find that we must live with roommates to start, until we further our careers and are able to afford a house. Now, if we are currently living with housemates in recovery, we might not want to live with roommates! However, living with roommates outside of recovery housing is very different, and often these group living situations are more independent. The trick is finding the right roommates and the right locations with the right amenities that we can live with for long periods of time.

First, we must consider what our needs are for our housing situation.

- Do you need to live near public transportation? Or if you have a car, do you have to keep your car in a garage or can you rely on street parking?

- How many roommates do you want? What qualities do the roommates need to have so that they will be compatible with you in a daily life setting?

- What price range can you afford? It is helpful to have a range of prices you are able to afford for a room to rent or half of an apartment. But be wary of roommates who charge too little for their room for rent! They might be charging very little because they have had trouble finding a roommate, and you have to consider the potential reasons why that would be the case.

- Can you share a bathroom? Do you need your own private bathroom? Keep in mind that having your own bathroom may cause your monthly rate to be a little higher.

- Is the apartment/room for rent close enough to your work or your school?

- Is the apartment/room for rent close enough to your support network?

- Is the apartment/room for rent furnished or unfurnished? (Furnished means that they have their own furniture, including lamps, beds, dressers, etc.) If it is unfurnished, can you afford to buy your own furniture?

- Is the apartment/room for rent in a safe neighborhood? Can you research the crime rate in that neighborhood?

- Can you live in a co-ed environment? Do you feel more comfortable with all female or all male roommates?

- How accessible are grocery shopping, doctor's offices, and other places you must go?

Budgeting for housing: How much should you spend for your housing options?

Keep in mind that the housing you choose must only take up a fraction of what you earn. You do not want to find a place that costs over 50% of your income, and if you can, you *should* find a home that costs less than that. If the housing you choose costs more than 50% of your income, you will put yourself in a position where you will not be able to afford basic necessities as the month goes on.

For example, if you make $1,200 per month, you do not want to find a home that costs much more than $600 per month, because having $600 spending money per month allows you at least $150 per week. If you pick a home that costs $800 per month and you have $400 left over, you will only have $100 to spend per week, and that will go fast! The more you spend in rent, the less you will have available to spend throughout the month. In the portion of this book which talks about money, we will discuss budgeting in more detail, but for now, just keep in mind that you must allow yourself to keep half or more of your earnings AFTER you pay rent.

Roommates

If you are lucky enough to find potential roommates from your recovery family, great! If not, you may need to find roommates whom you do not know personally, and must look elsewhere, usually online, via roommate apps, Craigslist, or other websites.

When choosing roommates, make sure that you know whether they are in a group living model or a more independent structure, and decide which you would prefer to live with. A group living model may involve regular house meetings, group dinners, and so on. Independent structures may involve less interaction with other roommates. Which one should you choose? It really depends on what you like! But keep in mind that if you don't really know these people whom you are to move in with, you might not want to commit extra time to being in their group.

Also remember that you will be around these people a LOT, and if they don't have a similar lifestyle, you will be less likely to want to live there for a long period of time. For example, if you are very religious or spiritual and your potential roommates like to party, it may feel like a toxic environment for you in the long term! Now that does not mean that everyone you live with must be the same faith as you are, but you do need to find roommates who have compatible lifestyles.

Location

Ideally, you want to find a rental place that is central to the places you need to go. You want grocery shopping to be easily accessible, doctor's offices to be accessible, and you want to be close enough to your support network, whether that is close to your survivor sisters you met in recovery, others whom you have met in recovery groups, or your spiritual or religious foundation groups.

You should try to find a central location that is also safe, but if you find that the only central locations that you can afford are in urban areas where crime rates might be high, you then want to find roommates who understand the risks of living in that area and have taken good measures to preserve their safety. That means they have taken precautions, like limiting the number of guests who visit, locks or double locks on each door leading to the outside, and have plans together as roommates on how to keep each other safe.

Challenge yourself to make a list of your requirements for your living situation, including what kind of roommates you want to live with, where you want to live, how much you want to pay for rent each month, and any amenities that are important to you.

The next section will discuss the steps it takes to find an adequate living situation, but for now, simply reflect on what kind of living environment you want to have, where there are acceptable places you may want to live, and what you want out of your housing.

PROMPT QUESTIONS:

1. What are your most important needs for potential housing?

2. Where, if anywhere, can you compromise? (For example, can you live with street parking? What if your kids can't live with you?)

3. What compromises have you had to make in the past in terms of housing?

4. When will you know that you are ready to move out of residential treatment housing into a more permanent home?

5. What are your fears about moving into your own place?

6. What are you most excited about in terms of moving into your own place?

AUTHOR'S EXPERIENCE:

At the time I was moving out of residential treatment housing, I still didn't have a car, so my number-one need was to be close to public transit. Another need was that I had to be able to afford the rent on a consistent basis. I think the number I gave myself was below $750. By the time I moved out, I had saved almost $3,000.

Oakland, California, is where I ended up in my early adult years. The city has a reputation for being a high-crime area. However, my roommates and I always worked together to keep each other safe. We had multiple locks on the front door and were able to lock our windows as well. We had set procedures for leaving the house after dark or before dawn. Part of staying safe was limiting the number of people who knew where we lived as well as limiting who was allowed into the house. The fewer people who knew who and what belonged in the house, the better.

CHALLENGE:

Challenge yourself to make a list of requirements for your potential living situation, including what kind of roommates you want to live with, where you want to live, how much you want to pay for rent each month, and any amenities that are important to you.

34

Finding Housing, Choosing the Right Fit

In this chapter, we will discuss what it will take to find places to live, including finding the right roommates, how to stay safe in rental housing interviews, what to expect during a potential roommate interview, and how much moving in will cost you.

Like when we apply for jobs, we may want to apply to as many housing options as possible, but unlike job interviews, we should be more selective as to which roommate interviews we choose to attend. This is because we are not going to public places of business; we are going to private residences, and we must keep our safety in mind. If you get a funny feeling about a potential roommate before you meet them, trust your gut and move on to the next housing option. You may have the option of meeting potential roommates in a public place like a coffee shop, but most likely you will be meeting them in their home.

What Will It Cost to Move In?

It will only cost the amount you will spend on monthly rent to move in, right? Wrong!

Many who are first-time renters find that there are many expenses required to move in to a new place besides rent, so if you think you have saved enough to move in by saving barely enough to pay your first month's rent, and that's it, think again!

Some expenses involved in moving in may include:

- Furniture, if the room is unfurnished, including your bed, dressers, lights, chairs, desk, etc.
- Cleaning supplies: You might not be able to share cleaning supplies with your roommates, and you will most likely be expected to help clean common areas
- Bedding, sheets, towels, and other household needs
- Groceries, including toilet paper and paper towels
- Pantry foods: You might not be able to share any pantry items, such as flour, salt and pepper and other spices, along with cooking oil, sugar, coffee, etc.
- Handyman materials, in case you need to fix up anything in your room

Also keep in mind that most places that you rent from may ask for first AND last month's rent, along with a security deposit. A security deposit is a one-time fee that will cover any damages that happen to the space you live in while you have lived there. If you do not incur any damages while you live there, you may get the deposit back once you move out. Sometimes landlords will ask for a fraction of the amount you will pay in rent for the security deposit, sometimes a few hundred dollars, and sometimes they will ask you for an amount equal to what you will pay for monthly rent. You will only pay this one time, but must keep this in mind when you budget for your move-in costs.

Credit Checks and Background Checks

If you are pursuing a room for rent in a shared house, it is highly unlikely that you will be asked for a credit background check. However, if you and a friend are looking to share a new apartment, be advised that you will most likely undergo a credit check, and potentially a background check. The reason for this is that your landlord will want to know if you are able to keep up with payments on time and in full. If you are still in the process of rebuilding your credit, it might be a better idea to rent a room in a house, where you will not be asked for a credit check. However, some apartment complexes do not go through that process.

What will happen in a potential renter interview?

As with employment interviews, it is important that you interview the interviewer as well as letting them interview you, although in this case, it is almost MORE important that you interview the person from whom you will rent. You want to be prepared to ask them questions to see if they will be a good fit.

Dress appropriately, show up on time, and be as polite as possible. Make sure you ask the important questions, such as how much the rent will be, if you can meet any other potential roommates, and ask if you can see the available room. You might not be able to see it that day, but if not, ask if you can see a room similar to the one you will ultimately be renting.

Some interviewers may ask you questions about:

- Your employment: They want to make sure you will be a good renter and that you can pay rent on time in full.

- Your daily habits: They want to know if you will be easy to live with.

- Your former roommates: Can they vouch for you that you are a good roommate? How did you get along with them? Keep in mind that they don't want to know all the drama that went on in the house; they just want to know that you could get along in group living. So do not talk badly about any former roommates if you can help it!

- Why you are moving out of your former place: Again, throwing others under the bus will just make YOU look bad. A better response than "My roommates were awful" would be that you are looking for a better location, bigger room, or anything that doesn't have to do with whether or not you liked your roommates.

Depending on the renter or landlord, they may ask you to present references of people whom you have actually lived with, and if possible, whom you have paid rent to. If you are in recovery housing, you can consider asking your house manager or program director if they would provide their contact info for your "rental" references. If you have no one you can ask, try providing employment references who can at least vouch for your character and reliability. It is better to have too many references than no references.

Safety

Before you look into finding potential roommates, please keep your safety in mind! You do not want to go to a stranger's place of residence by yourself, and if you do have to go by yourself, make sure a buddy knows exactly where you are going and when you will be back. It is better to assume you will need to be on your guard than to go to meet any stranger unprepared.

Because of this, it is understandable that many survivors may choose to live with only female roommates to begin with. That doesn't mean that all female roommates are safe to live with, but they are sometimes a lower risk.

RED FLAGS in Potential Roommates or Living Situations

Smell: Does it smell unclean? Like smoke? Urine? Do the renters have animals, and if so, is the smell of animal waste in the air? These are red flag smells to keep in mind. They indicate the kind of people you will live with, and if you don't want to live in that kind of environment, think twice before moving in there.

Substance abusers: Are there remnants of drug use in the home? Is there an excess of alcohol bottles? Do the interviewing roommates act aggressively or erratically while they interview you? The landlord may not currently be using drugs or alcohol while they interview you, but if you get a funny feeling while you talk to them, think twice before you move in with them.

Overly friendly roommates: Is the interviewing roommate flirting with you or being too forward? Do they go out of their way to touch you? Do you hear alarm bells go off in your head when you interact with them? And the BIG red flag: Do they offer a discounted rate for an exchange of a romantic relationship with them? If so, get out of there, girl! That is not a safe situation!

Bug activity: As the saying goes, for every bug you see, there are a hundred that you don't. If you see even one bug in the place you are viewing, it is likely that there are many more that you don't see. Anyone who has ever dealt with roaches and other pests knows that it is nearly impossible to eradicate a bug problem, and these bugs may follow you to your next home.

This section, challenge yourself to look at three potential roommate or rental ads, and ask yourself if they will be a good fit for you:

- Are the move-in costs within your price range?
- What do you know about the potential roommates?
- Is the rental place in a safe part of town?
- Can you see yourself living there for a long period of time?

Prompt Questions:

1. What are some costs that you predict you will have to cover when moving into your new place?

2. What would be your safety plan when going to a renter interview?

3. What red flags will you look for when you go to a renter interview?

4. What kind of things do you think you will be asked when interviewing for a rental? How will you respond?

5. What questions will YOU ask the interviewer? How will you ask these questions?

AUTHOR'S EXPERIENCE:

I really regret agreeing to move into an apartment that had a strong odor of cat urine all throughout the building, yet there were no cats in the apartment. Freaky. It was a sign that there were other issues when it came to the apartment. Soon I figured out that they had a mice and roach problem.

CHALLENGE:

Challenge yourself to look at three potential renter ads and ask yourself if they will be a good fit for you. Are the move-in costs in your price range? What do you know about the potential roommates? Is the rental in a safe part of town? Can you see yourself living there for a long period of time?

35

HOUSING MAINTENANCE

Once you have found a place to live, heave a big sigh of relief! The most stressful part is over, and you can now focus on making your room a safe haven to live in while you pursue other areas of independence. This section, we will go over moving, what to do once you move in, how to keep the peace in the home, and some respectful habits for living in independent-style group housing.

Moving

How long it will take: Keep in mind that moving is an ALL-DAY event, even if you are just moving the contents of one room at your recovery house to a new room for rent. Pack all your belongings as neatly as possible, and if you want to make the process easier, ask a friend to help you. Even if you don't have any heavy furniture to move, it might be helpful to have an extra hand to carry boxes and other belongings.

Transporting your belongings: If you have a friend who has a truck or van that can help you move, or if you have a car and your belongings can fit in your car, great! If not, you will need to think about transporting your belongings, because it would be too difficult to carry everything back and forth on the bus. Instead of renting a moving truck, which may be overkill for your needs, and expensive at that, try to use a rideshare app to take a few trips between your recovery housing and your new room or apartment. Some rideshare apps have an XL option, where they will send a larger car for a small fee. Consider using this option if you cannot afford a moving truck.

What to Do Once You Move In

Usually, you will trade your first month's rent and safety deposit for a house key when you are ready to move in. You may also sign a lease or renter's agreement. Make sure you understand all that is in the agreement before you sign, and if they do not have a copy for you to keep, take a picture of the document to keep for reference.

The first thing to do once you move in, before you unpack anything, is to inspect your room for any possible damages that occurred in the room before you moved in. Do you see dents in the baseboards? Do you see any mouse holes? Cracks in windows or doors? How clean is it? Take note of this, and if you can, discreetly take pictures of the room before you move any of your belongings in. This may help once you move out if you request your safety deposit back.

And before you are left alone in the house, make sure your key works for the front door. You do not want to accidentally have the wrong key and not be able to get in or out of the house! If you have a key to your bedroom door, make sure that one works as well.

Then, once you are settled in, start unpacking. Once you have moved in all of your stuff, try to decorate your room. Put up pictures, lights, and other things that make you feel at home. This will help you feel comfortable staying in this place for a longer period of time.

Check in with House Rules

Your roommates may not have official house rules written out and posted in the house, like a lot of recovery homes do. However, by simply asking other roommates about certain household habits, you can figure out what their unwritten house rules are:

- Noise level: Are your roommates early birds? Do they need music and television to quiet down at certain times so they can get to bed early? Or is it the opposite: Do they want the music and television to be quiet in the morning, in case they have evening/overnight jobs? How loudly can you listen to music or television? Are the walls thin between rooms?
- Guests: Are you allowed to have guests? If you are, are they only allowed to be in certain areas of the house, such as the backyard or your room? Can you have overnight guests?
- Sharing the bathroom: If you have to share a bathroom, can you figure out what times roommates take showers, and when you can take showers in the remaining time throughout the day? Is the shower noisy and could it potentially wake up other roommates? If so, what times are you limited to taking a shower each day? Or on the other hand, if you work early mornings or late nights and you must take showers around the time you work or get home from work, can you work that out with the other roommates?
- Cleanliness/housekeeping: Do your roommates pay for a maid service, or is the cleanliness of the house up to you

and your roommates? If it's the latter, do you have a rotating cleaning schedule, or is it simply that all roommates must clean up after themselves?

Good Cohabiting Habits

Until you know how relaxed or how strict your roommates are, you want to practice good cohabiting habits so that you can show respect to other roommates and the house in order to keep the peace in the home. There are always situations where roommates may have unrealistic expectations or are unreasonable to deal with, but for this chapter, we are only discussing how to deal with fairly reasonable roommates and how to respect them.

Here are some good cohabiting habits to keep in mind:

- Pay rent on time: Know what day you are expected to pay rent and always pay it on time. If that means you have to budget a portion of money from each paycheck you earn, then that's what you need to do. You do NOT want to get in the habit of paying late, as that might ruin your chances of being able to stay in that home.

- Keep a low profile: This means being respectful of noise levels both when roommates are awake and ESPECIALLY when roommates are asleep. This also means not leaving your things in common areas, especially if you notice others do not leave their things out in common areas as well. This means coming and going from the house in a quick and quiet fashion. And until you know your roommates better and can get a feel for the kind of lifestyle they live, limit the number of guests you invite over.

- Clean up after yourself: The fewer the people in the house, the less often you will have to clean, but as a rule of thumb, clean up areas immediately after you use them. This especially goes for the kitchen! If you're living with others who cook, you may want to use the same dishes and kitchen utensils that they do, but DO NOT leave community cooking utensils dirty, because others may want to cook with them. Also, do not leave the counters, stove, and sink a mess without cleaning up for the next person. You wouldn't want other roommates to do the same to you.

- DOCUMENT all additional payments: If your roommate is in charge of utilities or other bills, make sure you document when they ask you for money and how much you give them. You do not want to get into a situation where they ask you to pay the same bill twice in one month, and you want to know when to anticipate paying the bill for the next month.

If you are currently living with other roommates, challenge yourself to ask them what they look for in their housemates. What do they find respectful or disrespectful? And if you don't have roommates whom you can ask that, ask yourself how you would like to be treated by other housemates. How can you emulate the way you would like to be treated?

Next chapter, we will discuss how to deal with roommates who cross boundaries or are difficult to deal with, but for now, focus on the ideal living situation and how you can be a part of retaining a peaceful environment.

Prompt Questions:

1. What is the first thing that you should do when moving into a new apartment or room for rent? Why is it important to do this first?

2. Look at the "house rules" subsection. What are some house rules that you like?

3. What are some house rules that you DON'T like?

4. How can you tell what the house rules are if they are not clearly stated anywhere?

5. What habits can you practice to be an easy person to live with?

AUTHOR'S EXPERIENCE:

Every time I moved into a new place, I would spend a couple of days lying low and watching everyone else's habits to see when I could take a shower, use the kitchen, etc. After a while you will notice when it is safe to use the house as you need to.

Before I moved any of my belongings into a new place, I would take pictures of the rental. The floors, the walls, anything that could potentially get damaged, I took a picture of, especially if I saw that there was preexisting damage. That way, I would not be held accountable for damage I wasn't responsible for. Unfortunately, landlords can be shady, and I knew I had to protect myself the best I could.

CHALLENGE:

Challenge yourself to ask your current roommates what they usually look for in potential roommates. What do they find respectful? What do they find disrespectful? If you don't have roommates, ask yourself how you would like to be treated by other housemates. How can you emulate the way you would like to be treated?

36

Backup Plans for Housing

Perhaps because we have been in such toxic living situations through surviving exploitation, we may have very low expectations for our roommates now. Sometimes it is good to have low expectations for them, because fresh out of recovery, we most likely will not live in the most ideal situations and we still must get along with others as best we can. However, we do need to understand what kind of behavior crosses the line, how to mediate those problems, and in the worst-case scenario, how to exit the situation peacefully if necessary.

Interpersonal Mediation

Before immediately deciding to move out of uncomfortable situations, first try to mediate the problem at hand. Tell your roommates your concerns, and check in to see if there are some unwritten rules that you need to know about. There is a good chance that your roommates might not even know that they want things to be a certain way! This is the perfect chance for them to express themselves and have a good interaction that may keep the peace in the long run. Check out Chapter Nineteen to refresh yourself on proper conflict resolution, but for now, here is a refresher on household mediation.

Rules of thumb for household mediation:

- **Relax:** Take a deep breath and relax before you say anything. Don't be combative or aggressive when expressing your concerns or asking for help. Calm down and commit in your mind to handling the situation peacefully.

- **Make your respect for them your focus:** No matter how you feel about them, make sure they know you are just trying to respect them, and that's why you're coming to them with concern, not because you're angry at them.

- **Actively listen:** Make sure they know that you are hearing them out. If it helps, repeat back what they tell you. Don't be a right-fighter and dominate the conversation until you get what you want. The goal is to reach a compromise where everyone can get a little bit of what they want.

- **Know the desired means of communication:** Some roommates prefer texting while others prefer face-to-face communication. If you feel that there will be less conflict if you text, do that first. However, know beforehand that whatever you say in a text can be saved permanently, and you will not be able to take it back once the text is sent. Worse, some roommates can misconstrue what you say in a text as confrontational, when really it isn't. You can't express sarcasm in a text. Be aware of this!

- **NEVER get aggressive:** Once you let the peaceful conversation get combative, you put yourself in a dangerous situation. And since you may be one of the newest roommates, the odds will definitely not be in your favor if you are the aggressor.

What Crosses the Line?

Sometimes it is difficult to know when roommate quirks cross over into being toxic or inappropriate. It is important to know the difference. Here are some examples:

- **Being too friendly:** It's normal to joke around and be playful with other roommates, because that is what makes your house a home. But if they come on to you sexually or romantically, you may be looking down the barrel of household drama. In this situation you may be damned if you do and damned if you don't! If you do give in to romantic behavior with them, you may be inviting them too close into your life. If you don't, they might resent you, and this can put you at odds with them in the future.

- **They ask you for money:** Be careful about lending money, cigarettes, medications, or other necessities to any roommates. Sometimes, your roommate might just need an ibuprofen to get them through until they can go to the store themselves, but in some cases, they may be testing the water to see if they can ask for more or larger things later on. You do not want to get in the habit of lending them money, and if you have cash on you or keep it in your room, you do not want to let them know this. The best solution is to let them know that you don't have what they are asking for whenever they ask for it. A couple of drops of olive oil or a cup of sugar once in a while is not a big deal, but cash is.

- **Constant texting about household rules, etc.:** If your roommates text you once in a while about something that needs to be done in the house (for example, leaving your lights on or your alarm going off in your room when you are not there), that is not a big deal and probably the least confrontational way they can maintain the peace in the house. However, if they constantly text you about things around the house, and this exceeds more than an average of one text per week and especially if the texts are aggressive or rude, you can infer that these texts will escalate and create tension in the house.

- **Understanding common areas:** Sometimes, your living agreement may state that you are only to use your room and the bathroom, or a limited area of the house. This is common, but if you are allowed to use other common areas of the house, yet your roommates make you feel uncomfortable when you use those areas or go so far as to ask you to leave those areas when you are in them, your boundaries may have been crossed. Make sure you know the rules of the housing situation before you move in to a situation you don't want to live in, because the kind of people who ask you to leave common areas tend to be controlling.

- **Yelling:** If your roommate can't communicate with you without yelling or banging on doors or anything aggressive, you might find yourself in a tough situation that you should try to get out of.

Bottom line: The rules are rules and you probably can't change them, but when the rules are a reflection of the kind of person who lives in a toxic environment, you might want to keep your distance from them.

Preparing for the Worst

If you do find yourself in a situation where you do not feel safe in your home, or if you find that you are simply not a good fit for the household you are in, you must start planning ahead to find another room to rent with new roommates.

Typically, you will give your landlord a thirty-day notice for your move-out, which will give them time to find a new roommate and will give you time to find a new place to live. You will most likely still have to pay for that month. If they ask you to move out, make sure they have given you adequate time to move, usually thirty days, and stick to that time frame. And again, you will most likely still pay for that month.

Either way, you will need to start the entire moving process over. Start with searching for a room, move on to roommate interviews, and find a new place to stay. As difficult as this is, this is nowhere near as difficult as some of the things we survived in exploitation! Remember that you are still in charge of your life, and that you are more than capable of taking care of this situation.

While we don't want to constantly live in survival mode, we do need to remember how to protect ourselves, and there are a few things we can do to ensure our safety during this difficult time:

- **Keep an emergency fund:** As difficult as it is to save money while you are working an entry-level position, it is still possible, and this is something that will save you when you face an emergency. Think of how much you may spend on staying out of the house, in case you need to stay with a safe friend during this time, and what you will need to spend on finding a new place to live, including travel to interviews and costs to move in.

- **Keep some space from your roommates, and the house:** This can go one or two ways. The first option is to stay in your room as much as possible and keep a low profile in the household. If that is not a safe option, you can try getting out as often as possible, including staying at a safe friend's house if you are able. If you are able to stay out of the home, do not leave anything of value in your room. You may have to keep some valuables in your room, such as a television or computer, but if you do leave your place for extended amounts of time, do not leave any large amounts of cash behind, especially if you do not have a lock on your door.

- **"Keep the Peace" officer:** If you have concerns for your safety or that your roommates will retaliate once you try to move your stuff out of your room, call your local police department for a "keep the peace" officer. The officer you call will only be there to ensure that there is no physical confrontation while you move. They are not there to arrest your roommate or enforce anything aggressively. They will only react to any possible confrontation, and like their name entails, "keep the peace."

- **Prorated rent:** If you do find a place to move in before the month is over, ask your new landlord if you can move in early with prorated rent. Prorated rent means that you will only pay for the portion of the month you will be moved in for, and then start paying the full amount of monthly rent on the first of the next full month. This may help you get out of a bad situation and into a new situation quickly.

Remember that you got this! When you have survived exploitation, you have acquired all it takes to succeed in finding the right, stable home for yourself.

Prompt Questions:

1. How is interpersonal mediation different when it is not with someone you know well, and is instead with new roommates?

2. What kind of behavior crosses the line, in your mind, when it comes to housemates or roommates? Why?

3. What is your preferred form of communication when it comes to addressing issues? Do you prefer face-to-face communication or texting? Why?

4. What would happen in a living environment that would make you want to move out?

5. How would the discernment you acquired during exploitation prepare you for bad housing situations?

6. What is your plan if a housing situation does not work out? What will you do?

AUTHOR'S EXPERIENCE:

I had to move several times after I left residential treatment. Therefore, I always had an emergency stash of cash, just in case I needed it, and everywhere I went, I made friends, so I was lucky enough to have a couch to stay on between apartments.

Two major things that made me move were (a) my roommates were using drugs and acting erratically and aggressively, and (b) one of my roommates tried to have sex with me. Both were red flags and clear signs that I should move out as soon as possible.

CHALLENGE:

Challenge yourself to make your own list of household rules. What is important in your living situation?

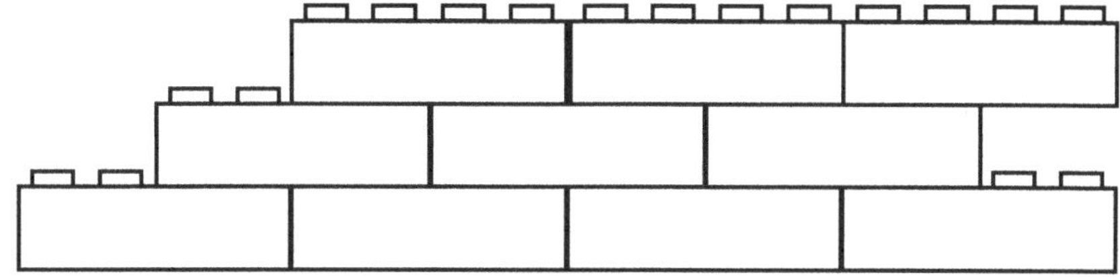

Health and Safety

37

Body Positivity

This book is designed to guide survivors through healing and gaining independence, and since we have spent the previous three months on gaining independence, from obtaining employment to finding a place to live, it is time to focus on healing. Perhaps what needs healing the most is what was exploited the most during our past trauma: our bodies.

Our bodies have gone through extensive trauma by the time we reach recovery. Not only may we have been physically abused by our exploiters, but by the very nature of sexual exploitation, we were sexually abused. Even if we gave consent to exploit our bodies in whatever way, we probably wouldn't want to engage sexually with any buyer if we weren't getting paid to do so. And if we didn't want to have sex with clients, yet we did anyway only because we needed the money, some consider this act as paid rape.

During exploitation, our worth was reduced to our appearance and how often and how much people would want to have sex with us. We learned to value how we looked more than our personality or strengths. And many of us find that after several months of rebuilding our lives, our looks were on the back burner and we now look nothing like we once did. Since we have had a previous pattern of equating our worth with how we look, what we see in the mirror may disappoint us.

But, if you are not feeling positive about the way you look now, you can encourage yourself to change your inner dialogue by putting a spin on the way you talk to yourself. One thing many survivors like to do is thank their bodies:

- Thank your legs for bringing you to recovery, for running from things that were not healthy for you, and for guiding you to a better place.

- Thank your arms and hands for working to get you help, for your ability to become employed or perform tasks at school, for reaching out for help and for helping others as best you can.

- Thank your head for figuring out how to get you to the place you are now, for continuing to think through difficult situations, and for the ability to plan ahead for your future.

- Thank your eyes for the ability to see through everything, for the way they guide us, for waking us up, and for seeing future possibilities.

- Thank your mouth for speaking words of wisdom, for the ability to communicate with others and to speak life into ourselves.

- Thank your gut for its intuition, for it letting us know what we need to do, and for nourishing our bodies.

- Thank your heart for the courage to improve your life and to get through all the challenges that you may face.

Our bodies do so much for us! We no longer have to use them in an exploitative way; we now can use them as the vessel to our future. We do not have to put our value on how our body looks but rather on all the things it can accomplish. Our bodies are strong.

Still, it is empowering to feel comfortable in our own skin, and unfortunately, we live in a society that is constantly cutting us down for the way we look. No one consciously makes the decision that they want to look radically different from the way they were born just for the hell of it, although everyone goes through weird phases. This need to constantly beat ourselves up about the way we look is more likely the product of long-term conditioning in a society where we are taught that we are inferior. Women are often told that if men don't find us attractive, we have no value. That is a lie, and it is fed to all women in our society from a very young age. Men and trans individuals also face a lot of harsh expectations from society, but no matter what the forced negative expectations are, the result is that we are not comfortable in our own bodies.

Perhaps because of this, we all subconsciously want to be the metaphorical person in the next room. Without realizing it, we see our brothers, sisters, or nonbinary folk as competition. While we don't always pay attention to the attention we personally receive, especially since we may already feel that we are inferior and undeserving of positive attention, we do see who desires everyone else, and how and why. We are born in a world where we want to be them and not ourselves, where we are already not enough.

It's okay to admire the person standing next to you and wish you were in their shoes, but just understand that for every person you envy, there is a person who envies you. No matter how big or small you are, there is always someone else out there who would want to look, talk, act, and feel like YOU. There is a person out there who wishes they were as slim as you, no matter how big you are, and there is probably someone out there who wishes they had your shape, even if you find yourself struggling to accentuate your build.

And as we may have seen in our past, there is a person out there for everyone, no matter what body type or look we have. With models like Tess Holiday, who is the largest supermodel ever, to Lupita Nyong'o, who has very dark skin and was voted most beautiful woman in the world, there is a HUGE range of what others may find attractive.

So, what's their secret? They let their beauty shine from within. They make a point to love themselves and accept themselves no matter who else loves and accepts them. That is pure confidence, and confidence is always attractive.

Eating Disorders

If you feel that you have an eating disorder, or if your life is chaotic due to the choices you must make centered around eating—whether you don't let yourself eat enough, you become obsessed with losing weight, or you intentionally throw up after eating—please consult a mental health professional immediately.

Bulimia, anorexia, and other eating disorders are mental health conditions that absolutely affect your bodily health. They can cause long-term medical problems, and in some cases, death. Please don't let an eating disorder rob you of your recovery, and do not let anyone tell you that bingeing and purging, or throwing up your food on a regular basis, is normal, healthy behavior. It may have been normal in the toxic environment of sexual exploitation, but it can lead to serious medical conditions, including cancer and even death. Additionally, an eating disorder at the very least will occupy your thoughts and impact your emotional well-being, which will distract you from your recovery.

Sexual exploitation recovery is designed to heal many areas of our life, because each survivor's needs are different. Just as some of us struggle with substance abuse in addition to our overall sexual exploitation recovery, some of us struggle with eating disorders. To find an eating disorder support group near you, visit ANAD.org. If you are working with a mental health professional, be honest about this and all other emotional challenges you are facing.

If you are still struggling with your own body positivity, challenge yourself to write a love letter to yourself. In this letter, tell yourself how much you love your eyes, from the way they look to how they serve you. Tell yourself how much you love your smile, your arms and legs, your gut, your head, your hair, and go into detail about how much you love them. Then read the letter out loud to yourself. Even if you don't believe how much you love yourself, it may help to look at this letter and read it to yourself until you DO believe it.

Prompt Questions:

1. What kind of expectations do you feel from society regarding your identity, gender, or role in the world?

2. How did exploitation change your attitude about your body?

3. What is your current attitude, good or bad, about your self-image?

4. Which body part are you most grateful for? Why?

5. What actions can you take to improve your self-image and confidence?

AUTHOR'S EXPERIENCE:

I actually do have an eating disorder, and my exploitation worsened it. I always felt an immense pressure to focus on my weight and overall appearance, so during exploitation, my ED got out of control. Unfortunately, when I went into treatment, my eating disorder got even worse, but at least I had the chance to fix it in a stable environment.

One thing I did was participate in a weekly ED support group. Another thing I did was follow body-positive and fat-positive people on Instagram. Watching other people work through their own body issues really boosted my confidence.

It is worth noting that "loving your body" doesn't work for everyone, especially when our bodies have been heavily criticized, especially by exploitation abusers. At that point, I try to work on body neutrality—not loving or hating my body, just accepting it for what it is, and appreciating it for doing all the functions to keep me alive. My body is always going to change, and to "love" it at one point may make the other points feel unlovable when they are not. Your body does too much work for you to have an opinion about it.

CHALLENGE:

Challenge yourself to write a love letter to yourself and your body.

38

Benefits of Healthy Nutrition and Exercise

It is very possible that most survivors did not have normal eating habits during exploitation. We may not have had the time to eat regular meals, or we may not have even been allowed to eat normal meals or allowed to eat certain foods, depending on the way we were controlled by exploiters. But we are survivors now, and we now can eat however we choose, and implement exercise in the ways we see fit.

We all know that good nutrition and exercise can improve the way we look, but it can do so much more than that. Healthy food and exercise can make us stronger and better able to face what life throws at us. It will also ensure that we do not face major medical issues down the road! Most importantly, it is a great way to gain control of our daily life.

Benefits of Diet and Exercise

Forget about losing weight or looking good. Maintaining healthy eating habits and exercising regularly provide the following benefits:

- It helps strengthen your body so that you are in shape and are better able to care for yourself, from protecting yourself to being able to do all the physical tasks in life with ease.

- It helps prevent long-term medical problems. If you have gained weight since you began recovery, you are not alone. However, you do not want to incur more medical conditions like diabetes or high cholesterol from binge eating too often or for long periods of time. Get in touch with your body, and learn your body's cues for when it is full or when it is hungry.

- It gives us more energy. If we eat healthy and exercise regularly, we will have more energy to complete daily tasks, and often we will also have more motivation to do those tasks!

- It often improves our emotional well-being as much as our physical well-being.

- It is a form of self-care. Eating right and staying active shows our body that we love it and want to take care of it.

- It helps us sleep. Working out regularly helps our bodies become tired enough to be able to get to sleep quickly and have prolonged, uninterrupted sleep.

If you are still growing in this area, please consider the following basic steps when trying to rework how you heal your body:

Ways to Start Exercising:

- Walking: Walking is perhaps the easiest way to start becoming active. You can start by walking a distance that could get you to break a sweat, or simply make the choice to walk more places than get a ride or take public transit. Making the choice to take the stairs instead of an elevator can also get you moving without carving out the time to work out!

- Yoga: Basic levels of yoga can be more restorative than aerobic. Yoga can help your body stretch and move in ways that you don't normally stretch and move throughout the day. It can also focus on meditation and positive self-talk, which can help as you strengthen your body.

- Running: If walking is too basic for you, running can make a huge difference in your active life. It takes no gym membership to go out and run, so running is free! And it is a great way to burn off calories.

- Swimming: If you have access to a pool, swimming can be a great way to get active. You can swim laps across the pool, or simply start by wading into the deeper end of the water, then watch your heart rate rise.

- If you have access to any apps on TV or on a computer, there are many free exercise routines at your fingertips.

Ways to Start Eating Well:

- Drink LOTS of water: Water helps every part of our body, especially with digestion. Drinking more water can help boost our metabolism and can even help us lose weight.

- Eat three meals per day: Many people have differing opinions on how much or how often one should eat, but if you are not eating three full meals per day, start doing so. Eating throughout the day instead of once or twice per day will help boost your metabolism and help with your appetite.

- Cut out one item: Without completely changing your diet, cut one unhealthy item from your daily meal plan. Soda? Try drinking water instead. Ice cream? Try only having it once a week, or replace your nighttime sweets with a piece of fruit.

- Healthy snacks: Instead of eating chips and cookies for snack, try eating veggies or fruit instead. Replace one unhealthy snack a day with one healthier snack.

- Protein is your friend: Protein is what curbs your hunger. The more protein you eat, the less hungry you will be. If you don't have time to cook meat for every meal, try eggs, or veggies and hummus. Hummus is chock-full of protein as it is made from garbanzo beans.

- Herbs and spices are ALSO your friend: If you find yourself not enjoying healthier food, try spicing it up! Garlic has lots of healing properties and is also very good for you. Use as much as you like! Try experimenting with new spices and watch your healthy meals improve in taste.

Medical Anxiety

As much as healthy nutrition and exercise can help you, they cannot replace medical attention from a doctor. If you develop a medical problem, seek medical attention! Only a doctor can help anything serious that may be going on with your body.

If you have medical anxiety because of your past in exploitation, or any other life trauma, it is best to come to every appointment prepared. Take deep, slow breaths before you walk in, and if you know what the appointment is going to be about, write down a few questions you may forget once you go into the appointment. If it helps, take a buddy into the appointment with you who you know can support you and help remember any important information that you might forget once you leave.

And remember that the doctor's office is there to help you, not harm you. No, doctors aren't perfect, but they are trying to boost your health so that you will be able to live a long and healthy life. It is okay to be nervous about seeking medical care, but just tell yourself that by going, you are becoming healthy and strong.

How Much Nutrition and Fitness Are Too Much?

Many people want to improve their health by changing their nutrition and exercise, and you can too! However, please do your best to pay attention to how much time and energy you are devoting to improving your fitness and nutrition. Incorporating healthy habits should feel easy and natural. So if you are constantly thinking about dieting and working out, so much so that you can't think of much else, and if these obsessive thoughts are coupled with negative body image and a lot of pressure on yourself, slow down! You do not want to unwittingly develop an eating disorder.

If you do feel that you have developed an eating disorder, of which some symptoms are laid out in the previous chapter, the best thing to do is to talk to a mental health professional and begin a treatment plan. Eating disorders are very serious and have serious consequences.

As you incorporate healthy nutrition and exercise in your daily routine, use positive self-talk to boost your vision for a healthier future. Tell yourself:

"I am getting stronger!"
"I am getting healthier!"
"I am nourishing my body and it is working!"

PROMPT QUESTIONS:

1. What is one benefit to diet and exercise that has nothing to do with looking good or gaining weight?

2. What is one easy way you can move your body?

3. What is one nutrition change you can make to help nourish your body?

4. When do you think managing your nutrition and exercise crosses over into being unhealthy?

5. Have you ever known anyone close to you who had an eating disorder? What did you witness from them, or what did they tell you?

6. How do you differentiate how you look from your overall physical health?

7. Regardless of how you look, what is your assessment of your health as it is right now?

AUTHOR'S EXPERIENCE:

Because I didn't take my health seriously when I was in recovery, I started drinking LOTS of soda, and I ended up becoming diabetic. Now I have to take injections of insulin every day. If I had done something really simple in the beginning by just limiting my soda intake, I might not have to deal with the same problems I have today.

I also get addicted to exercise, which can be unhealthy, so now I go on walks for my exercise. Not rigorous or long walks, just a walk once a day, and it actually makes a big difference in my overall health.

Drinking water was also a big change I made that helped A LOT.

CHALLENGE:

Challenge yourself to make ONE small change to your normal eating habits and exercise routine. This doesn't have to be life-changing, just a simple step in the right direction.

39

SAFETY AND CONSENT

Having lived through sexual exploitation, we may have skewed versions of boundaries when it comes to our bodies. We may be on the defensive, not letting ANYONE touch us at all in any way, or we may not feel that we can speak up for ourselves to avoid any sort of touching that we don't want to take part in, so we end up being passive. Now we are survivors, so we must take ownership of our bodies and protect them as best we can. When we protect our bodies, we are also protecting our hearts and minds.

What Is Consent?

Consent is when you give permission for someone to do something to you, or that you and another person both agree to do something together. In terms of touching, this means that whatever partner you are with will ask for permission to touch you, kiss you, hug you, or be intimate with you before they do so. Of course, this applies to sex, but we can practice consent with basic touching before we even get that far.

One way we can practice consent and set boundaries with new people is to ask them if it is okay to give them a hug before we automatically do so. And be prepared for them to say no, especially if this person is a fellow trauma survivor. Asking permission to hug someone does two things:

- It gives us a chance to practice consent
- It leads by example: showing others that you must ask before you touch

But what do we do when we are interacting with others who want to touch us without our consent? Here are two things you can try:

- When first meeting up with someone, we can put our hand out to shake their hand before they even try to hug us.
- We can use our voices. We can say something like, "I am sorry, I do not feel like hugging today." Or, if we want to be more direct, we can say, "I don't want to be touched today."
- Simply saying, "Oh, sorry, I am not a hugger!" is fine as well.

This seems so simple, but by doing this, we are letting the other person know that we will be touched on our own terms. If this person is going to be an intimate partner, it sends the signal, loud and clear, that they cannot initiate intimacy without your say-so.

Some intimate partners may be turned off by this and feel that you are being cold, but socially conscious people will understand these signals, and if they don't, they will be eager to learn what your signals are. Which person would you rather have in your life: someone who judges you if you don't want to hug them, or someone who respects your boundaries and still wants to get to know you?

This is important: No one should be able to touch you if you don't want to be touched, and if you don't want to be touched, it is your job to let others know.

We will go into detail about dating safety in Chapter Fifty, but for now, let's explore what to do when we are faced with our boundaries being crossed:

- You are out with a friend, and the more you two hang out, the more they hang on you, touch you, and hug you. You let them know that you are not in the mood to hug or touch, but they seem to ignore you.

  What to do: Firmly, clearly, and loudly tell them that you don't want to be touched, and that if they can't understand that, then you will have to leave. If they don't respect that, then you need to keep your word and leave.

- You're on a date with someone. You have been hanging out and having a good time. Your date asks to go back to their place to have some privacy, but you tell them you need to get home. They pressure you to go back to their place, and since they paid for the date, they say you "owe" it to them.

  What to do: Politely but firmly decline, and call a friend to pick you up, or ask the bartender to call you a cab. You want to stay away from people who think you owe them intimacy just because they paid for a drink or meal. Sounds like sexual exploitation? It certainly is close!

- You have practiced good boundaries and have told your partner that you do not want to touch from the beginning. They seem to hear you out, but as the hang-out goes on, they pressure you more and more to explain why you don't want to be touched.

  What to do: This is a teachable moment. Explain to them that you put a lot more value in conversation and personality than in how someone touches you. When you do decide to touch someone or let someone touch you, it will be a really important person who has earned that with you by being kind and patient and attentive to your needs and wishes. Remember, however: This is not an opportunity to let him in on all the details of your trauma. That is a conversation reserved for a later time in the potential relationship.

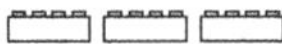

Facing Potential Threats

Ideally, once we set strong boundaries, the person who is attempting to cross our boundaries will hear us out, but as uncomfortable as the subject of sexual assault is, it is important to know that there are situations where we need to keep our bodies safe from someone who doesn't respect our boundaries. You can take a self-defense class at your local gym or clinic if you want to be able to defend yourself properly, but the most important things to remember when you feel you are in danger are:

- Your voice
- Your feet

Use your voice to make noise to attract attention to yourself so that (a) someone can possibly help you and (b) so that the person who is harming you will see the attention they're getting from the surrounding people and stop what he is doing. And, use your feet to get the hell out of there! Run to the closest safe place and ask someone to call the police for you.

Fight, Flight, or … Freeze?

(Content Warning: Sexual Assault)

We have all heard the term "fight or flight" before, which refers to when we are in a threatening situation, we either fight it out or use "flight" and leave the situation immediately. What happens when we are threatened and instead of fighting or leaving, we simply become paralyzed in fear?

This is a common reaction to sexual assault. Instead of fighting off our attacker, or perhaps because we cannot run away, we simply "freeze." We freeze because our mind tells our body that the only way to survive this situation alive is to stop everything we are doing and remain still and calm.

When this happens to assault survivors, they are often faced with guilt, asking themselves, "Why didn't I do something? Why did I just stay there?" The reason is that you were trying to make it out of the threatening situation alive. If this happens to you, do not feel ashamed. Simply get to safety as soon as possible, and file a report if you feel comfortable.

Challenge yourself to reflect on what your physical boundaries are. Do you like or dislike being touched or hugged? Are you okay with certain people touching you but not other people? It is very important for you to check in with yourself and know ahead of time before you get into situations where you must express these boundaries to others.

PROMPT QUESTIONS:

1. What does consent mean to you?

2. What is one way you can practice consent before you get into an intimate setting?

3. What signals would a future partner send you that would indicate consent? What signals would you send that would signal consent?

4. What are your personal boundaries? What about your physical boundaries?

5. What are the differences between fight, flight, and freeze?

6. How can you protect yourself when you leave residential treatment programming?

AUTHOR'S EXPERIENCE:

I would always practice setting boundaries by not letting just anyone hug me. If someone tries to hug me without my consent, I politely put my hand out for them to shake so that they don't touch me in a way I don't want to be touched.

"Freeze" from "Fight, Flight, or Freeze" was something I didn't understand before, but looking back, I froze a lot. I used to blame myself for freezing in situations where my safety was threatened, but now I understand that it was a part of trauma; it's a trauma response.

I have been learning more about the fourth F-reaction, fawn. This is when we react to a threat by being overly kind and compliant to our attacker. This is tricky, but it does not mean that we want to be kind to our attackers. It means that our brain tells us that fawning will help us survive the threat. I have heard this is common with survivors because they have dealt with sexual assault on a much greater scale than other individuals do.

CHALLENGE:

Challenge yourself to reflect on what your personal boundaries are.

40

SLEEP

Disordered sleep is perhaps one of the most common symptoms that sexual exploitation survivors report. Not sleeping enough, sleeping at inappropriate times, and having trouble getting to sleep or staying asleep are all things that almost every survivor experiences in recovery. This may be

- Because we have been attacked in our sleep
- Because we are fearful of our abusers
- Because we had an abnormal sleep schedule when we were exploited
- Because we had no sleep schedule at all

And the list goes on. If you are experiencing sleep issues that persist as you gain your recovery, know that you are not alone.

Fight-or-Flight and Sleep

If you think about animals of prey out in the wild, they probably sleep lightly because they have to watch out for possible predators who may try to attack them in their sleep. As survivors, we may have post-traumatic stress, which causes us to go into fight-or-flight mode more than usual. Some survivors go throughout their nighttime routine and get relaxed, but once they lie down, the worries start to surface.

We start to worry about our abuser or other possible predators. We worry about whether or not we will be able to do all we need to do to take care of ourselves. We worry about our safety. We worry about our home environment. And before we know it, several hours have passed and we haven't slept a wink. In this situation, we may feel like animals of prey, or at least our bodies are acting as if we are.

As distressing as this is, we can diminish these behaviors until they are under control and our sleep goes back to normal.

We diminish anxiety, fight or flight, and other behaviors that prevent us from getting to sleep with discipline that we implement into our nighttime routine. Below are some techniques that help us get to sleep.

- **Limited screen time:** Limit your screen time at bedtime, including your phone, computer, laptop, or tablet. If you do have to use your phone at bedtime, try turning the screen brightness down to halfway. You will see that, even at 50% brightness or less, you can still read off your phone in the dark, but it will not be so bright that it affects your sleep.

- **Have a bedtime routine:** Having a bedtime routine away from bright lights will signal to your body and brain that it is time for bed. Try taking a hot shower or a bath to relax your muscles, get a glass of water to keep by your bed, read, do some self-care, or watch a short, calm, and comforting show. Make sure that when you practice this routine, you turn the lights down!

- **Slow down your thoughts:** If you find one thought races into the next and your thoughts are spiraling out of control before bed, try to slow your brain down. You can do this by counting your breaths, or simply counting to ten slowly, then counting backwards, and repeating this until your brain calms down. When your mind wanders, bring your focus back to your breath.

- **Do NOT use your bed for work, study, or other engaging activities:** Your bed should be for sleep, and ONLY sleep. This is so that your brain registers your bed as a place to sleep, and so that you don't plop down on your bed ready to study when it is time to sleep. If you don't already have one in your room, invest in a desk.

- **Design your room for sleep:** If you have to, use blackout curtains on the windows, keep a white noise machine for bedtime, and make sure you have enough pillows and blankets for you to get to sleep.

- **Exercise daily:** A little cardio goes a long way. You may find that the more you work out during the day, the easier it is for your body to get tired and want to sleep at night.

Sleep Aids

If you find that you have practiced all of the habits above for a long period of time and you still can't get to sleep at a decent hour or at all, try using an over-the-counter sleep aid:

- **Zzzquil, or Benadryl:** The active ingredient in Zzzquil or Benadryl, Diphenhydramine, is commonly used as an antihistamine, which can help mild allergies, but it can also help you relax and fall asleep. Use as directed on the bottle or the package and allow for some time for it to kick in before you plan to sleep.

- **Melatonin:** Melatonin is a chemical that occurs naturally in the body at bedtime, but the over-the-counter version is made in a lab.

Melatonin is used for sleep, but keep in mind that it will only shorten the time it takes you to get to sleep by seven to twelve minutes.

- **Unisom, or Doxylamine:** Unisom, a common sleep aid, is used for extreme sleepless nights, not everyday use. Although it is over-the-counter and does not require a prescription, please use this sparingly as it has a lot of side effects, including constipation, and has adverse reactions with other medical conditions. In addition, if you take it too often, you can develop a tolerance for it, which will negatively impact your sleep in the long run. Even though you do not need a prescription for Unisom, it is best to talk to your doctor to see if they think it will work for your needs.

Be sure to use any over-the-counter sleep aid as directed by the package! However, if you have substance abuse issues, consult a medical professional before trying any sleep aids.

If you find that you have been practicing all good bedtime habits and you have tried over-the-counter sleep aids, but you STILL can't get yourself on a normal sleep schedule or you simply can't sleep at all, then it is time to talk to the doctor about what may work for you. There might be something that they can help you with better than any book, like this one, can. Try seeking medical treatment regarding your sleep.

This section, challenge yourself to make a bedtime routine that will signal to your brain that it is time to sleep. What will help you relax? Try reading, hot showers or baths, watch a show, and tuck yourself into bed. Then try to use this routine every night for one week, and see if your sleep improves.

PROMPT QUESTIONS:

1. How would you rate your sleep on a scale of one to ten, with ten being the highest? (Do you sleep too much or too little? How long does it take to fall asleep once you lie down?)

2. What is getting in the way of your ability to get good quality sleep?

3. Why do you think your sleep is the way it is?

4. What was your sleep schedule like during your exploitation? How did addiction or other factors play into your ability to sleep?

5. How has your past in exploitation or other dangerous lifestyles affected your ability to sleep?

6. What are some steps that you can include in your bedtime routine that would help you to fall asleep faster and stay asleep longer?

AUTHOR'S EXPERIENCE:

I have a very hard time sleeping because of my trauma, both because I have been attacked in my sleep and because my anxiety gets really bad once I lie down to relax. I have learned that my bedtime routine must include a few hours before I plan to actually sleep. It's not enough to take some sleep meds and lie down. For me, there is a whole process I must go through every night.

CHALLENGE:

Challenge yourself to create a bedtime routine that will signal to your brain that it is time to sleep.

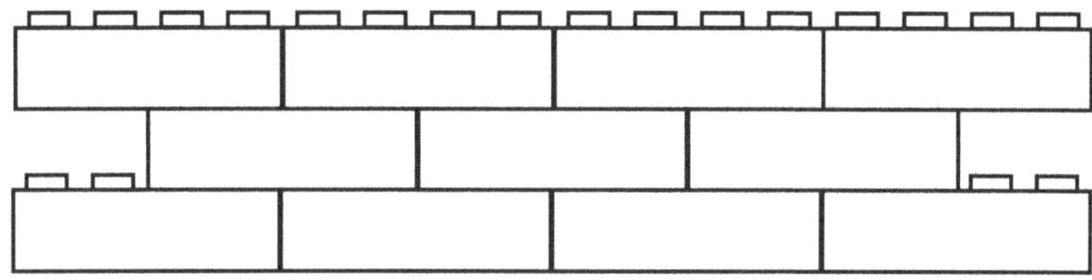

Money

41

Financial Anxiety

As you may have found in your exploitation recovery, it is extremely rare for anyone to go into exploitation for the fun of it. Even if it was initially something that piqued our curiosity, eventually we had to exploit ourselves to survive, and at the root of using exploitation to help us survive is MONEY. Perhaps we needed a lot of money fast, or perhaps we had criminal charges on our record that prevented us from getting legitimate employment, so we had a hard time finding a normal job. But wherever our story took us, the thing that kept us in exploitation was money.

And, if we weren't in control of the money we made during exploitation, especially if we had an abuser who controlled our finances, we might see money come in now and try to spend it fast, subconsciously because we fear that the money will be taken away somehow. Or instead, we might hoard money and not spend it even if we need to. Exploitation can give us all sorts of poor money habits and anxieties, no matter how long we were exploited, so now, as survivors of exploitation, we must be smart with money and gain control of our finances.

Flipping Our Attitude

Financial health begins with our minds. We must learn to not overreact when financial problems arise, and we must learn how to prepare for possible problems. This is when our calming, grounding techniques come into play in a serious way. We must remain calm both when money comes in, by not panicking and spending everything immediately, and remain calm when money goes out and we don't have much money left, yet we still have to make ends meet.

When we see bills come in, we can't look at this as a reason to be crushed, but rather as an opportunity to take care of ourselves. We should look at the bills, read them so we understand what we owe, and do what we can to make small payments that we can manage easily. When we are short of something we need, we must see it as an opportunity to be creative financially and stretch our money so that we can afford everything.

Money Problems Can Lead to Temptation

The main thing we need to worry about financially is that we won't be short in paying any of our expenses and thus be tempted to go back to exploitation. Not only does that stress the importance of budgeting, but we also need to be mindful of including extra spending money for things that will improve our quality of life.

Never budget only for the bare minimum of survival. Always leave some room in your budget for things that you just simply like and that make your life better.

If that means we budget to take ourselves out for ice cream once a week, or we want to go shopping once in a while, we must include that in our budget. We will discuss budgeting in more detail in the next section, but for now, just remember that you will want to give yourself wiggle room in your budget and plan to give yourself a budget that will make your daily life more comfortable.

In earlier chapters, we discussed how to afford basic necessities without spending much money, so review the section on cost-effective living when you get the chance. Not every survivor community has resources available like food banks and other necessities, although you should see what food banks are available just in case you need one. But do keep in mind that dollar stores or 99 cents stores have toiletries, food items, and household items at one dollar apiece. Consider also applying for food assistance from your local Health and Human Services center if you struggle to buy food every month. Ideally, we won't have to do any of these things, but in a pinch, food stamps and dollar discount stores can save us from going over budget, and therefore save us from the temptation to reenter sexual exploitation.

Believe it or not, many successful adults shop at discount stores in order to use their money wisely, even when they can afford more expensive stores. Part of gaining financial independence is deciding where you will splurge and where you will save. There is no shame in being smart and mindful of how to stretch a dollar. This will look different for everyone, but if you start to do it even while in a program, when you have $50 per month to spend, you will continue those habits as your finances increase.

Challenge yourself to make a list of specific times when money might be a source of anxiety, and make a step-by-step plan on how to relieve the anxiety and solve each problem. You might start with deep breaths and grounding exercises, go into looking at how much money you have, and piece by piece, put together a plan to pay for everything and then some. It takes a bit of practice, but if we prepare for the worst before it actually happens, it might not be so bad after all.

PROMPT QUESTIONS:

1. What is your overall attitude toward money?

2. How did exploitation change your attitude toward money?

3. Do you allow yourself a small portion of unmonitored spending money? Why or why not?

4. When it comes to finances, what are your biggest triggers?

5. When you are facing money problems, what can keep you on the right path so that you don't turn back to exploitation?

AUTHOR'S EXPERIENCE:

In all honesty, money still gives me a lot of anxiety. I'm not sure if that will ever go away or if that's just a part of life. Early on in my recovery, I was very tempted to go back to exploitation just to make ends meet. I didn't, however, because I had a strong support team, and I knew that exploitation was a slippery slope. If I were to go back, I would have to redo all the hard work I had done all over again.

It was important to me to always budget for at least one thing that I didn't necessarily need but that could improve my quality of life. If you don't allow yourself those freedoms, you may be tempted to overspend or ruin your budget in other ways.

CHALLENGE:

Challenge yourself to think of specific times when money might be a source of anxiety, and make a step-by-step plan on how to relieve your anxiety and solve each problem.

42

Basic Budgeting and Maintenance

Recovery gives us a chance to completely gain control of our finances. No, an entry-level job may not give us as much money as we are used to, but if we make some small adjustments and stay smart about how we spend our money, we can have everything we need and a few things we want.

This section, we will go over some steps to organizing and planning our budget, and although we have come up with some key steps, it is important to make it your own. YOU know where you need to spend and where you can make some sacrifices, so feel free to customize your budget in a way that will help you throughout the month. This section will only focus on the *basics* of budgeting.

Money Coming In

We start with our grand total per month. How do you calculate your monthly income?

- You can add up every paycheck you get through one month, which should already have taxes taken out, and that will give you a grand monthly total. If you want to get more of an average number, do this for a few different months, add all the monthly sums, then divide it by the number of months you're looking at, and you have your average monthly income.

- Or, instead of adding up check after check, try to start with your hourly rate. Multiply it by the average number of hours you work per week, then multiply THAT number by 3.4 (four weeks in a month, minus a percentage to go towards taxes), and you have your grand total for the month.

- If you have any other income from disability, Social Security, or even food stamps or government assistance, include this here.

Money Going Out

To organize your budget, take your entire monthly income and divide it among:

- Your needs: Rent, utilities, car payment and insurance, gas or bus fare, and groceries. Realistically, this may be over half of your total spending.

- Your wants: Daily craft coffee, lunch at work or school (if you decide to purchase lunch rather than take your own food from home, that is a "want"), clothes, toiletries. This should be less than 25% of your spending.

- And finally, a portion for savings or credit repair: This should ideally be 25% of your spending, but it might take a while for you to work up to that high a percentage.

Remember that these projected percentages are just *projections* in an ideal financial situation. If you have a low income with many bills to pay, it may be very difficult to save 25% of your income. Instead, try to pick a small percentage of your money coming in to save, and stick to that percentage for every paycheck.

Online bank account: If you have a bank account but do not have online access to your account yet, get online access to your bank account NOW. This is the easiest, most accessible way to keep track of all your spending. However, be aware that if someone tries to steal your phone, often the first app they will check will be your banking app. Make sure your phone is password protected, or better yet, fingerprint locked, so your bank information, and all your personal information, can stay private.

Needs

Needs include only the things you need to survive to the next month:

- Rent: As mentioned in previous chapters, rent should take up less than half of your total income. That will be your biggest chunk from your needs. If your rent does not cover utilities, include your utility bills here.

- Transportation: Whether you have a car or you use the bus, you should budget a portion of your needs for transportation, because you cannot survive without being able to get to and from work.

- Groceries: How much do you spend on groceries per week? Is there a way you can spend less and still get all the food you need? You cannot survive without food, so groceries are a need. (Eating at a restaurant is not a need, as it can be much cheaper to make food at home. However, if you are working multiple jobs and otherwise have a demanding schedule, it is okay to include eating takeout as part of your budget. Even so, it will still go under the "wants" section.)

- Living Necessities: While things like toilet paper, soap and shampoo, and cleaning supplies do not necessarily have to be purchased every week, and sometimes not even every month, you should keep a small portion monthly to take care of those needs.

Wants

Wants should include things that you do not need to survive, but that you would still like to have to make your life comfortable and livable. Some ideas are:

- Extra toiletries: We all need toilet paper and some soap and shampoo to get clean and be hygienic, but sometimes we want a fancy brand of shampoo, soap, or bubble bath, bath bombs, and scented candles to help us relax. Include these items in your "wants."

- Restaurants and going out: While we should *not* make a habit of eating out at every meal because that CERTAINLY adds up, we can budget to go out once in a while if we prefer it. Instead of planning to eat all your meals out of the house, pick one or two restaurants per month and look forward to that meal.

- Salon time: Some salon visits, be it for nails or your hair or whatever you want, can make saving worth the struggle. Be sparing with your spending on salon visits, but once in a while, if you save, you can treat yourself to the salon.

- Gym membership: Theoretically, we can get our cardio in while running around our neighborhood, which costs no money. If you feel you need a gym membership for whatever reason, include this in your "wants." (However, if you are an active athlete or if you are an aspiring fitness trainer, include your gym membership in your basic needs.)

- Coffee: Theoretically, we can make coffee at home for a low cost. If you feel that you need to buy craft coffee elsewhere, include this in your "wants."

Savings and Credit Repair

If you have no debt or credit issues, great! Start saving, because you want to have a financial cushion in case an emergency arises, or in case you are working toward a big purchase or investment. We will talk about this more in Chapter Forty-Four.

If you have debt on your record, a portion of your income should go toward credit repair payments. In a perfect world, we would have a portion of our income cover credit repair and have another portion go toward savings, but if you do have debt to pay, that should be your first priority. In the next chapter we will go over credit repair in more detail, but for now, just understand that a portion of your budget will go toward credit repair.

What to Do with This Budget

Sometimes, if you don't have to immediately intervene with your spending habits and are not in danger of going broke for too long, it may be smart to simply keep track of your spending habits for one month. Ask yourself:

- How much money is coming in this month?
- How much money is going out?
- What are some of my biggest expenses?
- What are some smaller daily expenses that seem to add up?
- Can I live without something? Or if not, is there a way I can save on a higher-ticket item that I need?

It may be helpful to watch your spending for a time and to see when money comes in, how much money is coming in, and how much is going out. Is there any room for savings? Can you cut down on any spending? What will work best for you?

Bank Accounts

Some of us come into recovery with delinquencies on our financial records, whether we have overdrawn our account and failed to pay it back, or we simply never paid our credit card bills and the credit account went to collections. Getting a bank account at that point is tough, because a quick background check may block the bank from opening your account. At this point, the best thing to do is to set up payments to whatever collections agency your account belongs to, until you can improve your credit. We will talk more about this later.

If you have no delinquencies or credit issues, yet you don't have a bank account, make sure you open an account at your local bank as soon as possible. You can have a banking agent help you set this up, but our advice is to not allow overdrafts (and overdraft fees) on your account. If you can, opt out of this and agree to have your card declined if you go over your funds. Getting declined is embarrassing, but it is definitely not as bad as being charged so many overdraft fees that you do not even see any of your next paycheck or deposit.

If the above factors have prevented you from getting a traditional bank account, consider obtaining an online account through a bank like Green Dot. There are pros and cons to accounts like these. For one, there is no brick and mortar location if you need assistance with your account, so you will be forced to stay on hold with outsourced customer service any time you need help. However, this is a safer option than being on a cash-only basis, especially if you are dealing with the totality of your income in cash. Keeping large amounts of cash can be risky. There is always the possibility that it will disappear or be stolen, while going through the proper channels can help you retrieve money in an account. Would you rather lose a debit card, where money can be recovered, or cash, that cannot?

In addition, an online bank account will, at the very least, show you a clear record of your saving and spending habits. What a great way to jump-start your finances!

STAY AWAY from Payday Advances

A payday loan, or payday advance, is a loan from a financial agency in which you pay a small fee (or sometimes, a large fee) and prove how much income you are expecting at your next paycheck, then the agency gives you an advance on your income. Sounds like a great idea? Wrong! This is a scam and a slippery slope. People have ruined their lives on payday loans.

Think about it: If you are spending one paycheck before it even hits your account, then once you get paid, you have to turn your whole paycheck in! What happens next time? You will have to get another payday advance. Next time? Another advance. And every single time you do this, you will have to pay the agency another fee. NEVER get a payday loan advance, and if you can help it, don't even walk in the doors of those kinds of financial agencies.

After gathering this data for your spending habits, challenge yourself to write out a written budget for the following week, or for your next pay period, and then when you can master your weekly spending, make a plan for the entire month. If you stay on top of things, you will see your financial situation improve.

PROMPT QUESTIONS:

1. How can you tell the difference between a need and a want?

2. Why are "wants" important?

3. Are you able to open a bank account? If not, what roadblocks are in your way?

4. What bad money choices will you stay away from?

5. What good choices will you be sure to make when it comes to your money?

Author's Experience:

Again, planning to spend on a small item or two that you don't need but that can improve your quality of life will keep you sane when money is tight. How you determine what those items would be is a little more difficult.

Please, please stay away from payday loans and multilevel marketing schemes. These are money pits that can ruin your life.

Challenge:

Challenge yourself to write out a budget for the following week, or for your next pay period. When you can master your weekly spending, make a plan for the entire month. If you stay on top of things, you will see your financial situation improve.

43

Credit Repair

This section, we will go over debt payment and credit repair. We will cover how to figure what you owe and how to take baby steps when paying everything off. Credit repair can be one of the most intimidating things when it comes to financial health, but saving often becomes the most important. In order to save big, you must repair your credit.

Why Repair Your Credit?

Future purchases: Anything you want to do in the future, as far as buying a quality car, a house, or even renting an apartment, will involve a credit check. You will want to have a high credit score or you will not be eligible to purchase these things.

Wage garnishment: On top of not being able to make large purchases, if your credit bills go unpaid for too long, you may be subjected to wage garnishment, and your tax return may also be affected. This means that collectors will take a portion of your check and you will be left with a fraction of what you earned. Imagine expecting a $500 check and only getting $250!

Steps to Credit Repair

The first step towards credit repair is to obtain a free credit report online. If you have never done this before, ask someone on your treatment team to help you. You will need some basic information, including your social security number and personal identification.

Once the report is run, you will see everything you owe. There will also be contact information for every collection agency or financial institution. Don't get sticker shock, though; you won't have to pay everything right then and there. Contact each creditor, explain to them that you are a victim of a violent crime, and that you are trying to pay your debts. Ask the agency about getting payments as low as possible. It might even help to relay to them that you are homeless and living in a homeless shelter, if you are in a residential recovery program, though you might have to prove this through written documentation from recovery home staff.

The great thing about calling creditors is that if you show good faith and make it clear you want to start paying off your debts, they will be happy to work with you! It can be scary to be in that vulnerable position, but remember that you are a strong, smart, resilient survivor and repairing your debt is nothing compared to everything else you have already survived.

Taking Baby Steps

Credit repair is not something that can be accomplished overnight, especially if we are working entry-level jobs, so take small steps every day. If you have to be on the phone with a bill collector, that's your step for the day. If you have to look up the number of creditors to call, take that step of searching who to talk to, and call them the next day. That's two steps in two days!

Sacrifices

While you are fixing your credit, you may have to make some sacrifices. You may not be able to apply for any credit cards and you may not be eligible to be on the lease at any apartment or rental property, which may force you to temporarily rent a room before you can rent an entire apartment. On top of those setbacks, you will still be expected to pay a certain amount per month toward your debt. This takes some discipline. Use this time to get back on track! But don't lose sight of the goal of having complete financial independence.

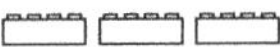

Challenge yourself to compile all bills from collectors and other debt payments. Put them into a large envelope. Every day, take one step toward tackling your debt, whether that means calling a collector or taking a trip to your bank to help you start making a payment. Then, write each day's date on the envelope and what step you took that day toward repairing your credit.

PROMPT QUESTIONS:

1. Do you know where your credit is at? Have you requested a credit report before?

2. What potential consequences could be your biggest motivation to repair your credit?

3. Have you had the experience of creditors calling you, or having your wages garnished? What did those experiences bring up for you?

4. Why is credit repair important?

5. What is your anxiety level when it comes to credit repair?

6. Can you think of any positive outcomes when it comes to repairing your credit?

AUTHOR'S EXPERIENCE:

I think the best thing to do with credit repair is to just suck it up and do it. Start taking small steps to work toward repairing your credit. Take another small step each day. And get any payments down as low as they will go. If you are still in recovery housing, you can prove your legal homeless status to help your case in getting your payments lowered.

The best thing I noticed about credit repair was that when you actually call a creditor and try to start setting up regular payments, they are super stoked that you want to start paying. I don't know why I thought that they were going to arrest me over the phone, when in reality, they worked with me pretty well as soon as they found out I wanted to start fixing my credit issues.

Challenge:

Challenge yourself to compile all bills from collectors and other debt payments. Put them into a large envelope or folder. Every day, take one step toward tackling your debt, whether that means calling a collector or taking a trip to your bank so they can start helping you make payments. Then, every day, write the date and what you did to repair your credit on the outside of the envelope or folder.

44

SAVINGS

After we have made steps toward fixing our credit, we must plan for the future. This is when we start to think about saving. Our savings account is what will give us long-term stability in life. Not only will it help our finances to have some discipline for saving, it will also help our stress levels, as we will not be worrying about what to do if we encounter a financial emergency. We will already have a cushion of money so we will be able to take care of tough situations.

This section, we will discuss what we might be saving for, including financial emergencies, and we will refresh ourselves on ways to save our money.

What Situations Might We Need to Save For?

After we have started making payments on our credit, here are some good things to save for, aside from saving for emergencies:

- Rent on a new apartment: first and last month's rent and security deposit

- A new car
- Vacation—because we all need some time to recharge ourselves
- Weddings, or other life-changing special events
- Starting a family

Having adequate savings allows us to completely improve our quality of life! This does take some discipline, however, and in order to make these life-changing purchases later on, you must commit to saving a certain amount from each paycheck. The hard part is not touching that sum once it comes in. You might want to work with your banker about having a savings account where, when your check goes into your account, a set percentage is withdrawn and goes into a savings account. If it helps, have them detach that savings account from your debit card, so the only way you can touch your savings is if you go into the bank in person.

Online-only Bank Accounts

Another option is to open an account with an online-only bank, such as Ally or Green Dot. Banks like Green Dot will accept you, with good or bad credit, as long as you are in good standing with their company. You will have access to savings, checking, and they will also give you a debit card. This will make your life so much easier, and safer, than being on a cash-only basis. Just keep in mind that there may be no physical locations for these banks, and often customer service is outsourced to different countries. To many survivors, however, this drawback is totally worth the benefits.

Emergencies: What constitutes an emergency?

Along with being a surprise event, an emergency must be something you cannot survive the next few weeks or months without paying for. This includes:

- Emergency dental work
- Car repair
- Medical emergency that insurance will not cover
- Having to move
- Home emergency issue: pest problems, damage to property

Avoid These When Saving

The following are things you should avoid when it comes to spending your savings:

- Avoid paying for another person's emergency, especially if you have an entry-level job and have worked so hard to save what little you have.
- Avoid telling anyone how much you have saved. Others may find out and try to exploit your good nature in order to get their hands on your hard-earned money.
- AVOID PYRAMID or MULTILEVEL MARKETING SCHEMES: No employer should require you to pay to be

an employee before you see any income. By the same token, you should not have to buy a product in order to sell it. Multilevel marketing schemes are money pits, and often you will never see a profit. You will only be encouraged to have more employees under you, so that you will be more valuable to the sales people YOU are under.

Ways to Save

So how do we figure out how much to save? Ideally, we would save about 25% of each paycheck, but sometimes it is tough to set aside that big a chunk from our income. So, another way we can figure out how much to save is by finding ways we can save throughout our daily spending, adding each amount that we save, and then saving that amount each month while committing to make those small sacrifices.

Making small sacrifices doesn't mean that you have to take away something you really need or want. It just means that you might want to be smarter about how you spend your money.

Ways to save with groceries:

- Avoid name brands: If you have a particular brand of an item that you really like, continue to get that brand. But if there is a store version of an item you usually get, try to get that item instead. If you do this for the majority of your groceries, you can save around ten percent off the top of your grocery bill.

- Government food assistance: If you haven't already, make an appointment with your local Health and Human Services office and apply for food stamps or food assistance. If you are accepted, you will get a generous amount of assistance per month, depending on your income.

- Food banks: Food banks offer free food items for those that qualify, depending on how low your income is. Although some food banks do not provide fresh foods, they usually provide things like rice, noodles, oil, and other necessities for no cost at all. This is great in a pinch and can save you lots of money in the long run.

Ways to save with toiletries, cleaning supplies, clothes, and nonfood items

- Dollar discount stores: Dollar discount stores, like Dollar Tree or the 99 Cents Store, can offer toiletries, cleaning supplies, laundry detergent and fabric softener, and other household items for only one dollar per item. They even have some name brand items for only one dollar apiece. Shop around in your local dollar discount store and see how much you can save! Think about it: If you only have $20 to spend, why get five items when you can get 20 items?

- Discount designer stores: Of course, discount designer stores, like Ross and Marshalls, can get you designer clothes at an affordable price. But did you know you can also get high-end shampoo, shower gel, and conditioner for a fraction of the shelf price? If you don't want to sacrifice your name brand toiletries, look for them at discount designer stores before you buy them off the shelf at their regular price.

- Thrift stores: Thrift stores are often ten years behind the current fashion trends, or more, but professional clothes for job interviews and special events never go out of style. You can find interview clothes here for a fraction of the regular price. And besides the clothes themselves, check thrift stores for furniture or household appliances before you buy brand-new items if you are trying to save a few bucks.

Ways to save with salon time

- Beauty school salons: If you are not able to perform your salon services on yourself, check out your local beauty school for salon deals. Experienced cosmetology students provide these services under strict supervision from their instructors. These services are professional quality for a fraction of salon prices!

Challenge yourself to think of three ways you can save money for the next month. Calculate how much you will actually save, multiply that by how many months are left in the year, and imagine what you can do with that grand total!

PROMPT QUESTIONS:

1. What big goal is on your mind that you would need to save for? Why are you looking forward to that goal?

2. How have you saved money in the past?

3. How was saving difficult in the past?

4. Why is it important to keep your savings to yourself, and not share with others what you have saved?

5. What small ways can you save so that later you can have a large chunk of change?

Author's Experience:

I usually save 10–15% from every paycheck for around six months at a time. At the end of those months I decide whether I am going to spend it or wait another few months. My time markers for these months are summer vacation and then Christmas.

I always get off-brand items to save money. When I calculated all that I would save by doing that, it turned out to be more than 10% of my grocery bill. Totally worth it!

Challenge:

Challenge yourself to think of three ways you can save money for the next month. Calculate how much you will save, multiply that total by how many months are left in the year, and imagine what you can do with that grand total!

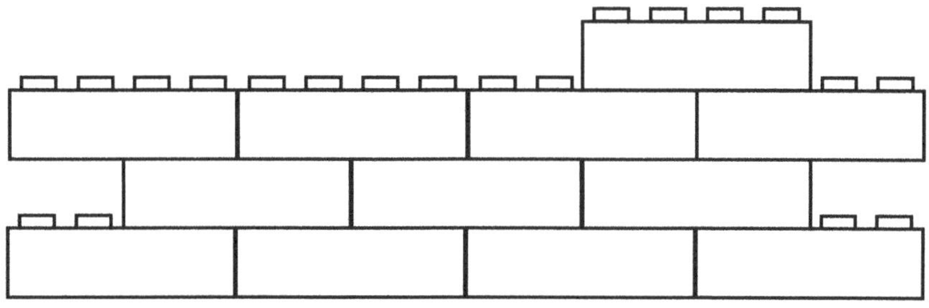

Reflection and Narrative Therapy

45

Understanding Narrative Therapy

Recovery from the trauma of sexual exploitation is hard work! Not only do we have to take many steps to get our life back on track; we also have to work hard at managing intense trauma symptoms, all while attempting to live a somewhat normal life.

As you look back at your past and everything that brought you to where you are today, do you ever wonder where you went wrong, or what you could have done to prevent the trauma that happened in your life? Do you see telltale signs that you could have been vulnerable to abusers, potentially long before you ever entered exploitation? Does this cause you to be less compassionate to yourself, or more compassionate? Does healing from your trauma affect the way you relate to others?

Sometimes, getting everything on paper, from start to finish, can help us understand what happened to us. We can look at our journey step by step, and if we do this with the purpose of being more forgiving and accepting of our former self, we can gain a lot of healing.

What Is Narrative Therapy?

Narrative therapy is a way to take our own personal feelings out of our story, and to look at our story objectively without making any judgments of ourselves. The goal is to write your own story, from everything leading up to your exploitation to your entry in recovery, while speaking in the third person, using "she," "her," and "they" statements instead of "I did …" "I went …" statements. This way, we can have an unbiased perspective of what happened to us. We can look at the facts without feeling all the trauma so intensely. And hopefully, after looking at the path behind us, we can begin to forgive ourselves.

Narrative therapy focuses on you becoming the expert regarding your own life, and also challenges your dominant problematic stories. You will look objectively at the story, but also "rewrite" places you are stuck with truth and compassion.

This is not an easy process. Narrative therapy involves confronting some traumatic memories, which may ultimately bring us healing, but while we are participating in writing our story, we may get triggered and become uncomfortable. This is one reason why this chapter is toward the end of the book: you should have approximately one year of healing before you confront something so heavy independently.

Preparing for Narrative Therapy

First, we must be honest with ourselves. Have we completed a large enough chunk of our healing that we will be ready to confront some triggering past events? Or do we need more time to heal?

It is also important to carve out a big chunk of alone time to get through this chapter. You will want enough time to write everything AND you want to have enough time to practice self-care after each writing session, or whenever you need a break from writing your narrative.

Remember that the purpose of narrative therapy is not to intensify emotions surrounding your trauma or cause you to blame yourself for the things that happened during your exploitation. Instead, it is to invoke self-compassion and forgiveness for yourself. This is an exercise in self-love and self-acceptance.

The ultimate goal is to move yourself past patterns or beliefs about yourself that inhibit you from moving forward.

Although some survivors have done narrative therapy and other similar activities on their own, it is best to do narrative therapy if you are regularly seeing a mental health professional, such as a therapist or a counselor. Narrative therapy can be triggering, and you may want to process all the emotions that come up with someone who is knowledgeable about mental health and trained in crisis management.

Chapters Forty-Seven and Forty-Eight will involve analyzing your narrative, while Chapter Forty-Six will involve writing your actual narrative with a few key prompts. Do not start your narrative today. Instead, reflect on whether or not you are truly ready for this type of therapy. If so, decide if you are going to write this on the computer, on your phone in a notes app, or in a paper journal. Finally, challenge yourself to think of some good self-care activities that will help you get through these potentially tough writing sessions.

PROMPT QUESTIONS:

1. How do you feel about putting your story into written form?

2. Are you far enough away from your past in exploitation that you can revisit some old memories in a self-empathetic way and write what happened step by step?

3. Why do you think it is important to write your narrative in the third person?

4. Narrative therapy can be intense. What self-care activity can you have on standby?

AUTHOR'S EXPERIENCE:

When I had left exploitation, I ended up writing out the entire experience in novel form. It ended up being 80,000 words long! But the time I spent writing my narrative, although it was not always easy, was super rewarding. It also helped me put my past behind me. Writing about myself in the third person helped me see myself as a close friend or loved one instead of having a shameful experience reflecting on my past.

CHALLENGE:

Challenge yourself to think of at least one good self-care activity that you can have on standby for when you write your narrative.

46

Writing Your Narrative

Are you ready to participate in doing your own independent narrative therapy?

If not, please just read through all prompts in case you want to do this in the future. This is a big step and should not be taken lightly, so you must be well prepared in order to do this. If you feel that narrative therapy would open more wounds than it would heal for you personally, it may be wise to give this some thought before you dive in. Remember, this process is meant to promote self-love and self-compassion, not to intensify our trauma symptoms in any way.

If you are ready, make sure you have carved a few hours out of your day to be alone and process, get your notebook or laptop or whatever writing tool you want to use, and have a self-care activity on standby. And before we start, make sure that you are able to take breaks as needed, even if you have to walk outside and get some fresh air.

Now, the first thing we need to keep in mind for this narrative therapy is that you will be writing in the third person. You will not be saying "I did, I saw" but rather "They did, their feelings were …"

This is so we can get an outsider's perspective on our own life, and so we can practice compassion as if our trauma were happening to our dear friend or loved one, rather than reliving it ourselves.

Read the following prompts that will guide you from before your trauma, during your trauma, and then out of your trauma into safety and recovery. If you feel the need to skip a certain prompt, that's okay. Skip it and move on to the next. Just remember to respond to each prompt in the third person, using your own name but remembering to use she, he, her, his, their, or they statements.

Sexual Exploitation Survivor Narrative Therapy Prompts

1. What was their birth-given name?

2. What was their childhood like?

3. When was the first time they experienced true emotional pain that only adults should feel? What did that event teach them, good or bad?

4. What led to finding their abuser or entering into exploitation? What was that experience like?

5. Is there anything they initially liked about being in exploitation? What was the appeal?

6. When was the first time they knew they were in danger in exploitation? What did that feel like?

7. Did they ever try to leave? What happened when they tried?

8. Were they ever injured? Did they get help or were they denied help? What was that experience like?

9. What was the lowest point they experienced while being exploited? What did that experience bring up for them?

10. When did they know that they needed to get out for good? What led them to that?

11. What was their exit strategy? How did their plan work?

12. Was entering recovery easy for them? How was it difficult?

13. Did they ever think of going back to exploitation? What stopped them?

14. What do they look forward to most now that they are exploitation-free?

Now that you have been through all the questions and answered honestly, release it. Close your notebook, or close the writing app on your phone or computer and walk away. Do not read what you have written. Say to yourself that this was your past, and that it's behind you. Next chapter we will look over all the questions and analyze what we have written, but for now, simply let that part of your life close.

Imagine yourself putting all those memories into a small jar. Put a lid on the jar and shut it tightly. Then imagine yourself putting it under your bed, or into the back of your closet, or somewhere safe. When you are ready, we will open the jar. But for now, let it remain closed and put away into a safe place.

And go on with your day. Do a self-care activity, eat some good food, and give your spirit a hug. You did some tough work today, and you should be very proud of yourself.

AUTHOR'S EXPERIENCE:

You might find that not every question applies to you. Know that every survivor's story is unique and do your best to make the questions fit your own personal journey.

My main self-care activity after writing in narrative therapy was having ice cream and watching cartoons. That comfort really helped so I didn't have to relive my past for too long. However, sooner or later, you will have to confront the emotions this exercise brought up for you. Discuss what you wrote with a therapist, or if you need a quicker release, discuss this with a close friend or confidant while you wait for therapy.

CHALLENGE:

Follow the questions laid out in this chapter and write your narrative.

47

Reflecting on Your Narrative

How did it feel to write your narrative? Was it healing? Did it trigger you?

We hope that the biggest thing you took away from your narrative is how far you have come. Even if you are merely a year into recovery, you should be so proud that you have made it that far! It is not easy to walk away from exploitation, especially when we are faced with life, having to pay bills or take care of children. All the while we are healing from a huge life trauma that changed how we thought about the entire world.

It is important, when you read your responses to the prompts, that you do not relive your experiences. Instead, read your responses as if they are happening to a close friend, your daughter, or someone else whom you love and would not want any harm to befall. You must remember that the purpose of narrative therapy is not to intensify emotions surrounding your trauma or cause you to blame yourself for the things that happened during your exploitation. Instead, it is to invoke self-compassion and forgiveness to yourself. This is an exercise in self-love and self-acceptance. That is the ultimate goal.

This chapter is also going to involve some of your own narration. If you don't want to write out all your new perspectives, you can grab a buddy whom you trust and simply discuss your thoughts with them, or you can keep your processing to yourself, silently.

Analyzing Your Narrative

Now, open your notes from your narrative. Without internalizing the words you wrote, read your answers as if a friend had written them and is letting you in on a deep, intimate secret. Then, ask yourself the following questions:

1. How do you feel when they talk about their pain in early childhood? Do you want to help them? What would you do as an adult if you knew how they felt, thought, and acted as a young child, or if you knew what they were going through?

2. Knowing what you know now, if you found that a friend of yours was going into exploitation, what would you say to them?

3. What do you wish someone would have done for you if you were that individual and the first instance of direct, undeniable abuse happened?

4. Do you think you would have accepted help at that point? Or were you so far deep that you wouldn't have listened, either out of fear or out of ignorance?

5. How did they gain wisdom that would help them rectify such a toxic situation?

6. Who was the hero in their story? Did they have to be their own hero? If so, how did they bring triumph to the darkness?

7. How is your life now compared to the narrative?

8. What advice would you give to the individual at the beginning of their story?

Now pat yourself on the back. Reflecting on your narrative is hard work! If you worked with a buddy, thank them for allowing you space to be vulnerable, because sometimes just hearing about someone else's trauma is hard work too!

Imagine yourself putting your traumatic memories back into your jar, shutting the lid tightly, and putting the jar away, knowing you can open it again if you ever need to. But for now, simply relax, do a self-care activity, and thank yourself for working through something unsettling that will ultimately bring you healing.

AUTHOR'S EXPERIENCE:

Looking at my narrative, I found that there was a huge difference between how my life was in exploitation and how it was in recovery. I also saw myself as courageous and strong rather than pitiful and weak. It was very healing.

CHALLENGE:

Challenge yourself to relax, do a self-care activity, and thank yourself for doing some hard self-work.

48

Rewriting Your Own Rules

Though we don't want to dwell on some toxic things we lived through while in exploitation, we must remember them enough to change the way we walk through life. Many survivors leave exploitation only to go back into it sometime later. We don't want that to happen again or too often, so we must set some rules for ourselves, with our past in mind, in order to guide ourselves through situations in the future that may be tough to handle on our own. We never want to put ourselves in a situation where we may be triggered to go back into exploitation, so setting some ground rules will protect us from those vulnerable situations.

The best part about this is that YOU will write your own rules. This chapter will simply guide you on some areas where you may need to set some rules, but the rules themselves will come from you. Think of this as your personal ten commandments or bill of rights. These "rules" will be your personal moral code to live by.

Some things to think about when setting your own rules:

1. How does your past affect how you will treat others? Do you aim to practice nonviolence? Do you vow to keep yourself guarded until you know someone well?

2. How will you hold yourself accountable? Are there certain things you will not do in life, regarding your personal space or intimacy?

3. Who do you aim to emulate? How will you set an example if you become a role model for others?

4. What backup plan will you keep in mind if you find yourself in a vulnerable position? What backup plan will you keep in mind if you find yourself in a bad financial situation?

5. Are there people you never want to see or speak to again? Are there people in your life whom you want to make more time for?

Now, write out five to ten rules you will hold close to your heart. Space will be left in this book for those answers, but feel free to write them somewhere where you can see them every day to keep them at the forefront of your mind.

My Rules:

1. ______________________________

____

____

____

____

2. ______________________________

____

____

____

____

3. ______________________________

____

____

____

____

4. ____________________

____

____

____

____

5. ____________________

____

____

____

____

6. ____________________

____

____

____

____

7. ____________________

____

____

____

____

8. ____________________

____

____

____

____

9. ____

____

____

____

____

10. ____

____

____

____

____

Author's experience:

I set clear boundaries when I left exploitation. There were certain people who I did not want to be around at all anymore. However, I did decide that I was going to make more time for my family. I already saw myself becoming an example for others, so I knew that to be a role model, I had to conduct my behavior by a certain set of standards. Making rules for myself became an empowering thing, not a limiting thing.

Challenge:

Challenge yourself to write out five to ten rules you will hold close to your heart.

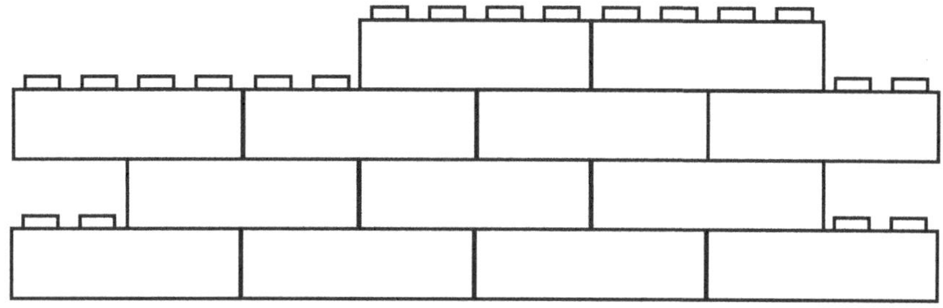

Dating

49

Pursuing Romantic Relationships

Many of us who have been exploited might have initially sought a romantic connection with a true partner in life, but ultimately were thrust into a very dangerous and toxic lifestyle, where we saw all kinds of people behave in despicable ways, including our exploiter, whom we may have seen as our life partner.

Exploitation might cause us to never want to date anyone again, for we don't want to be hurt. It is unrealistic, however, to think that we would never date anyone for the rest of our lives, and if we do find ourselves in a romantic situation, we must keep our wits about us. Furthermore, if we do find the right partner, our lives may be fulfilled in unimaginable ways.

Before we go on, please understand that it is totally okay to remain single if that is your choice. You do not have to date anyone in order to complete your recovery from exploitation. Just keep your ears open and absorb the information you hear this month and keep it in your back pocket in case a romantic opportunity ever arises for you.

How do you know you are ready to date?

As backward as it sounds, we should only consider seriously dating when we are independent and comfortable with ourselves and how our life is going even without a partner. We shouldn't have the feeling of needing a relationship, but rather have the burning desire to share our lives with someone who can bring the same amount of effort and positivity to our lives as we are bringing.

One thing to keep in mind, if you had any sort of romantic connection with your former exploiter, is whether or not you are still attached to that person. And be honest with yourself! Do you still have lingering feelings for them? And if so, are you simply looking for a rebound to get some temporary relief from that trauma? If that's where you are at, you might want to consider waiting to find the right person, because if you want to find a rebound, you are likely to find one, and that can lead to a dysfunctional relationship. Or, let's be real, a night you will later regret.

Codependency

Do you find that you do not feel like yourself unless you have a romantic connection with someone? Do you lean on your romantic partners a little more than you should? It's natural to want to lean on our partners for support, but if we are seeking out codependency, we will probably get it, and that can lead to old patterns of dysfunction.

It is important to understand that ultimately we will get the kind of relationship we are aligning ourselves with. If what we are aligning ourselves with is anything less than a happy, stable, functional relationship, we will unfortunately get exactly what we are asking the universe for. For example, if we are desperate for a relationship, chances are that we are going to match with someone else who is equally desperate. Is that your ideal romantic situation?

So, remember:

- Rebounds attract rebounds,
- Codependency attracts codependency,
- Desperate attracts desperate,
- But wholeness and stability attract wholeness and stability.

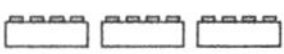

What are you looking for?

The key to finding a happy, loving, lasting relationship is to know what you want out of a relationship from the beginning and then choose to accept nothing less than what you want.

Here are some things to consider in your potential partners:

- **Commitment:** How much commitment do you desire?: Do you want to see this person every day? A few times a week? Do you want this person to ultimately live with you? Or is it more important that the person corresponds with you well by answering calls and texts when you call and text them, and can communicate well even when you're not there with them?

- **Intimacy:** Do you want to be intimate? Do you want to have intimate relations with your partner, or do you choose to stay abstinent until you are further along in your healing, for personal or spiritual reasons? Your partner must be someone who respects this and has similar ideas about intimacy.

- **Children:** Do you want kids? Maybe don't mention having kids on the first date, but if you already have kids, this is something that can make or break the potential relationship. What role do you want your future partner to play in their lives, if any? Are you looking for a partner who can ultimately be a second parental figure to your children, or do you want privacy and independence when it comes to raising your children? Of course, you may want someone whom your kids can eventually look up to, but that does not mean they must join you in decision making when it comes to your children.

- **Goals and Future Planning:** Does your potential partner line up with your ultimate goals in life? Do you foresee yourself having a family with your partner? Do you want to get married and/or have kids? Will you need your partner's support when pursuing a career or higher education? Do you want to be a homeowner? Though we can casually date someone who does not have the same goals, ultimately we should aim to date someone who has the same goals and visions for the future that we do.

With all these things, you can subtly investigate whether or not you align with this person through small talk when you are dating. Although telling a person on the first date that you want kids with them can be off-putting, you can make it clear to them what you want for yourself, whether they join you or not. The right person at the right time will align with you when you are confident about your goals and aspirations, because they will want the same things in their life.

Though we have seen some ugliness in our lives when it comes to romantic connections, we must be assured that there are good people out there whom we can easily end up with. Having a happy, loving, functional relationship can bring healing to our lives in ways unimaginable. When you have someone in your life who loves and respects you and is with you to give and receive support through thick and thin, you will see that it is okay to have faith in humanity again. A good relationship can give you an attitude of optimism that shows you the world is not a cold and lonely place, but a warm, full environment where we can be ourselves with anyone.

Challenge yourself to think of your dream partner. What kind of qualities will they have? What will they look like? How will they act? What kind of goals do you want your future partner to have? It is important to think about these things long before we rejoin the dating scene.

PROMPT QUESTIONS:

1. Do you see yourself dating anytime in the near future? What about the more distant future?

2. What are you looking for in a partner, in terms of commitment, intimacy, children or potential children, and goals or future planning?

3. What other details are you looking for in a future partner? Anything physical? Mental? Be honest.

4. Is there anything that you know you will avoid in the future?

5. How has exploitation affected the way you may act in romantic relationships in the future?

6. How will you know if you are ready to date?

AUTHOR'S EXPERIENCE:

I dated casually for around a year before I met my current partner. During that year, I constantly thought about what my ideal partner would be like. If someone I was seeing didn't fit that mold, I would move on to the next potential partner. I wanted to be with someone who was honest, funny, a hard worker, and independent. My current partner was all that and more.

I knew I was ready to date when I was completely financially independent. I knew if I had to depend on a guy for money or a place to live, I would be easy to control, and I did not want to be controlled.

CHALLENGE:

Challenge yourself to think of your dream partner. What kind of qualities will they have? What will they look like? How will they act? What kind of goals do you want a future partner to have? It is important to think of all these things long before we join the dating scene.

50

The Do's and Don'ts of Dating

Every sexual exploitation survivor has the experience of dealing with erratic and unpredictable romantic and sexual partners. It often doesn't matter how smart and savvy you are; potential partners can just be straight-out weird, and frankly, dangerous! Now that doesn't mean we shouldn't date at all, although some survivors make the choice to be self-partnered, but we should be careful and calculating when we are meeting potential romantic interests.

It will take a lot for you to decide if the person you are casually dating will become a good partner, so we will go over that in the next chapter. Right now, however, we are simply discussing if the person we are dating is safe to date and will not harm us. We are survivors, so we know how to get through some treacherous situations and come out just fine. But we are still independent individuals, and we must be smart to stay safe. That all starts with having a safety plan before you rejoin the dating scene.

Here are some rules of thumb for your safety that many survivors and other vulnerable individuals use when going out to date.

- **Use the buddy system:** It is often a good precaution to let a "buddy" know the name of the person you are going on a date with, where you will be meeting, and arrange a check-in time as to when you should tell your buddy that you got home safely. When choosing the buddy, make sure it is a person who can come to your aid if there is a major problem with the date. You can also arrange to be that "buddy" for the person helping you out, if that helps them agree to being your buddy.

- **Meet in a public place the first time:** Meeting someone at their private place of residence puts *them* in control of the date, and if they meet at your house if you haven't interacted with them elsewhere, you don't know what you're getting into. What if they are aggressive? Or what if you're just not into them. How do you get them to leave? Now they know where you live! Instead, try meeting at a restaurant, coffee shop, or other location to make sure that, if for whatever reason, they act in an unsafe manner, you are around other people and that you can seek help if an emergency arises.

- **Research your dates:** Often, those using dating apps have to have a social media profile in order to open their dating account. If that's the case, try to research your potential date's social media to make sure that this person is a safe person, and even more importantly, that they are who they say they are, which is also a safety factor. If you have their phone number, Google it. Maybe nothing will turn up, but you don't want to be caught off guard if there is something to worry about.

- **Watch your drinks:** This doesn't just apply to alcohol; watch ALL of your drinks. Never leave your drink unattended with your date. You don't want them to be able to slip a date rape drug into your drink. Unfortunately, this is still a fairly common predator tactic.

- **Intimacy:** Know what you want when it comes to intimacy, and have a plan to protect yourself if you do not want intimacy with your date. Intimacy can be a natural part of romantic relationships, but if your date wants intimacy sooner than you do, make sure that you can set boundaries with them. A good sign in a new partner is if they can wait till you're ready for intimacy, whenever that may be. If they can't, and they are pushy for intimacy, set clear, loud boundaries, and get help from your buddy in order to leave the situation.

- **Don't let ANYONE come back to your place until you know they are safe:** This is not a moral thing. This is a safety thing. Do not bring anyone to your place of residence until you are 100% certain that they are a safe person. When romantic partners go back to your place of residence, they are expecting to become intimate with you, and unfortunately, they will try to have sex with you whether you like it or not. You don't want a dangerous person to know where you live because you don't want them to try to come again, after the date is over, and potentially assault you, or at the very least, cause drama. If you want to be very careful, bring a buddy or someone significant in your life for your first in-home date.

- **Do not share about your trauma in sexual exploitation on the first date:** While eventually, with any long-term partner, you will want to be able to talk openly about your past, you should not talk about this to strangers, for you don't know if the person you talk to is dangerous and will try to reexploit you. Check out Chapter Twenty on social relationships to see how you can share about your past without sharing all the details. It can be very dangerous to share about your past with someone you don't know and haven't been able to feel out in a romantic setting.

The most important thing is to trust your gut. YOU know best when YOU feel right and when you don't. Just keep a plan in place in case you need an out from an uncomfortable or potentially dangerous date.

Dating DO's

Here are some DO's when it comes to dating:

1. DO Be SMART: Don't tell your date all your business before you know anything about him.

2. DO ask them questions about themselves and their life. As much as you may instinctively want to talk about yourself, you will make a better impression on your date if you make

a genuine effort to get to know them first.

3. DO relax: Though you want to stay safe, you won't be able to make smart decisions if you're tense. Loosen up! And if you get stuck in your nerves, calmly ground yourself with observations. (Look around the room: What are the colors of the walls? What do you smell? What does the floor look like?)

4. DO be yourself: You're not there to impress anyone else. You're there to find a good mate for yourself, and the only way you can truly do that is if you stay true to who you are.

Challenge yourself to make your own personal lists of Do's and Don'ts. What will you DO when you end up going on a potential romantic date? What won't you do? And as for your partner, what would they do to let you know they are a good match? What would they do, or not do, that would make you think they are not the one for you?

Prompt Questions:

1. What is your biggest safety concern when it comes to dating?

2. How comfortable are you with trusting your gut?

3. Why is it important to meet in a public place? Why must you be selective about who comes back to your home?

4. How is safety in exploitation different from safety in casual dating?

5. What would be a sign that your date is a safe person?

6. What would be a sign that your date is an unsafe person?

AUTHOR'S EXPERIENCE:

It's unfortunate to have to share this, but I did not take my safety seriously when I first started to casually date after exploitation, and I was sexually assaulted more than once. I realized that because the perpetrator wasn't selling or buying my body, I wasn't as concerned as I should have been about my safety. We have different standards of safety and respect once we leave exploitation and start recovery, and must protect ourselves accordingly.

CHALLENGE:

Challenge yourself to make your own personal list of Do's and Don'ts. What WILL you do when going on a romantic date? What WON'T you do? And as for your partner, what would they do to let you know they are a good match? What would they do, or not do, that would make you think they are not the one for you?

51

Red Flags in Dating

Often, when we have had the experience of surviving exploitation, one of two things happens during future relationships:

- We become hypersensitive to any possible disrespect in a relationship, to an extreme, so that we assume the other person is going to hurt us in some way, and then we go on the offensive and push everybody out of our lives, or …
- We have experienced such awful relationships that we let our partner get away with too much, for there is no way they could be as terrible as our former abusers. Then, they end up taking advantage of us.

Both of these patterns are a bit extreme, but nonetheless common, so the key is to stay aware of all possible flaws in the relationship without acting out of impulse. In this chapter, we will look at common red flags in potential partners so we know when to keep ourselves safe. We don't always have to be alarmists and run at the first red flag, but we should keep our composure until we are able to safely leave the date, so it is important to recognize what these red flags are. Check out Chapter Twenty-Two to understand more about abuse tactics, but for now, we will discuss red flags in a dating setting.

Red Flags

- **Urging you to drink:** If you meet at a setting where there is alcohol and your potential date pushes you to drink more and more, they may have ulterior motives in trying to assault you. Keep on your guard and leave when you feel safe. Or better yet, don't drink at all.

- **Having no car, no job, or living with their parents/on someone's couch:** You want your date to match up to your lifestyle and all that you've worked hard to achieve. You have worked your recovery for a long time now! You should match with someone who has a similar level of independence. Their lack of ambition and collection of chaotic choices may indicate that they live an unhealthy lifestyle which lacks stability, and you should keep your distance if so.

- **Not meeting you in person:** Being scammed in online dating is more common than you would think. Do not pursue any relationship when they cannot meet with you in person, or if they make excuses to not talk on the phone or video chat. Scammers often tell you that they love you very early on and long before they meet you … Don't fall for that!

- **Substance abuse:** If your date overdoes their drinking, or if they bring out illegal substances as the night goes on, this may indicate that they live an unstable lifestyle which can put you in danger. By the same token, drunk driving can also be a red flag. DO NOT get in the car with anyone who has been drinking.

- **Dropping backhanded compliments:** If your date has a way of insulting you and complimenting you at the same time, run! They are trying to see if they can manipulate you early on, and this manipulation can escalate as the relationship progresses. If they give you a backhanded compliment, call them out on it! Don't accept that kind of behavior.

- **Downplaying your accomplishments:** Again, this kind of manipulation can escalate, so you want to keep your distance from someone who does not respect all you have accomplished.

- **Being too interested in your past exploitation:** If you do choose to share with your partner about your past exploitation later on in the relationship, think about what an appropriate response would be. For example, a good response should be how sorry they are that you went through that, or how strong you are for overcoming all that trauma. But, if your date seems really interested in your exploitation and wants to know details about it, they may feel like they can treat you like your exploiter. This kind of person may secretly be an exploiter themselves, or a person who doesn't understand how wrong exploitation is. In any case, you should keep a healthy distance from this person.

When we do run into a person who acts in any of these ways—and given how popular the dating scene is, we probably will—we need to remain smart. Do not overreact and try to tell this person off. This can cause their behavior to escalate and they might try to harm you. Instead, keep your wits about you and formulate a good exit strategy for leaving the date safely. Call on the information you learned in the last chapter to stay safe and get home without any drama.

Dating can be a frustrating process, but it can also be fun. If it helps, keep a dating journal where you can independently process each date, what you liked or didn't like about that person, and what you wish would have gone differently. This may help you get fewer dates filled with red flags and more dates where you can get what you're looking for.

PROMPT QUESTIONS:

1. Outside of exploitation, have you ever run into a "red flag" date? What did they do that was so bad?

2. In your past relationships, what red flags have you seen that you either ignored or let slide?

3. What is one example of a physical red flag?

4. What is one example of an emotional/social red flag?

5. How can you properly set boundaries in casual dating? Do you feel like you're at that place yet, that you would be comfortable setting boundaries in a casual setting with someone you don't know well? Be honest.

6. What is an appropriate response to you sharing about your past trauma in exploitation?

AUTHOR'S EXPERIENCE:

I tended to be in defense mode when I first started casual dating. I was so sensitive to disrespect that I ended up leaving a couple of dates before they were over. But that was my right! The right person wouldn't disrespect me in any way, and I was willing to wait and be single until I found him, knowing that I might never.

I strongly recommend that you keep a "little black book" or journal record of what dates you go on, what happened, and how you felt about it. It will help you get less of what you don't want in potential partners and more of what you do.

CHALLENGE:

Challenge yourself to make a list of red flags that you have ignored in the past. What were they? Why did you let them slide? And finally, what would you do differently if, or when, you rejoin the dating scene?

52

Boundaries in Romantic Relationships

Once we are in a relationship, when we are fortunate enough to find one, we play the dating game by a separate set of rules. We are no longer trying to narrow down who is the best for us; we are now searching to see if our date can walk the talk. Often, a date might tell us what they think we want to hear to get themselves in the door with us, when really, their actions don't match up to their words.

In this chapter, we will explore boundaries when it comes to dating, looking at what to do when we are actually in a relationship. We must behave and think in a way we haven't before, for exploitation teaches us unhealthy coping skills and interaction patterns in relationships.

However, since we have the experience of surviving exploitation, we have a leg up on others in spotting unhealthy patterns. We know what kinds of games people play when they're trying to manipulate others, and therefore, we won't play those games again.

What does a healthy relationship look like?

The following traits are all positive qualities in a healthy relationship:

- **Healthy communication:** First and foremost, you should be able to communicate your wants and needs in the relationship with your partner, as should they with you. You must be able to do this without raising voices or making personal attacks. Everyone should feel heard, including you.

- **Having lots in common:** You should be similar enough to your partner that you mesh well with them, while being different enough to discuss opposing views. Having things in common, including the kind of music and movies you like, is a good sign. Often, opposites can only attract for so long, although there are exceptions.

- **Healthy relationships should be fun:** If you aren't having fun on your dates or in each interaction with your partner, why are you dating them at all? You might have found a good potential partner, but if you guys don't get along, have fun, and aren't happy when you are with each other, you might consider finding a different, more compatible partner.

- **Respect:** Every couple has disagreements, but it is how you two handle the disagreements that determines whether you will be compatible or not. Regardless of whether or not they agree with you, your partner should always respect your opinions and boundaries. Name-calling, yelling, and aggression are early signs that your partner may be a potential abuser.

  However, do not get discouraged if you get into a small but civil disagreement with your partner. This happens even between couples that have been married for decades. We all disagree with our loved ones at one point or another. Just make sure your partner maintains a certain level of respect when doing so.

- **Making time for each other:** Let's face it: Everyone has a busy schedule. But partners in a healthy relationship always make time for each other. No, you don't have to spend every waking moment with each other, but if your partner can't make time for you when you need it, they shouldn't be dating you.

If you are well into your relationship and you find that any of these major factors are not working for you, you should be able to talk to your partner about what you want to improve in your relationship. If they are not able to compromise or even hear your opinion, you should strongly consider finding another relationship. But if they are willing to work it out, grant them that chance. This shows resiliency and respect toward you.

Maintaining Intimacy Boundaries

As sexual exploitation survivors, we have been through a lot, and we need a partner who is patient with us. Some days we will feel okay with being intimate, and some days we won't. We need a partner who respects this and listens to us. As important as intimacy is, it cannot control the relationship.

By the same token, it is our responsibility to explain to our partner that this is nothing personal against them, and is not a reflection of how we feel about them. We need someone who is empathetic and understands that we are simply working through trauma and that we have good days and not so good days.

Does this mean that we will never get over our trauma? Absolutely not! But whether or not our partner understands our past is what can make or break your relationship. If our partner understands our trauma symptoms and helps us through them, they can be our biggest support system. If they don't, the relationship will never work.

Breakup Violence

Often, the term "ghosting" is talked about in a negative way, as if the person who does the ghosting owes their former partner something, even after the relationship is over. Realistically, ghosting, or the act of ceasing all contact with a person on all platforms, is the safest option when breaking up with someone. Confronting your soon-to-be-ex in person invites potential physical altercations, or at the very least, erratic behavior. It is best to break up with them remotely and then cut off contact with them however you see fit. Think about it: If a partner does something so upsetting that it would cause you to break up with them, you do not owe them anything.

Coming back to see your partner after you have broken up with them is a bad and potentially dangerous idea. If they need moral support or help getting over the breakup, they can get that from a friend, not you. Do not go to see your ex once you have broken up. Not in public, not in private, not ever. Breakup violence is a real thing, and you don't want to have accomplished all you did in recovery only to get it taken away from you because you gave the wrong person a second chance. Better safe than sorry.

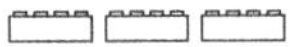

Remember that the most important relationship in your life is the one with yourself. You have conquered so much in your life to get to this point, and you should not give any of that up simply to be in a romantic relationship. If you don't find your ultimate partner in the first couple of rounds of dating, don't be discouraged! You have already proven to yourself how much you can accomplish on your own, and the right person will come into your life when the time is right.

PROMPT QUESTIONS:

1. Have you seen any examples of healthy relationships in your life? What about in film, television, books, or famous couples?

2. On a scale of 1 to 10, with 10 being a totally healthy relationship with respect and boundaries, and one being horrible communication and no respect at all, how would you rate your past relationships?

3. How high do you want that number to be in the future? What would a ten on the communication scale look like?

4. Thinking in terms of a committed romantic relationship, what are your personal needs?

5. All couples have their own personal disagreements. What would it look like to be in a relationship where you can have disagreements without getting aggressive or physical?

6. What would a future partner do to let you know that you can trust them?

AUTHOR'S EXPERIENCE:

When, and if, you move in with your partner, things change. When I had my first disagreement with my boyfriend, I panicked, but the difference between my exploitation and abusive relationships and my current relationship is that an argument didn't lead to name-calling, yelling, or physical aggression. Even though we were upset, we could keep our cool and resolve problems as they came at us.

CHALLENGE:

Make a list of the most important things you want in a relationship. What do you want your partner to do, or not do? How would they show you respect? What will indicate that he or she is a good partner, or that they aren't?

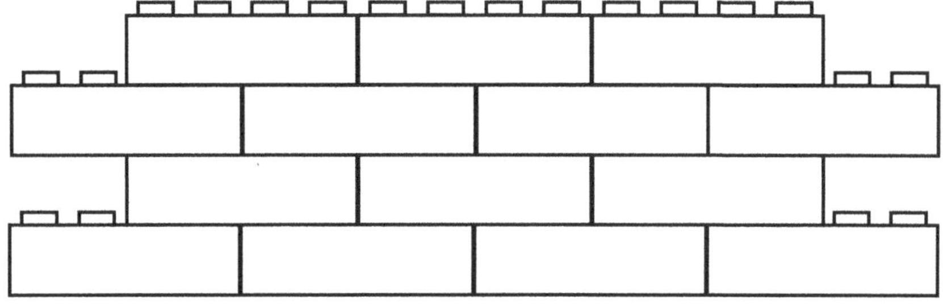

Mentorship and Advocacy

53

WHO ARE OUR MENTORS?

In my city alone, San Diego, there are an estimated 8,000 to 12,000 human trafficking survivors each year, generating millions of dollars in illegal revenue. Chances are that before my life is over, I will run into another survivor whom I haven't met yet. And as so many times before, I might be confronted with some tough questions from them, as far as what happened to me, how I got out, if it was easy, etc. I don't like answering those questions in general, but for a fellow survivor, I think it is important to have an open and honest dialogue, and it is best to know ahead of time how to approach those topics.

Not all of us survivors will find ourselves in positions where we will become direct mentors to other survivors, but most of us will lead those who come after us by example, whether we realize it or not. For this section of this book, we will discuss who our mentors are, what we can learn from them, and how to be a mentor to the sexual exploitation survivors or other trauma survivors who come to you after you have achieved stability and independence.

To be clear, not every survivor must become a survivor leader. Survivor leaders tend to live open lives and remain in the public eye, because it is their job to shed light on what it truly means to survive sexual exploitation, so that the world doesn't unfairly judge us. It is an IMPORTANT job, but it is not for everyone. There are many other ways to be a leader and advocate for fellow survivor sisters.

Even if you don't feel led to be an advocate, advocates and mentors can play an important role in your recovery, and it is important to identify who our mentors are and understand why and how they impact us. Keep your ears open during this chapter to learn more about their role in your life.

Who Are Our Role Models?

To learn how to be a leader, or to identify good leaders to follow and emulate, we must first look at who were our leaders in the past. Who have we looked up to? Who were our role models? If you're having trouble thinking of your past leaders, consider the following categories:

- Family: Who was the matriarch of your family? Who would you consider the head of your household growing up? How did they shape who you are today? Or, if you did not have a solid relationship with your family, did any other loved ones help you grow?

- Teachers: Maybe you didn't have the best experience in school, but one teacher stood out and inspired you to succeed. What did he or she do to inspire you?

- Historical figures: Many great leaders exist in history, including Harriet Tubman, Albert Einstein, Martin Luther King Jr., and many others. Which historical figure was special to you?

- Music Artists: Some artists entertain, while others use their platform to lead the world in a new direction. Which artist inspires you?

- Spiritual guides: If you are a Christian, how did Jesus lead his people? What kind of people did he help? Who did he surround himself with? This goes for other faiths, too. Who are your spiritual guides and what do they teach you?

Challenge yourself to make a list of five leaders in your life or the world you grew up in. Then, look at your list and see what these leaders all had in common.

- What were their strengths?
- Did they have any insecurities?
- How did they lead others?
- What was their approach to leadership?
- What did you like about them?

You may find that those whom you look up to are very different from those whom others look up to. That is because you are unique and you define your own strengths, weaknesses, and the qualities you strive to have. The leaders whom you look up to will determine how you, yourself, will set an example for others who may look up to you.

If you have made it all the way to Chapter Fifty-Three, you have been through so much training and hard work that you are likely to be someone whom others admire. And if one thing helps new survivors, it is to see more seasoned survivors doing well in life and achieving their goals, free from exploitation. You may not want to be a survivor leader, but you never know who wants to someday be in your shoes and is looking to you as an example of a strong survivor.

Prompt Questions:

1. Do you have anyone in your personal life or recovery circle whom you would consider a mentor? Why or why not?

2. Are there public figures, artists, historical figures, or well-known people whom maybe you haven't met, but you still look up to? Why or why not?

3. What leadership qualities do you possess?

4. What does it take to be a good leader?

5. Have you had experience with bad bosses, managers, or other leaders in the past? What was it that made them bad leaders?

6. Could you ever see yourself as a leader in any setting? Why or why not?

AUTHOR'S EXPERIENCE:

My role models tend to be strong-willed women, but sometimes I look up to men too. For example, E40 is a rapper from my hometown in the Bay Area. He started out in a very bad neighborhood and was extremely poor, but he used music to work his way up the ladder and became successful. However, he never sold himself out or sacrificed the quality of his work to make more money. I always admired his work ethic and his success. And of course I like his music.

Other examples include my mother, my grandmothers, and definitely other survivor leaders from my new home in San Diego. Some more public survivors whom you might recognize include Rebecca Bender, Cupcake Brown, and Harmony Grillo—all of whom have published books about their experience and their healing.

CHALLENGE:

Challenge yourself to make a list of five role models or mentors in your life. Who are they? Why do you look up to them? Then, look at your list, and see what they all have in common.

54

Helping Others Help Themselves

There is an old proverb:

"Give a man a fish, and you feed him for a day. Teach a man to fish, and you feed him for a lifetime."

Though our instinct as potential leaders may be to dish out advice to everyone who seeks it, it is important to remember that the most effective way to help others is to show them how to help themselves. It is the biggest gift you can give anyone, especially someone who stands where you once stood.

If you can help it, don't help others by doing their work for them. Instead, teach them or show them how to do what they need done. We can begin doing this by changing the language we use when mentoring others. Again, even if you don't assume a leadership role, make sure you don't have the expectation that those partnering with you on your recovery journey will do your work for you!

Here are some examples of how to help others help themselves:

- Instead of saying, "You SHOULD do this," try saying, "I try to do it this way," or, "Why don't you try this?" Be careful NOT to command them to do something.

- That being said, it is important to speak from your own experience. Using "I/me" statements not only prevents you from using commands or giving unwarranted advice, but also shows others your own proven method of getting things done.

- Always be encouraging: Even when someone may make a decision that you don't agree with, encourage them to do the right thing. And if someone is on the right track but just needs a boost in the right direction, give them that boost.

But regardless of the language we use, it is important to remember to not do others' work for them but rather show them how to do what they're trying to do themselves. Giving others your opinion, without telling them what to do, promotes autonomy and self-guided thinking.

Remember that the qualities of those whom you have looked up to should be qualities that you emulate yourself. If you admire leaders who are courageous, lead with courage. If you admire leaders who are movers and shakers, be a mover and a shaker. If those you look up to are reserved and soft-spoken, perhaps that is the way you should lead as well.

Ask yourself: What kind of things will a new survivor ask a more seasoned survivor? A new survivor might ask you questions about:

- How you found a job
- How you managed trauma symptoms
- How you stayed sober
- How you dealt with staff at your treatment program
- How you left your abuser

It is important to think about your answers to those kinds of questions before anyone ever asks you. How did you stay sober? What did it take to find a job? What emotional tools helped you the most in recovering from trauma? But remember, use I/me statements without telling any survivor how they must work their recovery, because every survivor is different.

Challenge yourself to think of the best advice you've been given. Think about who said it to you. Why did it have an impact on you? How did it change the way you saw the world? Chances are this advice was not given as a replacement for help, but rather encouraged you that you can do everything on your own.

PROMPT QUESTIONS:

1. Why is it important to help others help themselves?

2. What are some negative consequences that could happen if you do someone else's work for them?

3. What sort of language is important for you to use when helping someone out? What language should you avoid?

4. Has anyone from your past taught you how to do something without doing everything for you? Why was that helpful or not helpful?

5. Have you ever tried to help someone and realized that they just wanted you to do everything for them? What was that experience like?

6. What is the best piece of advice you have ever been given? Who said it? Why did it have an impact on you?

AUTHOR'S EXPERIENCE:

I was going to school at the same time as some of my other housemates who were in recovery. I had a survivor friend who was taking more classes than I was. She was always complaining about how much work she had to do, so I tried to help her, but soon enough, I realized that I was doing all the work for her!

This backfired, however, because when she transferred to a four-year university, and I was no longer there to help her, she started doing very poorly in school. Had I given her pointers instead of doing her work for her, maybe she would have graduated by now.

CHALLENGE:

Challenge yourself to think of the best advice you have been given. Think about who said it to you. Why did it have an impact on you? How did it change the way you saw the world?

55

DIFFERENT WAYS TO ADVOCATE

So many survivors who have gone through recovery find themselves wanting to help other survivors or to give back to the community in some way. And while we might have had a social worker, therapist, or police officer who has helped us and inspired us in a special way, those are not the only ways we can help other survivors.

Potential Mentorship and Leadership Roles

New survivors are going to directly communicate with:

- Survivor Leaders: Other lived-experience experts who speak at community engagements, facilitate support groups, advise nonprofit organizations, use social media to facilitate activism, and speak as experts on sexual exploitation to lawmakers and other important people.

- Social Workers: Social workers directly help survivors by assisting in case management and connecting them with services and service providers. They also can assist the unification of families if the survivor is separated from their children.

- Mental Health Therapists: Therapists are trained in how to treat trauma thought processes and behavior, and can directly help people overcome mental illness or addiction.

- Law Enforcement: Police are active agents in ending human trafficking, especially if your town has a human trafficking task force.

- Attorneys: Not only are attorneys potential lobbyists for the laws that will affect survivors, they can also help litigate for survivors' needs.

These are all valid roles in survivor recovery, and if you choose any of those paths, you will be able to have a direct impact on survivor lives. Any of these may also be resources to you in your recovery!

Other Potential Advocacy Paths

But what if the paths that are listed above are not for you? What if you are not cut out for law enforcement, litigation, or public speaking? There are still many ways to help survivors and have an influence on their lives, or even indirectly influence the lives of those who need it. Here are some career path ideas:

- Grant Writing: All social services organizations can use someone who is good with words to help them fill out grant applications for potential funding for their organization. This involves research and some basic math, but requires no public speaking whatsoever.

- Teaching: Maybe you don't want to mentor survivors directly, but if you think about it, teachers are the first people who can directly influence those who are potential exploitation survivors.

- Social Media Activists: Maybe you are a more tech-savvy person. Managing a professional social media account for a survivor organization, or simply starting your own advocacy page, is one way to help survivors.

Impromptu Advocacy

Beyond career paths, many of us will find that once we have survived severe trauma, others recovering from trauma will seek us out for help. Maybe a person whom you work with will need your help in some way, or will reach out to you because they see you as a strong person, regardless of what they know about your past.

I personally have had others reach out to me in the past in work settings. I did not tell anyone that I was a survivor, but I did open up to a few coworkers that I had experienced some domestic-violence-type issues. Not long after, a coworker told me they were worried that another coworker was going through the same thing, and after that, other coworkers came out of the woodwork seeking help for similar issues.

At the time, I was able to connect them with the right services because I was prepared to be an advocate, even though I wasn't a survivor leader, social worker, or any other professional advocate. I was working in food service, and yet I was becoming a mentor! Later on, I found out that a lot of my survivor sisters played the same role in their social circles. You never know when your expertise will be needed.

Confidentiality

If something similar happens to you and someone reaches out to you to advocate for them, it is important to recognize that this person views you as a safe person and confidant. You must honor that and keep their business private between the two of you. Then, help them research whatever resources they need, and encourage them to make the right decision for themselves and for their safety.

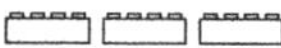

Challenge yourself to look at your personal career path, or simply what you do on a daily basis, and ask yourself: How can I use my daily tasks, talents, and interests to advocate for others and to be a positive influence on their lives? Be creative: You may be surprised by what ideas you come up with!

As the previous two chapters have emphasized, remember to lead others the way others whom you admire have led you, and remember that it is most effective to help others help themselves rather than do all the work for them. No matter how you lead others, your contribution to the greater good of other survivors does not go unnoticed. A little goes a long way!

Prompt Questions:

1. What does being a survivor leader mean to you?

2. Do you see yourself someday becoming a peer leader? Do you already fill that role?

3. Who has had the most impact on you in your recovery so far? Why has their role been important in your life?

4. What advocacy path, if any, feels closest to your own strengths and abilities?

5. How can you use your daily tasks, talents, and interests to be an advocate and have a positive impact on others' lives?

AUTHOR'S EXPERIENCE:

I looked up to many survivor leaders in my recovery, but public speaking is not my strong suit, so speaking engagements freaked me out. Instead I looked into grant writing. I can use my writing skills to advocate to potential donors about the good things that survivor-led organizations have done for me, and find the right funding for the right people in need. My work is mostly done behind the scenes, but I have a direct impact on survivors' lives.

CHALLENGE:

Challenge yourself to look at your personal career path, or simply what you do on a daily basis, and ask yourself: How can I use my daily tasks, talents, and interests to advocate for others and be a positive influence in their lives? You may be surprised by what ideas you come up with!

56

BOUNDARIES IN MENTORSHIP

In this section, we will discuss boundaries in any potential mentorship path. We will go over what it is like to see survivors go back to exploitation, what we can do in that situation, and how to protect ourselves if we are ever in positions of leadership for other survivors, or for the general public who are nonsurvivors.

When Survivors Falter

If you have made it this far into your healing, you have probably seen others not succeed in their recovery. Maybe you have already seen other survivors come into recovery, and for whatever reason, they fail, relapse in their addiction, or go back to exploitation. And for those of us who are extremely seasoned, often we will see OUR mentors, those that WE look up to, falter and take steps backward from all they've accomplished. Even some former survivor leaders have gone back to exploitation. It is hard to watch, and especially hard if these survivors are the ones who guided you when you needed help in the first place.

The truth is this: As of the year 2020, the national average of those who finish recovery and go on to their healthy next step in their healing is only 50%. That means half of the survivors you meet are likely to relapse with exploitation, and some may even pass away due to overdose, suicide, or other tragedies that sometimes come with exploitation. Consider yourself lucky if you have a handful of survivor sisters whom you can celebrate your recovery with, because many of us have watched a vicious cycle of recovery, then faltering, back to exploitation, then back to recovery, over and over again.

What can we do about this? For one, we need to be prepared for it. We need to be prepared for our own heroes to be imperfect. That is just part of maturing and growing up. But whatever you do, do not blame yourself for the shortcomings of others, even if you feel that you may have contributed to another survivor's failure. Know that everyone can only be responsible for themselves, and that we can put someone else on the right path, but only they can take each step themselves.

Showing Grace

One thing that we can do for a survivor who goes back into exploitation, if they decide to come back into recovery, is be encouraging and keep our door open for them. We may not approve of our friends going back to exploitation, but if they make the decision to start over and come back to recovery, we can say, "Yes, awesome! We missed you!" We don't want someone to remain in exploitation because they think we won't give them a second chance. We need to show them grace.

We must recognize how difficult recovery from sexual exploitation can be. So many survivors report that the thought in the back of their head is that at any moment, they could make a "quick buck" if they went back to exploitation. It is a difficult thought to live with, and for the last few chapters of this book, we will discuss how to combat that inner thought in more detail, but for now simply understand that the temptation is there for all survivors, and it is very difficult for many to ignore.

Keeping Your Guard Up

We must practice healthy boundaries around survivors who are struggling for a few reasons. For one, we must protect our own emotions if they struggle even more and end up going back to exploitation again, which is very possible, and pretty discouraging to watch happen. And two, we don't know to what extent they have been reexploited. We may have heard their testimony before, but often, reexploitation is worse the second or third time around. I know this because I have reentered exploitation more than once, and every time, it gets worse and worse. The violence gets worse, the substance abuse gets worse. So, we must remember that we don't know their whole story just because we know what happened to them before!

It is important to keep your guard up around struggling survivors WITHOUT being cold, especially if they break their recovery cycle by reentering exploitation and then rejoin recovery later on. This is nothing personal, but as they had learned to earn your trust before, they have to earn your trust again. If they value you as a survivor sister and a true friend, they will have no problem doing so.

Sometimes, being a survivor gets lonely, because so many girls don't make it out okay and improve their lives, and our choice to take our recovery seriously separates us from the fold. Do not let others' failures discourage you. Instead, give your own recovery recognition every so often, because you know how hard it is to improve your life, and yet you make the choice to do just that every single day.

Getting Compensated for Your Mentorship

If you are simply giving advice as one survivor to another, it is highly unlikely that you will be compensated, unless you are a professional mentor hired by a survivor agency. Survivors usually come into recovery without any income, making it impossible to compensate you for your mentorship. However, some organizations and agencies do hire lived-experience experts to advise new survivors on an array of issues, and those positions are compensated. The information here is for survivor leaders asked to speak publicly by nonsurvivors and other organizations or small businesses.

Be aware, however, that public speaking, especially about your trauma, is a really big step! Check in with your therapist or another confidant before taking on this responsibility.

Survivor leaders are often asked to speak to private or public groups, or to educate small groups of people. This often involves talking about your past, and may even involve the public asking tough or sometimes even inappropriate questions. Because you are going out of your way not only to travel to their event but also to educate others about a very personal part of your life, you must be compensated at the very least for your travel, if not for your time as well.

If an organization or business asks you to speak publicly about survivor issues, or asks for your testimony, but does not want to pay you, it is your job to educate them that expecting you to work for free is essentially reexploiting you.

Think about it: You are spending gas money, time, and emotional labor to be vulnerable about a private part of your life to complete strangers. If they don't pay you, you're paying THEM for a service you are already giving them, free of charge! Not to mention, you may reopen some old emotional wounds and then be sent on your way, coming out of that situation with less money than when you walked in. If that's not exploitation, I am not sure what is! To reiterate, always ask for compensation when asked to share your story by an organization, business, or community that reaches out to you.

Avoiding Inappropriate Questions

Unfortunately, many survivors who have spoken publicly about survivor issues have been asked some incredibly inappropriate questions in front of a live audience during the Q&A segment of their speaking engagement, and in some cases, in front of public news sources.

Some inappropriate questions include:

- How many STDs do you have?
- How many people did you sleep with per day?
- How much money did you make as a stripper?

Yikes! We don't know why people ask these questions, but we can assume this is due to misinformation and lack of education about sexual exploitation. If this happens to you, a good rule of thumb is to always bring the conversation back to empowering survivors. Don't let the conversation become degrading! Stick to a few of these key statements:

- "I am not here to talk about sex. I am here to talk about being a survivor of a violent crime."

- "We are here to talk about how survivors rebuild their lives, not what ruined their lives in the first place."

- Or simply, "With all due respect, you shouldn't ask survivors degrading questions like that."

Being a public speaker is tough, but it is even tougher when you must talk about a topic as sensitive as sexual exploitation! This path is not for everyone. But, if this is your path, just remember to keep the conversation positive and don't get derailed by inappropriate conversation.

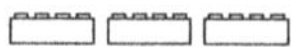

So, to summarize, if other survivors fail at their recovery, do not let it get to you. If they then want your help in getting back into recovery, welcome them with open arms, but do not be alarmed if they falter yet again once you offer them help, for this is a common cycle seen with many survivors. And above all else, guard your heart. Know that the most important survivor in your life is YOU, and you must take care of yourself first and foremost.

PROMPT QUESTIONS:

1. Why do you think only 50% of survivors of trafficking and exploitation go on to the next healthy step in their recovery?

2. How can you keep your guard up around other survivors, without being cold?

3. When is it important to show survivors grace? What would that look like?

4. Why is it important to be compensated for mentorship such as speaking engagements, peer support, case management, or other positions that should be paid?

5. What are some inappropriate questions that may be asked at a speaking engagement? How do you avoid these questions?

Author's Experience:

I am very lucky in that I first became employed in the survivor setting under Alabaster Jar Project, which employs a survivor staff. Therefore, I was already exposed to survivor leaders and saw them in professional settings on a daily basis. Unfortunately, and often from ignorance, people like to hire survivors as volunteers and never pay them. This is reexploitation. It's one thing to help out a vulnerable friend who is a survivor, but it's not okay to put in regular hours for a survivor organization and never see a paycheck.

Furthermore, if you are ever asked to share your story in a public setting, always require compensation for yourself. If you go speak about your past, reopen old wounds, and talk about some really hard stuff, then they don't even pay for your gas, how screwed up is that?!

Challenge:

Challenge yourself to research one survivor leader. Who are they? How do they advocate for survivors? And if possible, ask yourself, "What are their boundaries and how do they protect themselves?"

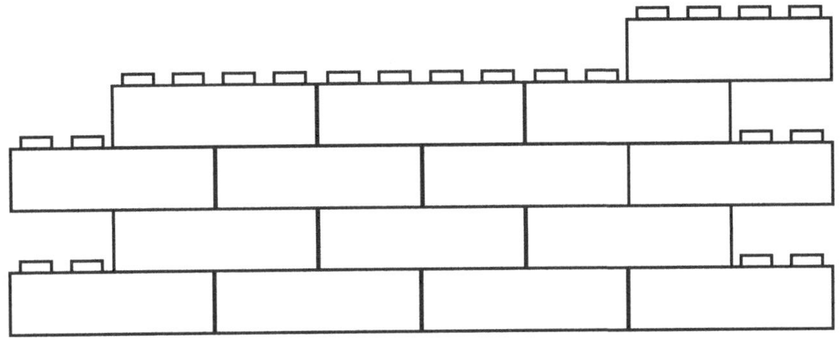

Staying Out of Exploitation

57

Reframing Life After Exploitation

Congratulations! You have reached the final few chapters of this handbook. After this month, you should take all that you have learned and apply it as you put your affairs in order to move on to the next step in living your independent life. But for now, while this book still has your attention, we are going to go over staying OUT of exploitation, because that is a temptation that you may live with for the rest of your life.

In all honesty, there is usually not one moment or one event that permanently drives someone away from exploitation. If we think back to how abusers work and all the psychological conditioning we went through in exploitation, we know that we were conditioned for months and possibly years to believe that the life of sexual exploitation was meant for us. We may have been told that it was our only option or that we were "meant" for the sex industry, among many other lies. And beyond that, we may have criminal charges that cause us to have limited job options, leaving us ever more tempted to go back to exploitation.

It is important for us to understand that—with everything working against us, all the mental torture and conditioning, all the trauma—we must CHOOSE every day to be a survivor of sexual exploitation, not a victim. It is a choice that we will make over and over until the temptation to return to sexual exploitation isn't so strong in our minds.

One way we make that choice is by reframing the way we look at life after exploitation. Changing the language we use when confronting our temptations can make a world of difference. When we speak positive, empowering words to ourselves, our thoughts and feelings begin to change. Think about it: How many times did your abuser have to tell you that you were dumb, or ugly, or any other lie, before you believed it? Probably not many times. Now, we can take a page from their book and tell ourselves that we are smart, capable survivors until it starts to sink in and we truly believe it.

Temptations

Another way to change the way we think, in order to leave exploitation behind for good, is to think of every possible temptation that may make us turn back to it, and reframe it so we know, deep down, that we should never go back. If we solidify these inner beliefs now, we will feel them deep down and know them by heart any time we are tempted to go back to exploitation. Sometimes, you just need to give yourself a pep talk! Next chapter, we will discuss how to put an action plan in place in case we face that temptation, but for now, here are some ways we can reframe all our temptations and issues that come with being a survivor of exploitation:

- **Money:** Money, and the need for it, is the number-one temptation for survivors to reenter sexual exploitation. Instead of fantasizing about how "easy" it would be to make some quick money if we go back to exploitation, we must tell ourselves that sexual exploitation is never easy. It is a slippery slope. We must remind ourselves that all the legitimate money we earn legally, WE are in charge of and WE get to keep. It can never be seized because it was made illegally, nor will it ever be taken by an exploiter.

- **Renegading:** "Renegading," if you aren't familiar with it, is the term that describes someone sexually exploiting themself without a pimp or any form of manager, specifically when it comes to sex trafficking and commercial sex acts. A lot of former survivors believe that this option won't be as bad as if they were exploited by a pimp, because *they* would be the one making the rules and wouldn't have to face any sort of unnecessary abuse.

  The problem with this theory is that renegades are more vulnerable without protection, including in the underground sex industry, to law enforcement, and to potential abusers who may try to exploit them anyway. If you find this option tempting, watch a few episodes of any true crime show and see how many renegade prostitutes are targeted by serial killers and other murderers. This is a VERY dangerous choice.

- **"Legal" sex work as an option:** Taking up exotic dancing or pornography after we leave other forms of sexual exploitation is just switching one toxic lifestyle for another toxic lifestyle. You don't know what the new form of exploitation is going to bring you, what drama, what trauma, what legal problems, and what forms of abuse. Worse, many strippers are often pressured by club members to perform sex acts in order to keep their jobs. This is a slippery slope!

- **Employment problems:** When we face problems at work that make us want to quit, we might be tempted to give up entirely. Instead of leaning toward sexual exploitation, we should try to take steps toward having a better job that we will be happy at. Is there a promotion coming up? Go for it! Is a different workplace hiring? Apply there! If you need to go back to school, take that step while you work at your current job. You have all it takes to change your path, so don't give up!

- **Family relationships:** Leaving exploitation and becoming a survivor doesn't automatically mean your family will accept you or that you will automatically get full custody of your children, and that can be very, very discouraging for survivors. Instead of letting this defeat you, know that you are on the right path, and as long as you keep taking steps forward instead of backward, your family relationships can heal gradually. But if you take steps backward and go back into exploitation, you are going to have to start the healing process for them, and potentially in the family court system, all over again.

- **Addiction relapse:** If you have a history of substance abuse in your past exploitation, a substance craving may lead you to reenter exploitation. At this point, you have to convince yourself that you don't want two relapses for the price of one by relapsing with your addiction and your sexual exploitation at the same time! You have worked too hard to do that to yourself. Get to a meeting as soon as possible, and consult with a survivor leader or drug counselor immediately. This can be a crisis situation.

- **Romantic relationships:** Especially if survivors worked with an exploiter or pimp in a romantic setting, that relationship can skew our perception of all future romantic relationships. As the bad memories fade, we might be left only with the good memories of our exploiter and compare every potential relationship to the one with our exploiter. Remind yourself that NO person who truly loves you will ever exploit your sexuality for their personal gain, no matter how loving they may seem. The right person will honor your autonomy. There are good people out there! You do not have to go back to your abusers to feel love, and you deserve so much more than that.

Challenge yourself to confront your biggest temptations of potentially going back to the life of sexual exploitation. What thought has remained in the back of your mind the whole time you have worked on your healing? Now, challenge yourself to reframe that temptation in a way that gives you healing and does not have you turn your back on all you have accomplished thus far.

A little self-encouragement goes a long way.

PROMPT QUESTIONS:

1. Do you think you will ever be tempted to go back to exploitation? Why or why not?

2. What temptations would be the strongest for someone in your shoes? Why do you think that is?

3. What temptations WON'T trigger you? Why would those factors be easier to deal with for you?

4. Have you ever thought of having a crisis management plan? What would that entail for you?

5. In your recovery, what have you done to help manage any crisis you have had earlier?

6. How did you handle a crisis in the past, before exploitation? Why was that helpful or not helpful?

AUTHOR'S EXPERIENCE:

Even though I was in recovery and was doing great in my independent life, money remained a trigger for me. I always had the thought in the back of my mind that if I was really hurting for money, I knew a way to make a "quick buck." When I would feel tempted to go back to exploitation, I would watch murder mysteries in which vulnerable exploitation victims would end up missing or dead. It's tough to watch, but I knew I could never put my family through that.

Though the thought of going back to exploitation can seem really strong at times, it does go away. I have several years, relationships, educational milestones, and career milestones that separate me from my past in exploitation. If I am ever in a desperate spot again, there are about one hundred things I will do before I even consider "going back."

CHALLENGE:

Challenge yourself to confront your biggest temptations of potentially going back to the life of exploitation. What thoughts have remained in the back of your mind the whole time you have worked on your healing? Now, challenge yourself to reframe that temptation in a way that gives you healing and does not have you turn your back on all you have accomplished thus far. A little self-encouragement goes a long way.

58

Creating an Emergency Plan

One step toward leaving exploitation for good is reframing every situation in your life that might make you turn back to exploitation, so that you know in your heart that it will never be a safe, fulfilling option for your life.

Another step toward that goal is having a concrete plan in place so that you will never have to go back to exploitation. This emergency plan will help guide you through your own thought process when you are triggered and will give you direct options of what to do instead of engaging in unhealthy behaviors. While we will lay out a pretty clear, concrete plan here, feel free to design and customize your own plan so that it will be most effective for you personally.

Building Your Emergency Plan

Emergency plans for sexual exploitation survivors must include:

- Name and contact info of a handful of safe people who can calm you down when you are facing crisis: You should ask permission ahead of time from those people to include them on your list and explain to them why you've chosen them. You must list two or more people here in case the first person does not answer your call or message.

- Professionals you can turn to: If you have a strong connection with a mental health counselor, survivor leader, social worker, or medical professional whom you trust, list their name and contact info here in case they may be able to lead you through crisis.

- Backup plan for money and necessities: In an emergency situation, money can be a big trigger that will make you reenter sexual exploitation. What will you do when you are low on money? Are there family members or other loved ones who could help you in the short term? Do you know of food banks in the area? Not a glamorous choice, but any expense that you can get covered for free will help you put money toward bills you are required to pay.

- Reminders: You should make a list of a few reasons you have left exploitation to remind yourself why it is so important. Is it your family? Your kids? Your independence? Your future? What key things remind you that it is important to stay out of exploitation?

- Emergency numbers: If you are experiencing a mental health or medical crisis, call 911 immediately. If you are feeling suicidal, the hotline is 1-800-273-8255, where trained counselors will know how to walk you through self-harm and suicide crises. If you are facing abuse from a trafficker or are in danger of being reexploited, the human trafficking hotline is 1-888-373-7888.

But, as said before, feel free to customize this list to your own personal needs. If worship music helps you get through tough times, list that in your emergency plan! If you need to watch certain shows or read a certain book to get your mind off your triggers, include them. Be creative with this. Challenge yourself to make your own personal emergency plan, even if you feel that you will never want to turn back to exploitation. You may not want to now, but you never know what life event may trigger a crisis response.

Recovery is not a straight line. It does not happen overnight. It's something that you work on for the rest of your life. After you leave whatever program you're at, you will become your own program director, making and acting in a plan that you will lay out for yourself to reach your goals. You become your own cheerleader, your own life coach, your own mentor. While it's important for those of us who choose the path of a survivor leader to lead others, the most important person you will lead in life is yourself.

Prompt Questions:

1. Who are some safe people in your life? Is there anyone on that list who can talk you out of a crisis situation?

2. What steps will you put in place that will help when you have a trigger regarding money?

3. What would you consider to be an emergency?

4. Have you ever faced an emergency in the past? What did you do to take care of the situation?

5. Is there anything you know you must do in crisis that is NOT suggested on the list?

AUTHOR'S EXPERIENCE:

To me, making choices to go back to exploitation is an emergency. It puts me at risk of violence, and potentially getting arrested and charged. I put plans in place to take all of my vulnerabilities into account. Money? I try to have a cushion of savings. Loneliness? I have people who can spend time with me when I really need it. Food and sustenance? I have mapped out different ways to get to food banks and other resources that I may need. An emergency plan is something that was suggested to me by another survivor leader, and I have always kept it up to date.

CHALLENGE:

Challenge yourself to make your own personal emergency plan, even if you feel that you will never turn back to exploitation. You may not want to now, but you never know what life event may trigger a crisis response.

59

Creating Your New Life

Recovery from sexual exploitation is not simply a matter of "giving up" old habits, old haunts, and toxic behaviors. It is also about gaining a new way of life and having complete control over it. There are so many things in life that we cannot do as long as we are exploited, and there are so many things in life that are better outside of exploitation than they are inside the beast.

Food

We can cook what we want to and how we want to, not because we have to. We can discover what foods we like. If we found a food we liked during exploitation that only reminds us of exploitation itself, we can now create new memories with that great food. Food tastes different when it's yours.

Clothes and Personal Appearance

Clothes may not seem like a big part of recovery, but how we dress and how we choose to present ourselves is the forefront of our identity. If we want to wear liberating clothes that make us feel good about our bodies, we can do that. If we want to wear conservative or comfy clothes that physically feel good to wear, we can do that. We can wear anything we want and we don't have to answer to anyone about it.

Family

We may never have the relationship we had with our family before exploitation, but maybe that's a good thing. If we wish to have a better relationship with our parents, now is our chance to be close to them as adults of sound mind. If we want our children back in our lives, after recovery from exploitation, we are now mature, healed adults who can be a better guardian to them. Maybe we can't get full custody of them right away, but we can always be a good influence on their lives.

Travel and Vacation

Maybe you don't get to travel as much as you did when you were hustling, but when you do travel you will appreciate it even more, because it will be by your own free will, something that you have worked so hard to be able to do, and you can be in charge of what you do and how you spend your time on your vacation.

Attitude

No one else will ever be in charge of how you feel or how you act. No one ever has to know what's on your mind again, as you can react to stressors however you choose. Your attitude is your choice from now on.

New Hobbies and Interests

This is YOUR world. Your NEW world. Challenge yourself to try something new, something you may not have even considered doing in the past because of time constraints or the limitations of exploitation. You might uncover a whole new side of yourself that you didn't even know existed.

Some ideas of new things and activities to try are:

Crafts and Homemade Projects

Scrapbooking, knitting, crocheting, candle making, sewing, and many other homemade projects not only kill time, but they take our focus away from our daily drama. When you finish a project on your own, it feels great, and sometimes it feels even better to share the fruits of your labor with your friends and loved ones.

Hobbies

Maybe crafting isn't your thing, but collecting things is. Maybe you'll enjoy collecting postcards or coffee mugs, or maybe photography can be a fulfilling hobby. Do you like coffee tasting? Craft cooking? Use your imagination!

Exploring Your Town

When our schedules fill up, we won't always have the time and means to travel, but we often find ourselves with time at the end of the week with nothing to do and nowhere to be. In that situation we can take advantage of our surroundings and explore what they have to offer. Maybe there's a new store, a new coffee shop, a new museum or zoo exhibit that grabs our attention. It's fun to throw yourself a staycation!

Take a New Class

This might not be a great option if you are taking a full load of classes, but if you have free time once or twice a week, you might consider taking a class in something you've always been interested in but have never tried. You can look for classes to take at your local community college, gym, art supply store, or local adult school. You may surprise yourself with your newfound talents!

But, in reality, you don't have to do any of this! The beauty of our life outside of exploitation is that our choices are completely up to us. We don't have to answer to an abuser, and soon we won't even be in the confines of a treatment program. We don't have to do anything we don't want to do. And we can do anything we want! That's our personal reward for working so hard at obtaining independence and emotional stability.

The more we step outside of exploitation and explore all the world has to offer, the more we learn to love life. The key to recovery is not giving up our old ways, but rather discovering completely new ways of living life, the way we want to live it.

PROMPT QUESTIONS:

1. Is there anything in your life that is better now that you are in recovery? Why do you think that is?

2. Is there anything new that you would want to try that you haven't tried before? What about it interests you?

3. How can your relationships improve now that you are in recovery?

4. What about before your exploitation? Is there anything you want to rediscover now that you are in a stable environment?

5. What is on your "bucket list"—what do you want to do before you pass away?

Author's Experience:

It may sound insignificant, but rediscovering cooking, and food in general, has been super rewarding since I started recovery. My exploiter did not let me cook, and he always ordered for me at restaurants. Now I can try whatever I want. I discovered that I really like poki and other raw fish dishes! As for cooking, learning that I could cook anything that I researched myself has greatly improved my confidence.

Also, my family relationships improved. I will never have the same relationships with them as before I was exploited, but in my case, that's a really good thing. Now I am of sound mind, with much more manageable mental health, and I get to know my parents, sisters, cousins, aunts, uncles, and grandparents as a fellow adult. It has been great.

Challenge:

Challenge yourself to think of one of three things:
Something you have never done before
Something that was tainted during your exploitation that you want to experience in a new light
Something you haven't done since before you were exploited.

And try to do one of those three. Have fun!

60

Remembering How Far You Have Come

Think back to before you opened this book, when you first learned about sexual exploitation and that you had been exploited. Remember thinking that finding safety and shelter was the first step of many, many steps you had to take to become the person you are today.

Do you remember who you were before that moment? Do you remember your identity in exploitation? Maybe you had a character or persona in that lifestyle, an act that you would put on to hustle and to hide the part of you that hated what you were going through.

Who was that person? What did they look like? What did they wear? How did they do their hair? Who were their friends? What did their voice sound like?

If you can, imagine that person clearly in your mind. All of their strengths, their weaknesses, their insecurities, their emotions … all that they were. Think of how they felt all the time, yet how they appeared to be tough, strong, or reserved and self-controlled.

Imagine that you, the person you are today, meet your former persona in a private setting. You two have decided to meet together without their exploiter or anyone who judges them (or you). With the deepest empathy in your heart for them, what would you say to them?

Now, take their hand in yours, look them in the eye, and say the following:

"I understand you and everything you did.
It's okay.
I forgive you.
I love you."

Give them the warmest hug, then tell them goodbye, and leave to go on with your life.

Empathizing with the person you once were will help you to understand what you went through and forgive yourself. It also helps us move on to the future of what life holds. Although you are at the end of this book, you are at the beginning of your new life.

Remember that you are a survivor and what that truly means. It means you are:

- Smart: Leaving behind the toxic lifestyle of sexual exploitation takes planning, strategizing, and analytical reasoning. Being a survivor shows us that we are capable of creating plans and sticking to them.

- Resilient: Surviving trauma means that we have stared some very scary situations in the face, and yet we have survived them. We are able to face challenges, take them on, and move forward.

- Strong: Making the decision to leave exploitation shows us that we can do what would make many people give up or surrender. Yet we have the strength to rebuild our lives anyway.

- Self-respecting: We recognize that sexual exploitation was not healthy nor safe for us and have made the decision to walk away from it. We respect ourselves enough to choose a different path that suits us better.

- Brave: It takes a lot of courage to walk away from sexual exploitation, knowing that we may risk our safety in doing so, but we did it anyway because fear is not something that we will let hold us back from the freedom we want.

Never forget the affirmations you told yourself at the beginning of this journey. Whenever you have a hard time creating your own affirmations, stick to the qualities that all sexual exploitation survivors possess:

I am smart
I am resilient
I am strong
I am worthy of respect
I am brave
… Because you are.

PROMPT QUESTIONS:

1. Is it challenging to think of your identity in exploitation? Why or why not?

2. Thinking back to your identity in exploitation, what do you think that version of yourself needed?

3. Has it hit you how much you have accomplished in your recovery? What are you most proud of?

4. What was the toughest lesson you learned in recovery? Why was it tough?

5. What was the most important lesson you have learned so far? Why is it important?

6. What advice would you give a new survivor starting their recovery?

AUTHOR'S EXPERIENCE:

In my recovery, I had several false starts, where I would try to nourish my recovery and pursue independence, yet I would fall back into old habits, and before I knew it, I was back into full-blown exploitation. In all honesty, I had to lose everything to really want my recovery to last. I was homeless, jobless, alone, depressed, malnourished, fearful . . . I was at the lowest point I have ever been in my whole life. Almost five years later, I am happier than I could have ever imagined. It's totally possible to completely change your life. You're already doing it!

CHALLENGE:

Challenge yourself to thank yourself in a special way for finishing all this hard work. Whether that means doing something nice for yourself, practicing self-care, or rewarding yourself with some prayer and meditation, thank your body, mind, and heart for all they have done for you.

If you or a loved one has been trafficked,
please call the National Human Trafficking Hotline at
(888) 373-7888 to get help today.

AFTERWORD

This book is intended to guide survivors of sexual exploitation through the first important steps toward healing from their trauma while restoring their independence and gaining self-sufficiency. However, there are many underlying risk factors that individuals have that may have contributed toward their exploitation that are not covered at length in this book. Often, once we are in a stable environment, those risk factors become magnified as we are finally in a safe place to process what led us to exploitation. For many, the biggest contributing factors to their cycle of sexual exploitation are substance addiction and a history of child abuse. For me, the risk factor that didn't come to light until after I spent a year in recovery was my very secretive eating disorder.

My hope is that the steps laid out in this book will lead you to a proper therapist and a support network that will help you tackle these intermediate issues that may not be directly affected by sexual exploitation trauma. I have found that a weekly support group coupled with one-on-one therapy with a counselor I trust has helped me start to heal from factors that are beyond this book's teachings.

My other hope is that YOU will pass on the healing you receive at the intermediate or niche level to other survivors who are still struggling, once you find the unique tools that will work for you. The best teacher is often someone who has gone through exactly what you are going through, and for someone else, that could be you!

ACKNOWLEDGMENTS

First and foremost, thank you to Susan Johnson for supporting me in finishing and publishing this book. I respect you as an ally and love you as a true friend. Thank you also to Alabaster Jar Project for coming behind us to make this idea into a reality as well as for shaping the survivor I am today.

Thank you to Stephanie Marshall Renick for your clinical perspective and expertise. I will always appreciate the extra time and care you put into this project for no other reason than you supported me and continue to support me and everything I do.

Thank you to Marjorie Saylor for putting your trust into this project and allowing me to teach from this book to survivors in our recovery circle. Thank you for always being supportive and encouraging about this project and all my writing endeavors.

Thank you to Roxanne Belle Hanson for being among the first people whom I shared this project with when it was only an idea. Your encouragement helped me believe in myself a little bit more and continues to lift me up. We miss you so much.

Thank you to Bethany Kelly of Publishing Partner for walking alongside Alabaster Jar Project so that this project could come to fruition. Thank you for your expertise, resources, encouragement, and survivor sisterhood.

Thank you to my family, especially to my mom, who never gave up on me, even when it was probably easier to let me go.

Thank you to Shannon, my boyfriend and partner, for being the first to read this book in its entirety. Thank you for being there for every idea and creative epiphany. I love you forever.

Finally, the warmest thank you to Grace House Residents, survivors at our weekly support group, and all the survivors who provided important feedback on early versions of this book. *Rebuild and Thrive* would not truly be a book by survivors and for survivors without your unique perspectives and insights. Thank you for being my survivor sisters. You are all my heroes.

ABOUT THE AUTHOR

Amanda Moon Ellevis is a survivor of trafficking and sexual exploitation. Currently, she is serving as a member of the survivor staff for Alabaster Jar Project, where she has created content for their web presence for roughly three years, including creating their blog, in addition to assisting with grant writing.

Amanda's heart for the exploited stems from her unique vulnerabilities as a young musician in the San Francisco Bay Area, as well as her experience being homeless. She hopes that this book will help other survivors identify unhealthy relationships and behaviors so that they can overcome the deep-rooted issues that bind them to exploitation, as well as gain a skillset that will lift them to higher levels of independence.

Amanda loves animals, especially bats, and loves to cook with her boyfriend, Shannon. Spending time with her family is among her most valued pastimes.

Made in the USA
Las Vegas, NV
15 June 2022

50280540R00275